GW00375211

QUANTITATIVE RESEARCH METHODS I ̄ ̄ ̄IAL WORK

QUANTITATIVE RESEARCH METHODS FOR SOCIAL WORK

MAKING SOCIAL WORK COUNT

BARBRA TEATER, JOHN DEVANEY, DONALD FORRESTER, JONATHAN SCOURFIELD AND JOHN CARPENTER

First published 2017 by
PALGRAVE

Palgrave in the UK is an imprint of Macmillan Publishers Limited, registered in England, company number 785998, of 4 Crinan Street, London, N1 9XW.

Palgrave® and Macmillan® are registered trademarks in the United States, the United Kingdom, Europe and other countries.

ISBN 978–1–137–40026–0 paperback

This book is printed on paper suitable for recycling and made from fully managed and sustained forest sources. Logging, pulping and manufacturing processes are expected to conform to the environmental regulations of the country of origin.

A catalogue record for this book is available from the British Library.

A catalog record for this book is available from the Library of Congress.

Printed and bound by CPI Group (UK) Ltd, Croydon, CR0 4YY

CONTENTS

LISTS OF FIGURES, TABLES, BOXES AND OUTPUTS

Figures

Tables

1

INTRODUCTION

Social work counts – every day social workers make a positive and lasting difference in the lives of many people. Whether it is supporting adolescents with life-limiting conditions, enabling an older person to remain living independently in their own home with a range of coordinated supports or providing therapy to a young child living with domestic violence, social workers practise at the very forefront of the challenges facing all of us in society.

In spite of the many different forms that social work can take, whether working with an individual, a group or a community, social workers draw upon a common set of values to guide their practice. At the heart of these values is a commitment to promoting social justice. Social justice can be expressed in many ways, but a key feature is the imperative for social workers and the organisations for whom they work to bring about positive change. Yet, as Sheldon and Macdonald (2008, p. 66) note:

> It is perfectly possible for the good-hearted, well-meaning, reasonably clever, appropriately qualified, hard-working staff, employing the most promising contemporary approaches available to them, to make no difference at all to (or even on occasion to worsen) the condition of those whom they seek to assist.

The point that Sheldon and Macdonald are making is that positive intentions, endeavour and good interpersonal skills, while very important, are insufficient in and of themselves to deal with the complex issues that many users of social work services encounter. There is a need for practitioners, managers and policy makers to draw upon information and knowledge to inform and shape what they do – whether it is a high-level policy or the focus of an intervention with a single service user. In this book we argue that a distinctive form of knowledge, quantitative research, makes a very important contribution to both understanding and responding effectively to the social problems that social work service users face. We should note that we will use the term 'service user' to refer to individuals who use or encounter social work services, and we acknowledge that this term may vary internationally where other terms, such as client, consumer, and patient (often within medical settings), are used in place of service user.

The Global Standards for Social Work Education, as agreed by the International Association of Schools of Social Work (IASSW) and the International

Federation of Social Workers (IFSW), includes having knowledge of social work research, skills in the use of research methods, including the consideration of ethics, and critical appreciation of the use of research and different sources of knowledge about social work practice (IASSW/IFSW, 2004). Although research is included in the global standards, the extent to which it is integrated and covered in the social work curriculum varies by country. For example, the Council on Social Work Education (CSWE) in the USA requires students across all accredited universities to engage in research-informed practice and practice-informed research (CSWE, 2015), the Australian Association of Social Workers (AASW, 2015) requires students to apply research knowledge and skills to inform and develop practice as well as conduct and disseminate research to inform practice, and the Health and Care Professions Council (HCPC, 2012) in England requires students to be aware of research methodologies and be able to evaluate research evidence to inform their practice.

The extent to which universities provide learning environments and opportunities to demonstrate such competencies or proficiencies can also vary within countries by university. Yet, a review of the international literature on the teaching and learning of research methods in social work by Sharland and Teater (2016) highlighted three main reasons to teach research methods, making future social work practitioners: (1) aware of research and how it can inform their practice; (2) consumers of research where they can critically assess research and its applicability to their practice; and (3) producers of research where they conduct research to evaluate their own practice. In achieving these aims, educators use a variety of methods ranging from lectures to raise awareness of research to requiring students to conduct service learning projects, empirically based dissertations (or theses) or evaluations of their practice. Interestingly, the review of the literature found that although qualitative, quantitative and mixed methods were covered in research classes, quantitative was covered less frequently or intensively, and where it did appear was more likely to be in the US literature over other countries, particularly the UK.

The review concluded with three key challenges to teaching research: (1) time and resource constraints in setting up, delivering and supervising experiential learning opportunities; (2) social work lecturers often untrained in terms of the skills and knowledge needed to effectively teach research methods to students; often lecturers lack knowledge in research methods themselves, particularly quantitative methods; and (3) 'Research reluctance' on behalf of the students where they experience anxiety, fear and/or a lack of confidence or motivation to implement research methods and interpret and apply research findings. Sharland and Teater (2016) conclude that 'more profoundly still, the literature makes reference to a deep-rooted climate of research resistance or ambivalence within the social work community, which can influence students' ability to see the relevance of research to practice' (p. 152). This concern is argued to stem from a lack of integration of research and practice

curriculum and 10 core teaching sessions that were produced during the project, but also includes other relevant additional material. While the book primarily focuses on quantitative research, many of the chapters are just as applicable to qualitative and mixed-methods research.

The book has 13 chapters that cover a number of key issues. Our overall aim is to support students and educators to appreciate the relevance and importance of quantitative research in understanding the social world. We also want to equip the reader with sufficient understanding of some key research and statistical concepts in order to be able to undertake a quantitative research study or to critically appraise the quantitative research literature. The book has a number of features that are intended to facilitate extended learning through illustrating concepts with reference to research examples from social work. Each chapter also contains a 'critical thinking' box that contains a discussion of a social work peer-reviewed journal article and some critical questions to answer in relation to the chapter topic. Finally, each chapter has further resources identified to support the reader to find out more about the topic.

In the next chapter we highlight how numbers and numeracy are a part of everyday life, and the role of statistics in understanding the social world. The chapter will introduce definitions of basic concepts such as data, variable and quantification using examples from everyday life. The chapter will then move to explore the importance of numbers in social work in relation to understanding the scale of social problems, the heterogeneity of populations of service users relevant to social work, the concept of effectiveness and the importance of being able to understand how numbers can inform both social policy and social work practice. Readers will have an opportunity to explore the social construction of statistics in order to become more aware of their strengths and limitations in different contexts.

In Chapter 3 we explore the issue of who is being studied. Understanding who research is about and who data were actually gathered from are key steps in evaluating any research study – whether qualitative or quantitative, and across all the social sciences. In practice, it may be particularly important for social work research because so much of our work is with groups who may be hard to involve in research. As a result our samples are often partial and may not represent the whole population in which we are interested. Yet understanding about samples and the potential for bias is not just a research question: it can also improve our understanding of practice and policy issues. It is particularly useful for developing a better theoretical appreciation of issues in anti-discriminatory and anti-oppressive practice. In this chapter we cover the definition of a 'sample', a 'population' and 'representativeness' and the difference between various types of research sample. Using examples related to substance misuse (how do we measure and define problematic substance use?) and children in public care (how do we measures outcomes for children in care?) the chapter will explore the ways in which different samples can influence research findings and how issues of sample bias in research can impact on anti-discriminatory practice and stereotyping in social work practice and policy.

This is followed by a discussion in Chapter 4 of what is being studied. This chapter looks at variables and their construction, with a particular focus on the development and use of standardised instruments for both research and practice purposes. Different standardised measures that might be used in social work settings are introduced, and key elements in understanding the contribution they can make and their potential limitations are presented. The chapter will consider descriptive research, introduce surveys and the use of routine data collection and will end with an introduction to concepts of reliability and validity. Construction and validation of measures will be critically considered.

In Chapter 5 we consider how quantitative data can be used to describe things. This might include research questions such as how common a particular issue is or the seriousness of a particular problem. The chapter covers in particular questionnaires and routine data as sources for quantitative research, and begins by considering routine information gathered by social work and social care agencies and its strengths and limitations for research purposes. This discussion is illustrated with examples drawn from government sources to illustrate the political importance of a critical understanding of routine data collection in social work. The chapter then turns to an exploration of the contribution that questionnaires can make, and an understanding of some basic issues in questionnaire design with examples from recent social work research studies. The information is intended to help readers who may wish to use questionnaires in small-scale primary research as well as those wishing to critically appraise them.

Chapter 6 explores the key issue of how to establish whether services provided for people make a difference, including the debates around this topic within social work and the social sciences. The most popular evaluative designs are introduced, with a particular focus on before-after, quasi-experimental and experimental designs. The broader evaluative research tradition is considered, including logic models and realist approaches. Throughout, key critiques are considered in relation to each type of evaluative design. The overall argument is that each method has strengths and weaknesses, and is likely to be appropriate for particular purposes in specific contexts.

In Chapter 7 we discuss how numbers can be used to describe a sample. In Chapter 3, we defined a sample as a subset of a population; although, as this chapter highlighted, the extent to which we can transfer knowledge of a sample to a population is contingent on the choice and rigour of our sampling methods. Through Chapter 7, we aim to demonstrate how a description of a sample, through the use of quantitative methods, can better assist in understanding the characteristics and needs of the sample and the population which the sample represents. This knowledge is relevant to social work practice as such an understanding can enable practitioners and policy makers to better understand the characteristics of a particular group of service users, tailor social work services to service users' needs, and begin to determine whether such services are effective.

In Chapter 8 we discuss how confident we can be that the findings from the research on a sample accurately reflects the true situation or condition of the population and that the findings are not due to chance. Through the use of specific statistical methods, referred to as inferential statistics, we are able to determine how probable it is that the findings from research on a sample are not due to chance, and, thus, are likely to reflect the situation among the population. In order to do so, we must understand the concept of probability. In this chapter, we will explore probability and the probability distribution, otherwise referred to as the standard normal distribution or normal curve. We will then move to discuss how we can use hypothesis testing to determine the probability that our research findings are not due to chance (or sampling error), and, thus, whether any research findings of differences between variables are 'statistically significant'.

Quantitative social work research requires researchers to gather data and then analyse the data in order to answer research questions or test hypotheses. The findings allow for researchers to tell a story about a sample, determine if social work interventions are effective or not and determine the extent to which the findings can be generalised to the larger population or across different situations. But, once we have collected our data, how do we know what statistical test to use to answer our research questions or test our hypotheses? How are we able to determine if variables in the data set are related, influence one another, or cause one another? In Chapter 9 we will explore how to look at the variables and the research question (or hypothesis) and determine the most appropriate statistical test to use. We will first look at the difference between parametric and nonparametric tests and then move to the difference between correlation and causation. We will then look at a number of statistical tests that are commonly used in social work research. Having knowledge of a range of parametric and nonparametric tests will enable social work practitioners to evaluate the validity of the social work research that they will use to inform their social work practice.

In Chapter 10 we extend the discussion of how variables are related by exploring how to predict a change in a variable (dependent or outcome variable) when there is a change in one or more other variables (independent or predictor variable), and the usefulness of multivariate analyses. Understanding the results from linear regression analysis can be helpful in predicting future circumstances, situations or outcomes given knowledge of specific variables and can, therefore, be helpful in planning social work practice interventions.

Chapter 11 then moves on to explore the very important topic of the ethics of social research and the implications for quantitative research, with particular reference to the principles of respect for autonomy, non-maleficence, beneficence and justice. Given the vulnerable populations that social workers work with, it is important that research can help policy makers and practitioners to better understand their needs and situation, while also guarding against any negative consequences for individuals participating in research.

In Chapter 12 we explore the growing area of secondary data analysis – or undertaking research without gathering any new data. In this chapter the potential benefits and limitations of these approaches are discussed, along with some of the opportunities and challenges. There are growing opportunities for this type of research and a need for social scientists who are able to undertake such work.

Our final chapter recognises that quantitative research has some limitations, and that studies using mixed methods can add greatly to an understanding of the scope and nature of social phenomena and the issues that social workers deal with. Supplementing quantitative data with qualitative data can enrich our appreciation of these issues, although care must be taken in ensuring that the specific methods chosen are complementary.

It is our hope that you find this book helpful in your work – whether by increasing your understanding and ability to read quantitative research or in supporting you to undertake some quantitative research. As social work academics and educators we are committed to producing and using research to inform practice, policy and teaching. Our ultimate goal is that high-quality research is both undertaken and applied in truly emancipatory ways that seek to promote the interests of social work service users.

2

WHY NUMBERS MATTER IN SOCIAL WORK

LEARNING OUTCOMES

By the end of this chapter you should be able to:

- Recognise the relevance of quantification in social work practice and policy
- Define some basic concepts such as data, statistics, variable and quantification
- Explain how statistics are socially constructed
- Discuss how statistics can help in understanding the scale and describing the characteristics of a social issue
- Describe how numbers can inform our understanding about the outcomes for service users from interventions

Introduction

Numbers are a part of everyday life, and our ability to engage with them is second nature to us. This also extends to the world of social work, whereby numbers are a necessary part of practice and policy, and our ability to engage with and understand numerical concepts and data should enable us to work more effectively with service users and to address social issues. In this chapter, we will explore in more detail *why* being able to engage with numerical concepts and data is important, and introduce you to some key numerical and statistical concepts (see Box 2.1) that will be developed throughout the remainder of the book.

Box 2.1: Concepts and definitions

Data: information that can be represented in numbers, words, symbols or images used as a basis for reasoning, discussion or calculation (example: the age of an individual person or his or her name)

Number: a unit of measurement

Quantification: the act of counting and measuring that maps observations and experiences into members of some set of numbers (example: the number of pages in this book)

Statistic: a numerical value or number

Statistics: the study of the collection, organisation, analysis, interpretation and presentation of numbers

Variable: something that can vary and can take on different categories or values (example: sex is a variable with three categories of male, female and intersexed; age is a variable constituting a number from 0 to infinity)

Numbers in everyday life

Ofcom, the UK government's independent regulator of telecommunications, reports that 93% of adults in the UK own a mobile phone, with 61% using a smartphone that has the capacity to connect to the internet (Ofcom, 2013). As such it is very likely that you, the reader, own a mobile phone. The mobile phone market is highly competitive, with a range of different companies making the mobile phone handset, and another range of companies offering the service for making calls, sending texts and mobile browsing. So how did you end up with the phone you have today? For a small minority of readers someone else may have given them the phone, but for most people they needed to consider a range of factors, such as those presented in Box 2.2, before choosing the phone they bought for themselves.

Box 2.2: Thinking of purchasing a mobile phone

What factors should you consider when purchasing a mobile phone?

1. Is there a particular type of phone I want?

2. What is the mobile phone reception like where I live/work/study?

3. Is there an initial charge for the phone – if so, how much?

4. Will I 'pay as I go' or take out a contract?

5. If I sign up for a contract, what is the minimum length I am committing to?

6. Is there a penalty charge if I want to change phones before the end of the contract?

7. How do I use my phone – how many minutes of talk time, how many texts and how much data will I need?

8. How do the costs compare between different mobile phone operators for the same phone and the same bundle of calls/texts/data?

9. Should I take out mobile phone insurance?

Answering all of the questions above requires quite a bit of detailed analysis, much of which is underpinned by the ability to use numbers to make calculations and comparisons. For example, one of the authors prefers a smartphone in order to be able to read emails and browse the internet when on the go. He does not have a preference for a particular make of phone, and is unlikely to change his phone regularly. He prefers a contract as he does not want to be stuck without credit when he might have an emergency! Thinking about his mobile phone usage, he tends to make low numbers of calls, but send more texts and use mobile roaming a lot. Therefore, which is the best deal? Being able to navigate all the competing deals between different companies means that he saved £200 over a two-year period when he bought his last phone.

Closer to your studies, how do you know whether your mark of 62% for a piece of coursework is good or not? Students are rightly concerned about the marks they receive for assessed work. Marks are important for students' final degree classification, but they are also important in providing feedback to students about whether they have grasped the key ideas from the teaching and independent study with which they have engaged. Students therefore look for additional information to guide their interpretation of their mark. This usually involves comparing the mark to marks for other pieces of assessment they have undertaken (even though the topic and the assessment task may have been very different); asking a friend what mark they received (and then making a judgement about whether their own mark is good enough based on their assumptions about whether their friend's mark equated with their assessment of their friend's ability); looking at the mark and the comments provided to see if they can understand what was good about their work and where there was room for improvement. All of this information might be helpful, but it also might just add to the lack of clarity. If the lecturer presented the information in a different format; for example, providing the class average and the range of marks for the class, then individual students might feel more confident about benchmarking their performance. Look at Exercise 2.1 to explore this in more detail.

Exercise 2.1: Is my work good enough?

Consider the following scenario:

You are given a mark of 62% for a piece of coursework. The lecturer also provides the class with information relating to the class average and the range of marks in the class. Would you prefer to be student A or student B? Why?

Student A achieved a mark of 62%. The class average was 68% with a range of 55% (being the lowest mark in the class) to 75% (being the highest mark in the class).

Student B achieved a mark of 62%. The class average was 58% with a range of 35% (being the lowest mark in the class) to 75% (being the highest mark in the class).

Looking at both examples in Exercise 2.1, each student may still have hoped for a higher mark but it is likely that student B will be more content with their performance than student A. Having this type of information reduces the need for students to make subjective judgements based on comparisons with previous assessments of different work or their judgement of their friend's ability.

Many individuals studying social work are very comfortable with numerical concepts and statistics. Some will have undertaken the study of mathematics or statistics at school or as part of previous educational courses. For other social work students, numbers are a bit of a puzzle, and in some cases may even be a little frightening. When applying to study social work, students understand that good interpersonal communication skills and the ability to form meaningful and supportive relationships with service users are key to delivering empowering and effective services. Very few think that a good understanding of numerical and statistical concepts is important as well. And yet our ability to engage with and understand numerical concepts and data is part of everyday social work practice even though we may not always realise this. At a basic level, social workers are interested in the nature, scale and impact of social issues affecting individuals, groups and communities, and what might be done to effectively empower and support people, and alleviate distress and suffering. There is a need to understand the scale and scope of these issues, as well as their impact on individuals. Consider the following example of domestic abuse.

'Research in practice' – domestic abuse

Over the past 20 years, there has been a growing recognition among politicians, policy makers and the general public that domestic abuse is a significant social, health and legal issue. There is a growing awareness and understanding of the impact of domestic abuse in both the immediate and longer term for victims and wider society. When violence between intimate partners emerged as a recognisable issue in the mid-1970s as a consequence of the pioneering work by women's groups, empirical knowledge was very limited. Over the past 20 years, a growing body of research has convincingly demonstrated the existence of different types or patterns of domestic abuse and what might be done to effectively address this issue (Emery, 2011).

Our increased understanding of the scale and nature of domestic abuse has come from a number of sources, including the voices of those who have suffered that have been collected and represented by support organisations for victims, such as Women's Aid in the UK; the publication of both qualitative and quantitative empirical research that has sought to capture experiences of domestic abuse and to measure the impact on victims; and the collection of statistics by central government.

One source of useful statistics is the Crime Survey for England and Wales (CSEW, 2015); which measures the extent of crime by asking people whether they have experienced any crime in the past year (there are comparable surveys in Scotland and Northern Ireland). In 2012–2013, around 50,000 households across England and Wales were invited to participate in the survey. Three-quarters of households invited to take part actually did so (approximately 35,000). The households were chosen at random and interviewers did not know who lived at the address until they visited. If more than one person lived at the address they would then randomly select one person aged 16 or over to take part in the study. Interviewers in the Crime Survey can only interview the person who was selected. If the selected person does not wish to take part then no one else in the household can take their place. Selecting one person in this way helps to ensure that the study represents everyone in England and Wales. The representativeness of the sample is refined further by weighting the survey to adjust for possible non-response bias and to ensure the sample reflects the profile of the general population (the issues of sampling and representativeness of a sample will be discussed further in Chapter 3).

From 2009, the survey has also included a separate survey to record the experiences of young people aged 10–15 years. This interview is shorter than the adult interview. Young people are selected to take part from households selected for the adult survey. Permission from a parent or guardian is always obtained before an interview is conducted with anyone aged 10–15 years. In 2012–2013, 3,500 young people were interviewed for the survey.

The survey includes a self-completion module on intimate violence, which is asked of adults aged 16–59 years. (Note the age range: research by Lazenbatt and Devaney (2014) highlights that those aged 60 years and above can still experience domestic abuse.) The module covers experience of emotional, financial and physical abuse by partners or family members, as well as sexual assaults and stalking by any person. In 2012–2013, the module included a special focus on the nature of partner abuse.

Typically the Crime Survey records a higher number of crimes than police figures because it includes the experience of crimes that have not been reported to the police for whatever reason. In 2012–2013, a range of information was collected in relation to experiences of domestic abuse (Office of National Statistics, 2014). The survey reported that:

- 7.1% of women and 4.4% of men reported having experienced any type of domestic abuse in the last year, equivalent to an estimated 1.2 million female victims of domestic abuse and 700,000 male victims;

- Overall, 30% of women and 16.3% of men had experienced any form of domestic abuse since the age of 16, equivalent to an estimated 4.9 million female victims of domestic abuse and 2.7 million male victims;

- The decline in domestic abuse between the 2004–2005 and 2012–2013 CSEW surveys was statistically significant. However, the current figure (5.7%) continued a fairly stable trend seen since 2008–2009;

- Women were more likely than men to have experienced intimate violence across all the main types of abuse asked about;

- In the year prior to the survey, partner abuse (non-sexual) and stalking were the most common of the separate types of intimate violence: 4.0% of women and 2.8% of men reported having experienced partner abuse (non-sexual); 4.1% of women and 1.9% of men reported having experienced stalking; and

- 2% of women and 0.5% of men had experienced some form of sexual assault (including attempts) in the last year.

From other data, we also know that domestic abuse accounts for 16% of all violent incidents reported to the police. It has more repeat victims than any other crime, with repeat victimisation accounting for 73% of all incidents of domestic violence (Kershaw et al., 2008). The Northern Ireland Crime Survey analysis of repeat victimisation revealed that 59% of all victims experienced domestic abuse from the same perpetrator on more than one occasion, with 35% victimised four times or more. Seventeen per cent of all female victims had suffered threats and/or force from a partner while they were pregnant. For over half of these women (56%), the violence had started during their pregnancy (Carmichael, 2008). Finally, in 2011–2012, 88 women and 17 men were killed by their current or former partner (Office for National Statistics, 2013).

Is this information relevant or helpful for social workers? Firstly, at a policy level this information highlights the prevalence of domestic abuse and the importance of developing strategies to prevent future abuse and reduce the likely reoccurrence. It also highlights the need for services to support victims and the need to respond to those who perpetrate such abuse. In this example, it is clear that gathering statistical information in this way can inform both our understanding about the scale and form of an issue, and therefore lead to the development of more robust and appropriate strategies and services. It is also helpful for practitioners, as it highlights that domestic abuse is likely to be a common experience for many users of services, even if it is not the primary reason for involvement. Receiving a referral about a woman's problematic use of alcohol, but realising that this stems from her experience of being abused and victimised means that our intervention is more likely to be effective as we are dealing with the substantive rather than the presenting issue.

Why is an understanding of numerical concepts and data relevant for social work?

Gathering and analysing data about social issues, whether through routinely collected administrative data (e.g. police statistics on recorded crime), surveys (e.g. of individuals' experiences of crime) or quantitative research (e.g. to measure the impact on children of exposure to domestic abuse) can provide us with a more rounded understanding about the scale, scope and impact of the issues that we as social workers deal with. However, an understanding of numerical concepts and data can also be helpful in working directly with individuals, groups and communities. Look at Exercise 2.2 for more examples.

Exercise 2.2: Numbers and social work practice

These are three everyday examples of how numbers permeate into how social work is practised in different settings and contexts:

1. In giving evidence in court for a care application the defending barrister asks the social worker what the likelihood is of the child experiencing future harm – is it possible or probable? What is the difference, and why is the distinction important?

2. A community mental health team is undertaking a review of a service user with schizophrenia and severe depression. The service user's self-care has deteriorated significantly and the team is considering whether electroconvulsive therapy might be a suitable form of treatment to recommend to his next of kin. What research evidence on the effectiveness of electroconvulsive therapy should inform the decision about intervention?

3. A community development association is seeking funding to roll out a scheme of home visitation to elderly people on a large housing estate. The application requires a quantification of the need for such a service. What type of information would be most useful in making the case for funding?

The three examples in Exercise 2.2 highlight that being able to understand numerical concepts and use data can help social workers in fulfilling their role in very diverse employment settings. The examples also highlight that numbers are, in themselves, only part of the information that needs to be considered when undertaking assessments and planning interventions. Social workers need to make judgements and decisions that are informed by professional codes of conduct, the wishes and feelings of service users and the evidence of the nature of an issue and how an intervention is likely to make a positive difference while reducing the likelihood of a service user experiencing harm.

Being able to gather, interpret, use and communicate quantitative data is an essential skill that requires a body of knowledge in order to understand what the numbers mean. That is the primary purpose of this book – to help readers to develop both the confidence and competence to engage with and use numerical data and concepts. Without such knowledge and understanding social workers (and other helping professionals) are less effective in working with service users and with social issues. This is not to say that quantitative data are the only information that social workers require – rather, quantitative data can address questions and assist understanding about issues that could not be answered in other ways.

Using the second of our examples in Exercise 2.2 highlights the interplay between ethics, evidence and the involvement of service users and their families in decisions that affect their lives. The induction of a seizure (fit) for therapeutic purposes by the administration of an electrical stimulus (electroconvulsive therapy or ECT) remains a common treatment option for people with schizophrenia. The electrical stimulus is administered via electrodes attached to the scalp through which a variable frequency electrical stimulus (shock) is applied to the brain. The procedure is usually modified by the use of short acting anaesthetics and muscle relaxants. This is important as the former reduces apprehension and the latter reduces the likelihood of the unwanted consequences of inducing a seizure, such as injuries to the head, back and limbs caused by the resultant vigorous muscle convulsions that would occur if a muscle relaxant was not used. There are, though, still side effects of ECT. During the administration of ECT some individuals lose control over their bladder and bowel. Immediately after receiving ECT, many people have a headache and some aching in their muscles in the short term. They may feel fuzzy-headed and generally out of sorts, or even nauseous. Some individuals become distressed after the treatment and may be tearful or frightened during recovery. For most people, however, these effects settle within a few hours, particularly with reassurance and support from relatives and nursing staff, simple pain killers and some light refreshment. In the longer term, memory problems can be a side effect for some people. Surveys conducted by doctors and clinical staff usually find a low level of severe side effects (approximately 1 in 10 of all individuals who receive ECT suffer them), although patient-led surveys have found much more of a problem, with severe side effects in maybe half of those having ECT. A small number of people report more distressing experiences, such as feeling that their personalities have changed, that they have lost skills or that they are no longer the person they were before ECT. They say that they have never got over the experience and feel permanently harmed (Waite and Easton, 2013). So, given these side effects, what are the potential benefits of this form of treatment?

One way of trying to answer this question is to undertake some research. While this may improve our understanding of an issue and offer a view as to the effectiveness of an intervention, practitioners are right to be cautious about basing their practice, or developing policy, based on one isolated study. It is much better to be able to look at a number of studies on the same issue to gauge whether there is a consensus about what works, and if so, how and why. The ability to assess the quality of research and the robustness of the findings of any piece of research is an important skill for social workers. However, for many people they have neither the time nor the resources to search for all the relevant literature and to begin to make sense of it – one of the challenges in comparing research studies is that they are likely to have been undertaken in different ways, with individuals and groups in particular places. As such, many practitioners and policy makers find systematic reviews a very useful resource.

A systematic review is a comprehensive review of the research literature focused on a specific research question that tries to identify, appraise, select and synthesise all high-quality research evidence relevant to that question. Systematic reviews are particularly useful when there have been a number of studies on a specific topic but each is too small to provide a conclusive answer (see Box 2.3). The first step of a systematic review is a thorough search of the literature for relevant research publications. The quality of each individual research study is assessed, and then the findings from the different studies are synthesised to allow some conclusions to be drawn about the key findings. Most systematic reviews focus on quantitative studies and therefore use statistical techniques to combine the data from different studies in order to identify more clearly the overarching findings of the combined studies. More recently, systematic reviews of qualitative research have also begun to appear. While systematic reviews are a very powerful and useful tool for overviewing the state of knowledge on a particular topic, not all systematic reviews are conducted to the same standard (Moher et al., 2007). As a consequence, guidelines have been developed to improve the quality of systematic reviews, and collaborations, such as Cochrane (www.cochrane.org) and Campbell (www.campbellcollaboration.org), have sought to provide a very robust process of quality assurance of reviews completed to a common standard.

In relation to our practice question, a systematic review conducted to Cochrane standards was undertaken on the research outcomes from 26 studies that included over 798 participants who had schizophrenia and had been in receipt of ECT. The review concluded that 'courses of ECT can, in the short term, result in an increase in global improvement for some people with schizophrenia' (Tharyan and Adams, 2005).

The development of psychological and pharmacological (drug) therapies over the last 50 years has seen a reduction in the use of ECT. However, for some individuals these other interventions have limited efficacy, and as such ECT still has a use, even though no one is certain how ECT works. As Blease (2013) notes, refinements in how to use ECT and a greater focus on the smaller group of individuals who are most likely to benefit from this form of treatment has seen somewhat of a renaissance of its use in the UK.

Box 2.3: The logo of the Cochrane Collaboration

The logo of the Cochrane Collaboration features a simplified version of a 'blobbogram' (sometimes also referred to as a forest plot). The example used in the logo relates to the results from an important meta-analysis, which looked at an intervention that saved premature babies' lives. We know that babies born prematurely have a higher probability of dying. Doctors in New Zealand experimented with giving a short, inexpensive course of a corticosteroid to women about to give birth too early. Seven studies were undertaken between 1972 and 1981 on the effectiveness of this intervention. Two of the studies showed some benefit from the steroids, but the remaining five failed to detect any benefits. As such, the intervention was felt not to be worthwhile. However, in 1989 a meta-analysis was undertaken pooling all the data from the seven studies. The Cochrane logo displays the results from this meta-analysis in the form of a blobbogram. Each horizontal line represents a single study: if the line is more to the left it means the steroids produced a better outcome than a placebo, and if it is more to the right, then it indicates that in that study the steroids performed worse than the placebo. If the horizontal line for a trial touches the vertical 'nil effect' line in the centre of the diagram then the trial showed no clear difference one way or another. Finally, the longer a horizontal line then the less certain we can be in the outcome of the individual study. The blobbogram above shows that there are five not very certain studies – long horizontal lines, mostly touching the central vertical line of 'no effect'. However, they are predominantly to the left of the vertical line, suggesting that there may indeed be a benefit from administering to pregnant women at risk of giving birth prematurely a short course of steroids, even if each study in itself is not statistically significant. The diamond at the bottom of the diagram shows the pooled answer through combining the data from the seven studies. There is, in fact, very strong evidence that steroids reduce the risk – by between 30% and 50% – of babies dying from the complications associated with being born prematurely. Because no systematic review of these trials had been published until 1989, most obstetricians had not realised that the treatment was so effective. As a result, tens of thousands of

➤

premature babies have probably suffered and died unnecessarily (and needed more expensive treatment than was necessary). They died even though the information was readily available from 1981 to indicate what was needed to increase their chances of survival. This is just one of many examples of the human costs resulting from failure to perform systematic, up-to-date reviews of the already available results from completed research.

Source: www.cochrane.org/about-us/our-logo

Research indicates that any effect from ECT is more likely to be due to the resulting fit rather than the electrical current. The electrical stimulus appears to change patterns of blood flow through the brain and the metabolism of areas of the brain which may be affected by depression or schizophrenia. There is evidence that severe depression is caused by problems with certain brain chemicals. It is thought that ECT causes the release of these chemicals and, probably more importantly, makes the chemicals more likely to work and so help recovery. Recent research has also suggested that ECT can help the growth of new cells and nerve pathways in certain areas of the brain (Waite and Easton, 2013). One way of testing whether an intervention is effective is to compare the outcomes for two groups with similar characteristics – one receiving the intervention and the other receiving what they believe to be the intervention (a placebo) – and then comparing the outcomes.

In the case of ECT this usually takes the form of comparing the outcomes for two groups of individuals where everyone is told they will be receiving ECT, everyone is given the anaesthetic and muscle relaxant, but only one group receive the actual electrical stimulus. There is some evidence that individuals who received the electrical stimulus have better outcomes on a range of measures compared to those who received the placebo treatment, but that the difference is 'modest', and that those receiving the placebo treatment still appear to have better outcomes compared to similar individuals who did not go through the sham ECT procedure (Blease, 2013).

In the ongoing debate about the merits and demerits of the treatment, the opinions of patients who have undergone ECT and their relatives have rarely been sought (Chakrabarti et al. 2010). Clinicians and researchers have traditionally focused on aspects such as efficacy, side effects and the mechanism of action. However, the realisation that mere clinical efficacy of ECT did not necessarily predict patients' perceptions or satisfaction with the treatment has eventually led to several investigations of the knowledge, attitudes and experience of the procedure among patients. When their views have been sought research has shown that a majority of individuals who have received ECT perceive it to be helpful and most are willing to undergo the treatment again (Chakrabarti et al. 2010).

The World Health Organization (2005) states ECT should only be administered after informed consent has been gained. The issue is, therefore, how might staff ensure that individuals are in a position to be able to weigh the potential benefits and risks associated with this form of treatment compared to not receiving the treatment, typically at a time when there are concerns about their capacity to consent or to act in their own best interests. This is where the skills and knowledge of a social worker can come to the fore in involving individual service users, their relatives and the multidisciplinary team in a meaningful and authentic discussion. This, though, is predicated on the social worker having the ability to:

- communicate sensitively and clearly with service users, relatives and colleagues;
- form therapeutic working alliances with other members of the multidisciplinary team;
- understand the research evidence about the issues under consideration;
- communicate complex ideas and information in ways which are easily understood by service users and their relatives; and
- facilitate service users and their relatives to discuss and consider the information with which they have been presented.

This will in part be informed by the social worker's understanding and use of numbers and statistical concepts. For example, if a service user is to weigh up potential benefits and risks they will need to be able to conceptualise these. Some key questions might be:

- What proportion of individuals with symptoms similar to mine undergo ECT?
- What proportion of individuals who receive ECT report side effects in the short term (first 24 hours), and what are the nature of these?
- What proportion of individuals who receive ECT report side effects in the longer term, and what are the nature of these?
- How different are the outcomes and risks of alternative forms of treatment compared to ECT?

While other members of the multidisciplinary team have a significant role in discussing these issues with individuals and gaining consent (as ECT is a medical procedure), this example seeks to highlight that an understanding of numerical concepts and quantitative research underpins aspects of person-centred, ethically informed and relationship-based social work practice.

The social construction of statistics

We often need to be able to count a phenomenon to understand the scale and presentation of an issue. However, what we count, in what way and for what purpose is not neutral. By better understanding how statistics are collected and used we can be more thoughtful and careful about the interpretations we place on them. Mark Twain (1907, p. 471), in his autobiography published in the *North American Review*, stated that 'figures often beguile me, particularly when I have the arranging of them myself; in which case the remark attributed to Disraeli would often apply with justice and force: "There are three kinds of lies: lies, damned lies, and statistics"'. Sometimes statistics are used in ways which are deliberately misleading, but it is just as likely that individuals misinterpret what a statistic means (Box 2.4). In later chapters, we will explore in detail different types of statistics and statistical tests and their uses, but in this section we will discuss some important considerations about how statistics are constructed. An understanding of the way that statistics are constructed will be helpful in critically appraising how numbers are presented and what they might mean.

Box 2.4: Misinterpreting statistics?

In January 2013, the then UK Labour party leader Ed Miliband stated that 'only crisis-hit Spain has higher numbers of young unemployed people than the UK' and that 'we are in the relegation zone when it comes to youth unemployment'. Indeed, although comparative figures in this area are a little shaky (e.g. do you count a student with a summer job or not?) the comparison at the time showed more under-25s were out of work in the UK than in any other European country bar Spain. However, the comparison is meaningless. The UK has a lot more of everything compared to most European countries – including people (the UK has a population of 63.7 million compared to Spain's population of 46.7 million people). What matters if you are making a comparison with other countries is not how many under-25s are unemployed, but what percentage of them. In that regard, the UK is 10th best out of 27 countries (Benedictus, 2013).

'Research in practice' – crime statistics

In thinking about how statistics are constructed we will return to crime statistics as an example. We will explore four dimensions: the definition of an act as a crime; the detection/counting of that act; the response to that act; and the recording of that act.

Firstly, what is counted as a crime is tied up with how we define a crime and who does this. From the social constructionist perspective, crime is a way of classifying behaviour defined by individuals with the power and authority to make laws that identify some behaviour as offensive and render those who perpetrate such behaviour subject to accountability and/or punishment. In Western societies, legislators and courts, enforced by state agencies (such as social services and the police), have the power and authority to define crime and/or administer punishment. What behaviour they define as a criminal act reflects both the values and interests of those who make the law and the collective norms and values of the society, or at least the most vociferous or powerful parts of it (Henry, 2009). The extent to which the norms and values of a society represent those of the whole society or some universal human values is open to debate, because what counts as crime in different societies can vary significantly with a few exceptions.

In their study of many different cultures, anthropologists Kroeber and Kluckhohn (1952) highlighted that there do seem to be some universals. Kroeber and Kluckhohn claimed that among its own group members, no culture could be found that accepts: (a) indiscriminate lying, suggesting that all societies value honesty; (b) stealing, such that all societies value rights of property ownership; (c) violence and suffering, suggesting that all societies value peaceful coexistence; and (d) incest, such that all societies restrict sexual intercourse to nonfamilial adults. However, what constitutes an offence can change over time. For example, it is only recently that domestic abuse has been defined as an issue warranting the intervention of the state, and for which legal remedies and sanctions, both criminal and civil, should be available (Laing et al., 2013). In spite of the prevalence of domestic abuse there are actually very few specific domestic abuse laws. What criminal laws do exist focus primarily on physical violence rather than the wider range of controlling and psychological behaviours that constitute the majority of domestic abuse.

Next, we have already discussed the mismatch between the experience of being a victim of domestic abuse and the number of recorded instances of domestic abuse. This can be for two main reasons – firstly, many instances of domestic abuse are never reported to the police. Data collected from victims show that 80% of the worst incidences of domestic violence are never reported to the police (Carmichael, 2008), and data collected from 22,000 16–59 year olds for the England and Wales Crime Survey indicate that only 31% of women and 18% of men who had experienced an incident of domestic violence (a combined rate of 24%) reported having told the police (Office of National Statistics, 2013). For those who did not report the abuse to the police, the most common reasons given were that the abuse was too trivial or not worth reporting (42%), it was a private, family matter and not the business of the police (34%) or the victim did not think the police could help (15%) (Smith et al., 2012).

The other main reason is that the police have to interpret an incident as firstly being about domestic abuse and then as a specific crime. For example, in Northern Ireland the police publish regular statistics about the number of incidents that police officers respond to that involve domestic abuse. During 2013–2014, this amounted to 27,628 incidents, but only 12,720 crimes were recorded as domestic abuse under the headings of 'violence against the person offences' (70% of the recorded crimes), 'theft and criminal damage' (28%), 'breach of non-molestation order' (0.7%) and 'all other offences' (0.5%) (Police Service of Northern Ireland, 2014). Even when the police record an incident as a crime, this does not automatically result in their undertaking an investigation or the matter proceeding to trial, and it is estimated that less than 5% of all instances of domestic abuse results in a prosecution (Devaney, 2014). In asking respondents what happened when they did report the issue, 18% of respondents reported that the police took no action, with perpetrators being warned in another 39% of instances. Perpetrators were arrested in 31% of cases, and only 12% of offenders were charged with an offence (Crown Prosecution Service, 2012).

In summary, using statistics to measure a phenomenon is actually quite difficult, and care needs to be taken with how we interpret and use statistics if we are unclear about what has been collected and in what way. That is not the same as saying that statistics are useless. Rather, we need to be careful about the conclusions we might draw based on statistics as we are rarely able to count or study all the cases of some social problem (e.g. the educational performance of looked-after children). Instead, researchers typically collect some data from a sample of cases and generalise from them. Generalisation involves some basic processes: the problem must be defined, a means of measurement determined and a sample that is representative of the population being studied must be chosen. These are elementary steps in social research. But even the most basic principles can be violated and, surprisingly often, it may not be noticed when this happens. So, in terms of looking at the educational attainment of children who are looked after, consideration needs to be given to how to define who is looked after and what is an educational outcome, and how we determine whether the outcome is good or not.

Summary

In this chapter, we have argued that social work and social work practice will be stronger as a consequence of our ability to engage with and understand numerical concepts and data. Numbers can illuminate the scale, scope and impact of social issues and inform how we respond in ways which are ethical, empowering and effective. Statistics and quantitative research complement the knowledge to be gained from the experiences of service users, the practice wisdom developed over time by colleagues and ourselves, and the wide array of qualitative research that social work and other academics have published. Therefore, learning how to read and interpret numerical information, underpinned by an understanding of how statistics have been calculated, can ensure that we are able to critically engage with discussions and debates on issues that affect the lives of our service users.

Critical Thinking Box

Read: Masson, H., Hackett, S., Phillips, J. and Balfe, M. (2015) Developmental markers of risk or vulnerability? Young females who sexually abuse – characteristics, backgrounds, behaviours and outcomes. *Child & Family Social Work*, 20(1), 19–29.

There is increased awareness of the sexual abuse of children. However, much of what we know and understand is based on the sexual abuse of children by adult males or male adolescents. We know less about the sexual abuse of children by young females. This article presents information on 24 young females aged 8–16 years who were referred to specialist services in England during the 1990s because of their abusive sexual behaviours. It details the characteristics, backgrounds and behaviours of the young females and compares these with the males in the total population studied and with findings from the limited international literature on young females who present with sexually harmful behaviour.

● Why are the findings from this study important?

● What are the similarities and differences in the age and gender of victims of the females compared to males in the study, and why is this important to understand?

● What other differences are there between the types of sexually harmful behaviour displayed by females and by males?

● What are the limitations of the sample size of this study?

Further resources

Thoburn, J., Robinson, J. and Anderson, B. (2012). *Returning Children Home from Public Care*. London: Social Care Institute for Excellence. Available at: www.scie.org.uk/publications/briefings/briefing42/ (accessed 15 October 2015).

Webber, M. (2011). *Evidence-based Policy and Practice in Mental Health Social Work*, 2nd ed. Exeter: Learning Matters.

3

WHO IS BEING STUDIED?

LEARNING OUTCOMES

By the end of this chapter you should be able to:

- Differentiate between a population and a sample
- Identify and define the different types of both probability and non-probability samples
- Assess the potential for bias in the ways that samples are selected
- Recognise the importance of representativeness and generalisability as key research concepts
- Justify the importance of careful selection of samples in order to promote anti-discriminatory practice

Introduction

Perhaps the most important question to ask of any study is – who is being studied? It is rarely possible to study everyone in the group you are interested in (e.g. all children in care; everyone with a particular disability), therefore researchers need to find a smaller group (known as a sample) who are representative of the larger group (the population). This gives rise to two very important questions:

- Who are researchers trying to study? (sample type)

- Who did they actually study? (response rate)

The key concern with sampling is whether it is possible to make a statistical inference from the sample to the population. In research terms we should differentiate between the definition of population in the general sense and the research sense. In a general sense the population is often understood as referring to everyone in society, whereas in research the population is more typically an object (such as individuals, households, communities) which shares the same characteristic as the issue we are interested in; for example, all young people in care. It is fundamental to being able to read and appraise a research study to be able to define the population that a study is interested in, and whether the sample is likely to be representative of the diversity of people within that population. If the sample is representative of the population then we can have greater confidence that we can generalise the findings from the sample of people studied to the entire population of people who are in a similar situation. This also allows us to use statistics to measure whether our findings are significant, and if so how confident we can be in drawing conclusions from the research. We will return to these concepts in later chapters.

It is important to remember that the issue of the representativeness of a sample of participants in a research study is not just a research question – it is also an issue of social justice. We need to know who might not have been involved in the study, and why not. For example, if research is conducted by postal survey into the levels of disability within a community in order to inform service development, it is highly likely that most people who are homeless will not be able to participate, even though there may be high levels of disability within this group. Without knowing their particular range of needs, services might not be developed in a way that meets them. They may have greater levels of certain types of disability that may have contributed to their homelessness, or been caused or exacerbated by the experience of being homeless.

Therefore understanding who is being studied and who might be potentially excluded is an important part of critically appraising research and using research findings to inform practice and policy.

Defining the sample

In order to be able to design a study a researcher must be able to define the population that they are interested in studying, and then to consider what the range of characteristics are within that population that should inform who is part of the sample. The ability to be able to draw conclusions from a sample and to then apply this to the whole population of interest is called generalisation. The ability to generalise findings from a study to a larger population contributes to the external validity of a study and increases the potential for a good study to be relied upon to inform practice and policy decisions.

A key stage in selecting a sample is to determine a sampling frame. This is a listing of all the units in the population from which the sample will be drawn – this could be individual people or places, such as residential units. For example, if we were interested in adult alcohol dependency it would be important that we are able to differentiate between the population of adults who use alcohol, those for whom their use of alcohol is problematic but who are not dependent, and those who are clinically dependent on alcohol. It is estimated that 9% of the population in England drink more than the recommended daily amounts of alcohol, with 18% of men and 12% of women having drunk heavily (at least twice the recommended limits) on at least one day in the previous week. The

NHS estimates that around 9% of men in the UK and 4% of UK women show signs of alcohol dependence. However, it is estimated that only 6.4% of dependent drinkers access treatment in the UK (Alcohol Concern, 2014). It can therefore be difficult to know exactly who fits within these different subgroups and whether there is a straightforward way of identifying everyone who fits into a particular subgroup. Without this knowledge it is more difficult to construct the sampling frame.

Exercise 3.1: Surveying alcohol use

Consider the example of adult alcohol dependency. You are interested in undertaking a survey of the levels of alcohol misuse within your community to inform service development:

- Who is your study population?

- Which community members might be more difficult to reach with a survey?

- What would you do to ensure that the survey was more inclusive of the entire range of individuals within the community?

Without being clear about these subgroups it would be possible that we might include people in a study that we did not intend to, or exclude people who should be included, and therefore our findings and the conclusions drawn would be compromised. There is therefore an important relationship between a research question, the population to whom the question applies and the sample of participants included in a research study.

The implications of bias for sampling

All research is prone to bias. In research terms, bias refers to a preference or predisposition to favour a particular outcome, with the result that the research conclusions are systematically distorted. While some research is intentionally distorted to present the findings that are most favourable to the researcher or a funder, most bias is unintentional. For example, interviewing parents of a child with a disability about their support needs might be partial if the research was only undertaken with parents who attended a focus group held in a day centre. Might parents without any support be able to attend?

In terms of sampling, bias simply means that those who are selected to be studied are not typical or representative of the larger population they have been chosen from, whether the bias is conscious or not. Bryman (2012) states that sampling bias can arise in three ways:

1   If a non-probability or non-random sampling method is used there is a possibility that human judgement will in some way mediate the recruitment and selection process. This has the potential to increase the likelihood that some members of a population have a greater likelihood of being selected than others. The use of random sampling, as described below, eliminates the potential for this form of bias.

2   If the sampling frame is not comprehensive, is inaccurate or is impaired in some other way, then the sample cannot claim to be representative of the population of interest, even if probability/random sampling has been used.

3   If some sample members decline to participate or cannot be contacted, then this may mean that those who do respond may not be representative of the wider population. While it may be possible to make allowances for some issues, for example stating to what degree the sample differs from the population in aspects such as age and gender, it is more difficult to state this for factors such as attitudes and experiences as there may not be a baseline for the entire population being studied.

For example, the Children's Commissioner for England completed a report into the experience of children who are sexually abused within familial situations (Children's Commissioner for England, 2015). There is a challenge in trying to establish how many children have experienced sexual abuse, as we do not know the population very well and there are issues in trying to make contact with children to survey them, even if we know who they might be (see appendix A of the Commissioner's report). We will now discuss these issues in greater depth.

Sample types

If the results of a study are to generalise to the intended population then the researcher must be careful about how the sample is selected. The optimal way of doing this is to identify the population and then draw a random sample from that population. In a random sample every individual in the population must have an equal chance of being selected for the study – this is sometimes referred to as probabilistic sampling. A study that uses a truly random sample allows for the greatest confidence in generalising from the research study to real life. In order to be able to draw a random sample it is necessary to know who is part of the population and to have a means of being able to contact them to seek their agreement to participation. Every unit in the population (such as a person, address or organisation) is assigned a unique number ranging from 1 to N (with N being the total population size). Random numbers between 1 and N are then drawn (typically using a random number generator available on most statistical software packages and some calculators) until the required sample size is achieved. This is called simple random sampling. In practice, though, this approach can be cumbersome and time consuming. An alternative approach that is simpler and more convenient is systematic random sampling. In this process every member of the population is assigned a number from 1 to N (with N being the total population size) in ascending order. The process then involves choosing a sampling interval and then selecting every n*th* case – for example, every fifth member of the population. The process is continued until the desired sample size is achieved.

However, being able to generate a completely random sample of partici-pants from the population of interest is far from straightforward, and often not possible. This can be for a variety of reasons. For example, we may be interested in better understanding the educational outcomes for children in public care. However, it may be impractical, due to cost, to undertake the research across the whole of the country. However, we also know that the backgrounds and situ-ations in which children come into care differ across the UK. Therefore if we only undertake the research in one part of the country it is more difficult to have confidence that the findings are equally applicable in another very different part of the UK.

Additionally, we might want to ensure that the diversity within a popula-tion is reflected within a sample – for example, ensuring that the gender and ethnicity of children in public care is represented, as well as the diversity of living arrangements. In such a case it may be appropriate to use a stratified sample (sometimes also known as a quota or proportional sample) to ensure that there are sufficient units of analysis (in our case children) that we can study and draw inferences from about the whole population. For example, there are over 80,000 children in public care in the UK of whom 12% are living in a residential unit rather than in family-based care arrangements. If we used a simple random sample of n = 1,000 we would expect to get 120 children living in residential care but, by chance, we could get fewer than that. We might then not have very large numbers of children who are living in residen-tial care who are female and of a particular ethnicity. If we stratify our sample we can do better. Stratification would mean that we identify the characteristics we are interested in (e.g. living arrangements, gender, ethnicity) and then decide how many individuals we want in each category. Once this is decided we can then randomly select potential participants from within these sub-groups, therefore still protecting the randomness within each subgroup but ensuring an overall sample that is more likely to be representative of the diver-sity within the population.

In practice, though, most research studies use a non-probability sample. This can be for a variety of reasons, such as not knowing who is part of the population of interest (e.g. all people who are substance dependent) or the costs associated with undertaking a study using a random sample who may be geographically dispersed. This does not mean that non-probability samples are not representative of the population. However, it does mean that non-probability samples cannot depend upon the rationale of probability theory. At least with a probabilistic (random) sample, we know the odds or probability that we have represented the population of interest well. We are able to estimate the confidence we can have in the inferences that we draw through the use of statistics. With non-probability samples, we may or may not represent the population well, and it will often be hard for us to know whether we have done so, and if we have, how well. In general, researchers using quantitative methods prefer probabilistic or random sampling methods over non-probabilistic ones, and consider them to be more accurate and rigorous. However, in applied social research there may be circumstances where it is not feasible, practical or theoretically sensible to do random sampling. Non-probability sampling methods can be divided into two broad types: convenience or purposive. Most sampling methods are purposive in nature (i.e. we choose to sample a group for a specific reason, such as we know they are likely to take part in the research, or to have something to tell us) because we usually approach the sampling problem with a specific plan in mind. The most important distinctions among these types of sampling methods are the ones between the different types of purposive sampling approaches.

The most straightforward form of non-random sampling is convenience sampling. This refers to studies where the researcher chooses participants based on their availability rather than their representativeness of the wider population that they are part of. For example, if we are interested in understanding the educational outcomes for children in public care it might be easiest to study all the young people living in a particular residential unit. While this will generate some information that might be useful, it is unlikely that the young people in one residential unit are representative of all young people living in residential care even within a single local authority, let alone all children in public care. Typically, convenience samples are used in many qualitative studies; for small-scale studies when time and finances are limited; or whenever a researcher might want to carry out some preliminary work to test some aspect of their research design ahead of a larger-scale study.

The other category of non-probabilistic sampling is purposive sampling. This can be very useful for situations where a researcher needs to reach a targeted sample quickly and where sampling for proportionality is not the primary concern. With a purposive sample, the researcher is likely to get the opinions of the target population but it is also likely to overweight subgroups in the population that are more readily accessible.

To deal with this last issue, researchers sometimes use non-proportional quota sampling. In this approach the minimum number of sampled units required in each category is specified. The researcher is not concerned with having numbers that match the proportions in the population. Instead, they simply want to have enough to assure that they will be able to talk about even small groups in the population. This method is the non-probabilistic version of stratified random sampling in that it is typically used to assure that smaller groups are adequately represented in the sample. Developing our previous example, this might involve ensuring we include children in care who are living in different types of arrangements (residential care; stranger foster care; kinship care; at home with parents) and ensuring that within each of these groups we have some boys and girls, and some children from different ethnic backgrounds. We might want to ensure that we have a minimum number of children who are in every subgroup rather than trying to match this to the proportions we know are in the care system.

Finally, many of the issues that social workers are interested in are often of a hidden or sensitive nature. In these cases it may not be possible to readily identify the population who share the characteristics of interest. In such instances snowball sampling may be appropriate. This approach begins by identifying someone who meets the criteria for inclusion in the study. They are then asked to recommend or recruit others who they may know who also meet the criteria for inclusion in the study. This can be a very useful approach for exploratory studies that are seeking to shed light on an issue without necessarily seeking claims to be representative of the wider population or definitive in the conclusions drawn. Without such approaches it may be very difficult to undertake research on some of the most marginalised groups in society, and therefore their needs and experiences would be less well understood.

'Research in practice' – outcomes for children in care

The UK government was interested to know whether the outcomes for children in care in England were affected by the types of family placement they lived in, and whether the types of family placement chosen for children might also be influenced by other factors such as their age upon entry to care and the reasons for the need for care.

A longitudinal study by Biehal and colleagues (2009) followed up children in England who were in foster care in 1998–1999 and who, three years later, were still settled in the same foster placement or had been adopted (either by a stranger or by their foster carer). The sample included 196 children who were surveyed by means of a postal questionnaire to their carers/adoptive parents and current/last social worker. In-depth interviews were also conducted with

37 children and their foster carers or adoptive parents. The study assessed the uses and outcomes of long-term foster care, adoption by carers and adoption by strangers, comparing:

- placement stability
- children's psychosocial functioning and educational progress
- planning for permanence, including factors which promote or inhibit the use of adoption
- the nature of contact with birth families
- children's and carers' perceptions of permanence, belonging and contact
- local policy on permanence for children in care.

The study provided valuable, comparative data on three alternative permanent placements which helped to guide policy and practice on planning for and supporting permanent placements and on improving outcomes for children in care.

Sample size

A common question in most social research relates to the number of partici-pants required to make a sample 'big enough'. While a larger sample size may ensure that findings are more accurate, it also means that the research is likely to be more costly and time consuming.

Depending on the nature of the research it may be that a certain minimum sample size is required in order to be able to undertake some meaningful and robust statistical analysis of the findings. For example, in evaluating whether an intervention works it is typical to have an effect size specified. In statistics, an effect size is a quantitative measure of the strength of a phenomenon. Reporting effect sizes is considered good practice when presenting empirical research find-ings in many fields of research. The reporting of effect sizes facilitates the inter-pretation of the substantive, as opposed to the statistical, significance of a research result, but it is dependent on the size of the sample and its representa-tiveness of the population being studied.

Before a sample size can be calculated, a few things about the target popula-tion and the sample need to be determined. The first of these relates to the size of the population of interest, although in many cases it may be that the popula-tion size is either unknown or an approximation. No sample will be perfect, so a researcher needs to decide how much error is permissible. The more important the decisions, the greater the onus on reducing the likelihood that the findings are attributable to chance and on preventing errors resulting in the sample not being sufficiently representative of the population. If the issue or population has been studied before, this prior information can be used to reduce the necessary sample size. This can be done by using our knowledge of the prior mean and variance estimates, and by stratifying the population to reduce variation within subgroups within the population.

Overall the sample size selected must make sense. This is where trade-offs usually occur. Researchers want to take enough observations to obtain reasonably precise estimates of the parameters of interest but also want to do this within a practical budget and timescale. The important thing is to quantify the risks associated with the chosen sample size, and for researchers to be explicit about this in the reporting of their findings.

Response/participation rates

Even when considerable care has been taken in constructing the sample to take part in the research, this means little if the response or participation rate is such that the sample is no longer representative of the population. Most social research involves the principle of autonomy, meaning that participants should ordinarily have the option of giving voluntary and informed consent to being directly involved in research (e.g. being interviewed or observed) or indirectly involved (e.g. their information, such as in case files). As such, it is likely that in almost all studies some people will choose not to participate for a wide range of issues including lack of time, lack of interest or even a fundamental opposition to the focus of the study. While researchers can do much to encourage potential participants to take part in research, such as explaining the importance of the research, ensuring that the demands of the research on time will be low, or through offering remuneration such as vouchers to recognise people's input, it is unlikely that most studies will get a 100% response rate. For studies with non-probabilistic samples, this is less important than in studies where a probabilistic sample is essential. A low response or participation rate can give rise to sampling bias if the non-response is unequal among the participants regarding exposure or outcome. Such bias is known as non-response bias.

The response or participation rate in research studies can be affected by a number of factors including the design of a study. For example, various studies have indicated that respondents are more likely to disclose sensitive information, such as experience of domestic violence, when screened using an audio computer-assisted self-interview where the research participant listens to an audio recording of the questions and enters their answer directly into a computer, rather than being interviewed face-to-face by a health care professional (Klevens et al., 2012).

A further issue that can affect participation/response rates involves, paradoxically, some of the safeguards that might be built into a research study to protect potential participants. While we will address ethical issues in greater depth in

Chapter 11, it is worth reflecting on the potential implications of undertaking ethical research on participation rates. For example, it is common for many forms of social research to involve the recruitment of participants through organisations providing support or services. These organisations can sometimes be called 'gatekeepers', as along with assisting in recruitment or providing access to data, they also can be involved in deciding who is approached to be involved, or whether certain types of information or data can be accessed (Punch, 2013). As Hayes and Devaney (2004, p. 329) note:

> It would be a perverse consequence if, in trying to protect the rights of vulnerable individuals, that their lived experiences were lost, and those responsible for formulating policy and delivering services knew less, rather than more, about the needs and views of the marginalized in society.

Exercise 3.2: Using routinely collected data

Social researchers are increasingly interested in making use of information that has been collected by organisations through their direct work with service users. This information may be stored in case files by social workers or on computer systems.

The analysis of secondary data (secondary meaning that it has an additional use to the primary reason it was collected in the first place) saves time that would otherwise be spent collecting data and, particularly in the case of quantitative data, typically means that larger and higher-quality databases can be accessed as this would usually be unrealistic for any individual researcher to collect on their own. In addition, it also allows for the analysis over time of social and economic change that would be impossible to study without conducting a new survey each time.

Example: A researcher wishes to study whether the characteristics of children subject to a child protection plan change over time. The researcher wishes to access social work case files on individual children to gather information about their demographics (such as gender and age), characteristics (such as who they live with) and circumstances (such as the reason for their need for a child protection plan).

Consider the following questions:

- Should the permission of service users be sought to allow a researcher to access the information held by an organisation about them for a research study?

- Would your answer change if the researcher only had information that was anonymised?

- What might be some of the implications for the robustness of the research if some information was withheld from secondary analysis because a service user or gatekeeper declined access to particular case files?

Sampling error

When there is an error in the findings from the research due to the differences between the sample of a study and the population being studied, this is referred to as a sampling error. This can arise in both probabilistic and non-probabilistic sampling. A non-sampling error is an error in the research findings due to a difference between the population and sample that arise either from inadequacies in the sampling approach, such as an inadequate sampling frame or non-response, or from such problems as poorly worded questions in a survey or a flaw in the analysis of data. Such errors are important for researchers to minimise, as they impact on the ability to generalise the findings from a study to the wider population that are the focus of the study. As a reader of research it is therefore important to be able to ascertain what steps a researcher has taken to reduce the likelihood of these types of error arising, and any limitations that they faced in sampling.

Other approaches to sampling

Some social research is interested in studying phenomena over time and then drawing conclusions from the data (Bryman, 2012). We might be interested in studying behaviours and looking at whether and how they change over time, and whether the nature and frequency of some types of behaviour can be altered by an intervention. For example, we could be interested to know whether older people who have dementia and who are living in residential care are more or less agitated at different times of the day, and whether this is related to the regime of the residential unit. We therefore might record incidents of agitated behaviour, and note what happened immediately preceding this. In this example the sample is the incident within a particular time frame (such as a 24-hour period). We can also observe and record in short periods of time – for example for five minutes once every hour. In this case we then note everything that is occurring during this five-minute period, which could include periods when the residents would not be agitated. We might want to know when residents are settled in order to be able to compare to the times when they are agitated. In this example the sample is the repeated observations within a particular time frame (e.g. over a 24-hour period). We can also observe and record over a longer time frame – in our example this could be a whole day of 24 hours, and do this at different times of the week or month to see, for example, whether the patterns at weekends or in winter differ from weekdays or summer. Finally, we might decide to time sample, making repeated observations at the same time over a longer period of time – for example, studying the residents every day at the same time (such as lunch time) over a week. Each of these approaches has a particular benefit, but also limitations – the key is to choose the approach best suited to answering the specific research question. We will explore this further in subsequent chapters.

Critical Thinking Box

Read: Blomberg, H., Kallio, J., Kroll, C. and Saarinen, A. (2015). Job stress among social workers: Determinants and attitude effects in the Nordic countries. *British Journal of Social Work*, 45(7), 2089–2105.

Blomberg and colleagues (2015) state that little is known about social workers' job stress in a comparative sense, and whether job stress might negatively affect their views of clients within the welfare system. The researchers sought to examine these issues on the basis of cross-sectional survey data collected from professional social workers in four Nordic countries that have similar welfare systems and where workers engage in similar tasks. The research team measured job stress using two indicators: workload and role conflicts. The results indicated frequent problems with job stress in all four countries, although they are especially pronounced in Finland. Social workers with limited work experience, as well as those working within the public sector, suffered the most, both from an extensive workload and from role conflicts. The findings also indicated that social workers' attitudes towards clients within the welfare system are to some extent related to their level of job stress.

The data used came from nationwide surveys among professional social workers in Sweden, Finland, Denmark and Norway. In Finland in autumn 2007, all social workers who were members of the Union of Professional Social Workers and had an email address (approximately 70% of the members) participated in the study. 1,299 of the 2,078 trade union members who received the electronic questionnaire completed it, resulting in a response rate of 62%. In Sweden, electronic questionnaires were also sent in the autumn of 2007 to randomly chosen members belonging to Akademikerforbundet SSR (The Union for Professionals, a trade union for university graduates with a degree in social science, behavioural science or social work): 2,809 out of the estimated 4,600 social workers who received the questionnaire completed it, resulting in a response rate of 61%. In Norway and Denmark, questionnaires were sent (in the spring of 2008) by mail to randomly chosen members of the Norwegian Union of Social Educators and Social Workers and the Danish Association of Social Workers, respectively, as it was not technically feasible to create an electronic survey: 1,200 members per country were sent questionnaires.

In Denmark, 743 trade union members completed the questionnaire, whereas in Norway 703 members completed it, resulting in response rates of 62% and 59%, respectively. The majority of professional social workers in Denmark and Norway are members of the union in their own country.

- What additional information might assist you to make a judgement about whether the sample chosen to be surveyed was representative of social workers in each of the countries?

- What additional information might assist you to make a judgement about whether the response rate of the survey would support the generalisation of findings to the whole social work profession in each country?

Summary

In summary, the importance of understanding how a sample has been selected and who has responded needs to be understood in order to make an informed judgement about how representative the sample is of the population being studied, and therefore how robust the findings are likely to be. The way a sample is chosen can increase or lessen the likelihood of bias in the recruitment and selection of research participants, but it is also important to understand who has responded to the invitation to take part in the research, and who has declined. In critically appraising a research study, understanding the characteristics of the sample and its similarity or difference to the population of interest allows a reader to make a more informed decision about whether the research findings have the potential to be generalised.

Further resources

Bryman, A. (2012). *Social Research Methods,* 4th ed. Oxford: Oxford University Press. (See Chapter 8 – Sampling.)

Research Methods Knowledge Base [online]. Available at: www.socialresearch methods.net/kb/ (accessed 15 October 2015).

4

WHAT IS BEING STUDIED?

LEARNING OUTCOMES

By the end of this chapter you should be able to:

- Define a variable
- Describe reliability and validity and identify their importance in quantitative research
- Evaluate the quality of quantitative research based on knowledge of reliability and validity
- Assess the strengths and limitations of validated and standardised instruments for research and practice purposes

Introduction

In the previous chapter we considered who is being studied – the 'sample'. This chapter examines what is being studied. In quantitative research the 'whats' are known as variables. A variable is simply something that can be measured, and that varies. Quantitative research involves examining the relationship between variables. For instance, gender can be assigned a number (say 1 for male and 2 for female) and so can height (say 170 centimetres). So it is relatively straightforward to test in any given sample whether there is a difference in the height of men and women. It is also possible to say what the size of this difference is on average and to describe it in a variety of other ways (which are explored in Chapters 8, 9 and 10).

Of course, it is not usually of interest to social workers to explore the differences in height between men and women. Yet variables allow us to explore things that are likely to be important to social workers. For instance, instead of the relationship between gender and height we might want to explore the relationship between gender and other variables. This would allow us to investigate questions such as:

- Are women more likely to be depressed?

- Do boys suffer more long-term harm from child abuse?

- Are men more likely to be diagnosed with schizophrenia?

- Do women or men benefit more from counselling for alcohol problems?

These are potentially interesting questions, but quantitative analysis of the relationships between variables allows us to ask perhaps even more interesting and relevant questions for social work. For instance:

- Women are in fact more likely to experience depression (see Brown and Harris, 1978 and much subsequent research) but what are the factors that are linked to this that may interact with gender? For instance, what is the impact of caring for children? Social class? Isolation? The quantitative literature provides a wealth of evidence about such issues.

- It is possible that boys are more likely to suffer long-term harm from abuse. There is a relatively strong body of evidence suggesting that girls tend to be more resilient when exposed to a variety of potentially difficult childhood experiences, from divorce to serious alcohol or drug problems in parents (Velleman and Orford, 1999; Forrester and Harwin, 2008). Further study has allowed researchers to unpack some of the potential reasons for this, including girls doing better at school and being more likely to share problems with friends and a tendency for boys to 'act out' while girls internalise low self-esteem and emotional trauma. As a result it is possible that the problems of boys are more visible, because they can cause disruption in classes or neighbourhoods while the harm that girls experience is private and therefore not picked up in research studies (Overbeek and Andershed, 2011). This example identifies some of the complexity involved in developing and using variables in a field like social work – and is explored in more detail below.

- Men are more likely to be diagnosed with schizophrenia, but quantitative research can also identify that there are differences between men and women diagnosed with schizophrenia. For instance, women tend to be older when diagnosed and the symptoms tend to be more severe in men (Dickerson, 2007).

- In general, men and women seem equally likely to benefit from counselling for alcohol problems. However, the picture is more complex than it may seem because women seem to experience significantly more barriers to treatment. In particular, looking after children makes accessing treatments – and particularly residential treatments – more difficult for women because women do most of the childcare in society (Green, 2006).

These are all examples of quantitative research that explores relationships between two or more variables. The reason we do this is because it allows us to have a deeper and more nuanced understanding of important social work issues. By the end of this chapter, you should not only understand why variables and the measurement of variables is potentially helpful for research, but also how you might use such approaches in your practice. After all, a key element of social work is assessment, and the process of developing and measuring variables has much to teach us about assessment. Potentially even more important than knowing about how variables are created, we hope you will develop a critical understanding of the limits of any variable.

Some things are relatively simple to measure. For instance, people's height is comparatively easy to measure. Yet few things are that straightforward. We have used the example of 'gender' so far in introducing variables, and treated it as a dichotomous variable (i.e. people are either male or female). This is not the whole picture. People can move from one gender to another, or feel uncomfortable with the gender they find themselves to be. On this basis, campaigners have argued that surveys should offer more categories than simply male or female. This is not yet the case in the UK, though in the 2011 Indian Census an 'Other' category was added to gender (Times of India, 2 February 2011).

The point here is that even for something such as gender, measurement may not be as straightforward as it might first appear. Imagine how much more difficult this can be with complex variables we often want to measure. For instance, in the examples above research measured the following variables:

- depression, social class, isolation and caring for children;

- child abuse and long-term harm;

- schizophrenia and the severity of symptoms associated with it;

- alcohol problems and whether alcohol counselling reduces alcohol-related problems.

These are important things to measure. In this chapter we outline how researchers can approach measuring things that are important but that may be difficult to measure. A particular focus is the importance of developing measures that are reliable (for instance, they get the same score when different people measure the same thing) and that are valid (in particular, they successfully measure the thing you really want to measure). A critical appreciation of research instruments with reliability and validity is then provided which will also introduce how you might use research instruments in your everyday practice.

'Research in practice' – stress and anxiety in newly qualified social workers

As in most chapters, we will illustrate the points made through examination of a piece of social work research. For this chapter we explore a complex piece of research aimed at evaluating a new approach to supporting newly qualified social workers (NQSWs) in England (Carpenter et al., 2011). For this chapter, we look at one element of this study, namely how stressed and anxious NQSWs were.

Finding out how stressed NQSWs are, and whether this is affecting their emotional and mental well-being, is an important question. Indeed, measuring the levels of stress and anxiety in child and family social work has become a key element in several studies, with increasing recognition that workers appear to be very stressed. This is likely to be linked to the high levels of 'burn-out' identified in social workers, which in turn probably contributes to the high turnover of staff in the area of child protection. Yet while this is an important area to study, how can we measure how stressed or anxious somebody is?

One way might be to ask people how stressed they feel, for instance on a scale from one to five. A problem with this approach is that we cannot be sure that these numbers actually mean anything. If I say I am at 'three' and you say you are at 'two', perhaps your understanding of 'three' is what I mean by a 'two'. Stress and anxiety are important concepts, yet they are difficult to turn into measures that are reliable (for instance, ensuring that when you and I give a score they mean roughly the same thing) and valid (meaning that the score is genuinely measuring the thing we want measured – in this case stress and anxiety, rather than, for instance, general happiness).

To address this, Carpenter and colleagues applied a commonly used measure called the General Health Questionnaire. There are longer and shorter versions of this measure, differentiated by the number of questions. Carpenter and colleagues used the GHQ-12, so-called because it features 12 questions. The GHQ-12 is one of the most widely used research instruments in psychology or psychiatry. In this chapter we use it to illustrate the properties needed in a research instrument; we then constructively critique it before returning to its use by Carpenter and others to help us understand the stresses and strains social workers find themselves under.

Basic concepts: reliability, validity and standardised instruments

Many things are relatively straightforward to measure or to count; for instance, the number of people using a service, the time it takes from referral to somebody being seen or the money spent on a new day centre. Even measuring such apparently straightforward things requires agreement on definitions – for instance, does popping in for a piece of advice count as 'using' a service? Equally, money spent on a new centre may or may not include some benefits provided in kind such as a building formerly used for some other purpose. Given this, as mentioned earlier, how do we measure important things that are not so easy to measure, such as levels of stress and anxiety, or levels of behavioural problems?

Quantitative research involves identifying attributes of an individual (or an organisation or other entity) and operationalising them. The operationalisation of an attribute is a variable. So, for instance, the following might be attributes of individuals. For each, think how you might operationalise it into a variable:

- Height

- Intelligence

- Beauty

- Anxiety

Height is relatively easy to measure, using centimetres. Intelligence requires some agreement about what intelligence is, and fierce debate continues to rage on this issue. The degree to which one exhibits the signs of intelligence can then be tested (such measures are called intelligence quotient or IQ tests). Beauty is perhaps even harder to 'measure', though researchers have tried to do so by having multiple raters see if they agree (and there is apparently relatively high level of agreement). Finally, what about anxiety? How might we operationalise this as a variable so that we could see how stressed and anxious NQSWs are?

To do this with credibility we need to address two core issues. We need to develop a measure (and here we are talking about a series of questions) that is reliable and valid. Reliability and validity are central concepts in quantitative research.

Reliability

There are in fact several types of reliability, and the type of reliability that is important may vary depending on the nature of the attribute you are measuring. Table 4.1 describes the two main types of reliability in social work research. A key type of reliability is inter-rater reliability. This is the degree to which different people using a particular measure agree. This is often a foundation for using a variable at all. For instance, imagine you and your friend want to look at the relationship between height and gender but you discover that when you measure people you get very different heights to when your friend measures people. This would then make it difficult to be confident that you had measured correctly.

There are some attributes that are relatively easy to get agreement around. For instance, if we decide to measure height using a measuring tape we would tend to find a relatively high level of agreement, though we would not find complete agreement. For all sorts of reasons – from people slouching to those

Table 4.1 Types of reliability

Type of reliability	Description
Inter-rater reliability	The degree to which two different people rating something give the same score. This is not an issue for some measures (for instance a questionnaire such as the GHQ-12) but can be very important for other measures (for instance, where different observers are coding for something).
Test-retest reliability	This is the degree to which multiple tests of something are consistent. Again the degree to which test-retest reliability is important will depend on the nature of the attribute being measured. We think of intelligence as something relatively consistent, so high levels of test-retest reliability are expected of IQ tests. Stress may vary over time so we would not perhaps test for this.

doing the measuring using the tape in different ways – we usually find some level of variation. This can be reduced by training or protocols (which set out how measuring should be done) or by introducing a new technology to ensure accuracy. For lots of other potential variables, it is, in fact, very difficult to get agreement on what is being observed. To take an example from the field of education, Robert Coe examined ratings of the quality of observed lessons using the Ofsted framework (lessons were rated 'outstanding', 'good', 'adequate' or 'inadequate'). Even when the observation was carried out by experienced teachers – who each thought they knew what they were looking for – the level of actual agreement was very low. For instance, Coe's analysis suggested that if one observer rated a lesson 'inadequate' there was a 96% chance that a second one would *not* agree (Coe, 2014). This type of finding about reliability is really important; it contributed to Ofsted stopping the rating of individual lessons.

It is worth reflecting on the implications of this research finding for social work. First of all, if observation of lessons is so unreliable, how reliable do we feel that the following might be?

- the rating of a direct observation by a practice educator;
- the marking of an essay;
- an Ofsted inspection of children's services;
- your assessment of risk or need for an individual or family.

Understanding reliability is not simply about having a better insight into research. Once we realise how much we vary in how we operationalise concepts, this then has major implications for our understanding of practice and policy.

It is also worth thinking about how reliable measures are in social work studies. (Top tip: if you have to do a critical analysis of research it is always worth thinking about how reliable the coding of variables might be.) There are many social work studies that make crucial decisions about important variables – such as whether a child has suffered harm or been abused, whether an outcome was positive or not – without providing evidence on the reliability with which such important and difficult judgements are made. If you find such a study, treat it with particular caution!

Inter-rater reliability is not the only type of reliability. One other is worth considering: test-retest reliability. This is simply the extent to which the same 'thing' measured over time remains the same. A key issue here is whether one might expect the variable to remain the same. For instance, one would be suspicious of a measure of height that seemed very different over a year for adults (and equally suspicious of one that did not show variation for children). So, the type of variation one might expect to find might influence the level of test-retest reliability one might hope to see. For instance, would one expect high or low test-retest reliability for: intelligence? Anxiety? Gender?

There are some other types of reliability mentioned in research, but for the vast majority of purposes it is inter-rater reliability that is important. For a smaller proportion it may be test-retest reliability.

Validity

Reliability is a necessary ingredient for a quantitative variable, but it is not sufficient on its own. The validity of a measure is more complicated and probably ultimately more important than its reliability, though you cannot have a valid measure that is not reliable! Or, put another way, reliability is like the foundations of the building, while validity is the building itself. So what is 'validity'? Validity is the degree to which the variable is capturing the attribute it aims to operationalise. In plain language: does this capture the thing you want to measure?

This is a complex issue to explore, because there are different senses in which a measure may be 'valid'. Table 4.2 provides descriptions of different types of validity, with examples of how they might apply to IQ tests. IQ tests are a helpful example, not only because IQ testing is something more social workers will come across in practice, but also because there has been more testing of 'intelligence' than anything else, and it therefore provides a wealth of insights into the opportunities and the potential pitfalls involved in developing valid and reliable measures.

To further complicate matters, we need to think about the validity not only of individual variables but also of whole research studies. This is because the same questions apply to both, namely to what degree are they capturing the things they wish to capture. Here we consider validity of variables, or the instruments we develop to measure attributes, while the validity of study designs is considered in Chapters 5 and 6.

Table 4.2 Types of validity in measuring variables

Type of validity	Description	For instance (applied to IQ tests)
Face validity	Does this *seem* like a credible measure? For instance, do the questions in a questionnaire seem likely to be related to the attribute they aim to measure?	On the face of it do the questions in an IQ test seem likely to relate to intelligence?
Content validity	Does the operationalisation capture the range of the attribute? Measures that do not have sufficient variation, or do not include key elements of the attribute to be studied, lack content validity.	Do experts agree that the key areas of 'intelligence' are captured in this test?
Criterion validity	The degree to which the variable correlates with other measures relevant to the attribute. These can be either predictive or concurrent tests of criterion validity (see below).	(See below, under concurrent validity and predictive validity.)
Concurrent validity	A test of criterion validity that compares a measure with another established measure for an attribute.	For instance, does a new, short IQ test correlate well with a longer one that has established validity?
Predictive validity	A test of criterion validity that establishes that the measure predicts a later event or score that theory would suggest it should predict.	Do scores on IQ tests predict the sort of things we think intelligent people will do (e.g. reach higher levels of achievement, command higher salaries) or those with less intelligence may struggle with (e.g. obtaining or retaining a job)? See commentary for discussion.

The weakest and least important form of validity is 'face' validity. This is the degree to which questions or other measures seem likely to measure the variable they aim to measure. Face validity is often the starting point for developing measures in research, but it is little more than that. What is needed for robust research is evidence that what appears likely to be valid actually is. For this, more complex forms of validity are needed.

Content validity examines the internal coherence and usefulness of a measure. One way to explore content validity is by looking at the pattern of responses to a questionnaire or a categorisation scheme. A variable that found that everyone being studied was in the same category, or one where some categories were constantly used and others not used at all, would probably require revision. For instance, the government returns for children's services have eight categories for 'reason for involvement', but the fact that more than 75% of all cases come under one category (abuse and neglect) immediately makes the eight-category approach questionable. In simple terms measures or categories should capture most of the relevant information for the attribute being studied. If everyone receives a very similar score, or most people are categorised in the same way or if a high proportion of instances are defined as 'other' and do not fit the typology being developed then this would call into question the content validity of the variable. At a more general level content validity can be tested to establish the degree to which questions within a questionnaire or other measure are related to one another.

The questions in a valid measure will tend to agree with one another. This can be quite a complex area, with specialist researchers focusing on developing measures that have not just final scores but also sub-scales within the question-naire. One example might be IQ tests. IQ tests aim to measure something we call 'intelligence'. They typically have sub-scales that look at verbal reasoning, numerical reasoning and other areas such as spatial reasoning. Validity testing for such a measure requires a process of testing out whether individual ques-tions (a) relate to the overall construct being measured (in this case the score in the IQ test) and (b) whether they relate to other measures within a sub-scale. If a question does not relate strongly to the other questions then it is unlikely it is a good measure of the thing being measured. For instance, one might put the question 'How many uses can you think of for a brick?' into an IQ test. If it relates weakly to the other questions then it is probably actually measuring something different. In such a case, either the question needs to be dropped (for instance, perhaps it measures creativity rather than intelligence) or the whole instrument needs to be adapted (for instance, adding a 'creativity' sub-scale or even replacing much of conventional IQ testing with more of a measure focused on creativity).

To address such issues there are statistical procedures that explore the inter-nal validity of measures, by which we mean the degree to which questions agree with one another and the extent to which overall measures have discern-ibly different components. Questionnaires that have been through this process of psychometric development are more robust, as unhelpful or poorly designed questions that do not relate well to the other questions will be removed.

The internal validity of a measure is important, but the ultimate test is whether it relates to other variables in the real world. This is known as criterion validity, and has two main elements: concurrent validity and predictive validity. Put simply, criterion validity answers the following question: does a score on a measure predict or relate to the sort of things you might expect it to? The ulti-mate test for any measure is that it is linked to other variables in meaningful ways. IQ tests are a good example. How can one test whether scores on verbal reasoning or spatial awareness are signs of 'intelligence'? The simple answer is by seeing whether they predict the types of things that we associate with intelligence. There is thus a large literature that finds that scores on IQ tests are related to levels of educational achievement, salaries or whether people are in employment, which in turn is used to justify the use of IQ tests. However, it is worth noting that this is a very complex literature. IQ test scores have increased with each generation. They also appear to disadvantage some groups and their relationship with achievement is complex – many high achievers do not appear to show high IQ as children. Some of the evidence is far from complete: for instance, class is more important than IQ in predicting future salary. It is likely that hard work is more important than simply natural ability, though this is very difficult to research.

In social work we are usually working with variables that are relatively hard to measure. For instance, the emotional welfare and behavioural problems of children or the level of stress and anxiety people are experiencing. How do measures for such 'things' establish the validity of the measures? One example is the Strengths and Difficulties Questionnaire (SDQ). The SDQ asks questions about a child's behaviour and emotions. It consists of five sub-scales (emotional, conduct, hyperactivity, peer relationships and prosocial behaviour). The scores on the SDQ have been extensively validated by seeing whether they predict (or correlate with) other measures and behaviour or other measurable events. For instance, high scores on SDQ are closely linked to independent clinical judgements (Goodman and Goodman, 2011). Furthermore, scores predict whether children will get in trouble at school, be referred to Community Adolescent Mental Health Services or receive a conviction (see the Youth in Mind website (2012) for a summary of research and a range of references). In fact, taken as a whole the validation suggests that the SDQ is very good at identifying children who may be at risk of problems relating to their emotional welfare or behavioural problems. This is a crucial form of external validation.

Critical Thinking Box

Read: Carpenter, J., Patsios, D., Wood, M., Shardlow, S., Blewett, J., Platt, D., Scholar, H., Haines, C., Tunstill, J. and Wong C. (2011) *Newly Qualified Social Worker Programme Evaluation Report on the Second Year (2009–10)*. London: Department for Education.

As noted above, Carpenter et al. (2011) were interested in the level of stress and potential burn-out in newly qualified social workers (NQSWs). To measure this they used the GHQ-12. Knowing what we know now about reliability and validity, how might we think critically about the positives and negatives in the use of this measure?

The GHQ-12 has been used extensively in research with a very wide variety of populations. Scores on the GHQ-12 can be expressed either as an average number in a population or as a percentage who might be considered to be 'at risk' of developing clinically significant symptoms. The fact that it has been used in a lot of different studies means that findings can be compared. This is useful and interesting in its own right. The shorter version of the GHQ-12 has been found to correlate fairly well with longer versions (concurrent validity), and these have strong evidence that they predict likely problems fairly well (predictive validity). The GHQ-12 has been less thoroughly tested but it does seem relatively good at identifying people at high risk of anxiety or related problems that may require treatment.

On the other hand, the GHQ-12 is very sensitive to current mood. Any given individual can get different scores if they complete it at different times (having done so, this author can vouch for the wide range of responses that are possible). This is deliberate: the coding scheme asks people to consider whether they are experiencing issues such as poor sleep more or less often than not. It is therefore very sensitive to change. As such, the GHQ-12 is not particularly useful for identifying level of stress for any given individual. However, it is reasonable to use it to measure levels of anxiety/social phobia in a population.

Carpenter et al. refer to the GHQ as a measure of 'stress'. Interestingly, that is not strictly what the GHQ measures. In fact, it is a tool 'to detect those likely to have or be at risk of developing psychiatric disorders; it is a measure of the common mental health problems/ domains of depression, anxiety, somatic symptoms and social withdrawal' (Jackson, 2007). As such, Carpenter and colleagues, along with many others, are using the GHQ to identify when stress seems to be leading to problems. Of course, some people develop mental health problems without being under stress, while others do not despite being under enormous levels of stress. Carpenter et al. are probably wholly justified in considering overall levels of risk of depression/anxiety as an indicator of level of stress within a population; however, this is worth considering in analysing the validity of the measure they use.

Carpenter and colleagues compared the GHQ-12 scores of new social workers in their first year of employment for three cohorts of workers. They found that about a third had scores at the clinically 'at risk' level at the start of their new job but that this had risen significantly in all three cohorts, with the highest proportion being 40%. This finding highlights the very high proportion of workers experiencing high levels of anxiety/ stress. However, it needs to be seen in context: almost a fifth of the general population are identified as 'at risk' by the GHQ-12, and one might expect higher levels of anxiety in workers setting out to do local authority child and family social work.

Validated instruments and social work practice

Validated instruments – also called standardised instruments – have been developed to provide reliable measures in relation to specific issues. Scores obtained using them have been shown to predict important outcomes. They are therefore crucially important tools for quantitative research, as well as being possible aids for social work practice. For both research and practice they essentially serve two functions. The first is that they can allow us to compare how serious a particular issue is compared to the general population. For instance, a score on the SDQ or the GHQ-12 allows us to ascertain whether the child or adult concerned has a behavioural problem or level of anxiety that puts them at high risk of serious problems (this is the sense in which they are 'standardised' – their scores can be compared to that found in larger samples, and often the general population). In research this can be useful in describing a sample: in practice, using a validated research instrument in an assessment would allow a worker to support (or perhaps challenge) their own judgement, for instance by finding that an individual's GHQ score suggested they were currently highly anxious and 'stressed'.

A second use is to compare change over time. For research this is particularly important for evaluative research. For instance, if one runs a training programme to help social workers manage the stress of the job how can one know whether it has worked? Asking people is fine – but people tend to be positive about training they have done. The GHQ-12 given out before and after the training would provide some more robust evidence on whether the stress of workers was reduced by training.

The same principle applies to practice, and it has two obvious applications. First, have I made a difference? One way of measuring this is to use an appropriate standardised measure. For instance, if you are working to reduce a child's challenging behaviour, the SDQ could be completed before and after the work to see whether parents or other carers, the young person and possibly teachers see a difference. A second practical application of validated and standardised measures is to measure capacity to change. Harnett (2007) set out a detailed approach to this, and his approach has recently been identified as a model for good practice by Ward et al. (2014). In summary, the area where change needs to be assessed is identified, a standardised instrument appropriate for that area is administered and it is administered again at the end of an agreed time period.

Exercise 4.1: Validated research instruments in practice

There have been calls for social workers to use standardised questionnaires more in their work for at least 40 years (Goldberg and Warburton, 1979). Yet to date social workers have shown considerable reluctance to do so. One attempt to include instruments came with the launch of the Assessment Framework. The framework came with supporting materials, including access to various standardised instruments that were suggested as likely to be helpful for workers. The questionnaires were:

1. Strengths and Difficulties Questionnaires

2. The Parenting Daily Hassle Scale

3. Home Conditions Scale

4. Adult Well-being Scale

▶

5. The Adolescent Well-being Scale

6. The Recent Life Events Questionnaire

7. The Family Activity Scale

8. The Alcohol Scale

These are all still freely available (see 'Further resources' at end of this chapter). Have a look at them and then consider:

● Why, in general, do you think psychologists often use such instruments but social workers rarely do?

● Do you think these reasons are good reasons for not using them?

● How might you use them in your practice?

Exercise 4.2: Screening for alcohol problems – are you at risk of having an alcohol problem?

One of the instruments provided for child and family social workers as part of the materials accompanying the Assessment Framework was the AUDIT. This is on the face of it surprising – the AUDIT is in fact a screening tool for risk of alcohol-related problems. It is unlikely that workers would be using it for this purpose in child and family social work. It also relies on honest answers. It is therefore far more widely used by health professionals to help individuals identify whether their drinking may be at a level likely to cause them or others problems.

To complete the AUDIT you need to know what a 'standard drink' is (see DrinkLess, 2015) – but it is approximately equivalent to the smallest drink of a particular type, for example a small glass of wine, half a pint of beer or a single shot of spirits). If you know this you can complete the AUDIT yourself in two minutes online:

http://patient.info/doctor/alcohol-use-disorders-identification-test-audit

You can compare your result with the general population and identify whether you should take any further action (see Babor et al., 2001, particularly p. 22).

Questions to ask yourself:

● How easy or difficult was this process?

● Would it provide you or others with useful information about alcohol use?

● What are the pros and cons of this way of exploring alcohol use?

Summary

This chapter has focused on how variables are constructed. The importance of reliability and validity in developing and using measures has been reviewed and some of the key elements of each concept have been explored. The importance of thinking about reliability and validity when critically evaluating research was then illustrated in relation to some recent studies. The application of validated instruments into everyday social work practice was then explored.

Further resources

The instruments accompanying the Assessment Framework in England are available at: www.teescpp.org.uk/Websites/safeguarding/files/Content/1828003/Scales%20 and%20questionnaires.pdf (accessed 2 August 2016).

Campbell, A., Taylor, B. and McGlade, A. (2016). *Research Design in Social Work*. London: Sage Publications.

5

HOW TO DESCRIBE ISSUES USING NUMBERS

LEARNING OUTCOMES

By the end of this chapter you should be able to:

- Identify the key elements and principles for descriptive quantitative research that measures the extent or severity of an issue
- Explain how routine information is gathered by agencies and assess its strengths and limitations for research purposes
- Assess the contribution that questionnaires can make, and identify some important considerations in questionnaire design
- Appraise the contribution that repeat measures over time can make for improving our understanding of social issues

Introduction

This chapter builds on the description of key concepts such as reliability and validity to consider how quantitative data can be used to describe things in practice. This might include research questions such as how common a particular issue is or how serious a particular problem tends to be. The chapter covers in particular questionnaires and routine data as sources for quantitative research. Existing data sets are covered in Chapter 12. The chapter begins by considering routine information gathered by social work and social care agencies and its strengths and limitations for research purposes. This discussion is illustrated with examples from government sources to illustrate the political importance of a critical understanding of routine data collection in social work. The chapter then turns to an exploration of the contribution that questionnaires can make, and an understanding of some basic issues in questionnaire design with examples from recent social work research studies. The information is intended to help students who may wish to use questionnaires in small-scale primary research as well as those wishing to critique them.

Introduction to descriptive research using numbers

Up to now a range of important methodological considerations, such as sampling, reliability and validity, have been considered in relation to quantitative research. The next few chapters turn to consider how quantitative research can help us understand the world better by applying these principles in different types of research study. As such, this chapter provides something of a bridge between the consideration of key concepts and the application of these concepts in different types of research design. The focus of this chapter is therefore descriptive quantitative research. This will usually be research that considers:

- What is the *extent* of a particular issue? For instance, how many people are affected by an issue such as depression or physical abuse?

- How *serious* is the issue? For instance, how seriously does an issue such as depression or physical abuse affect people?

These are often important questions – as illustrated in this chapter. It is therefore important to have a critical appreciation of the ways in which the fundamental principles of good research design can be applied in such studies. This chapter therefore provides an opportunity to explore the application of principles of reliability, validity and sampling (outlined in Chapters 3 and 4) to descriptive research. However, in practice most quantitative research looks at relationships. This in essence takes descriptions of different samples or the same sample over time to say interesting things, for instance about the relationship between different variables (e.g. does poverty make it more likely that an adult will experience depression?) or the same variable over time (e.g. do people feel better after being allocated a social worker or attending a particular service?). Most of the rest of the book is concerned with how such comparisons can provide important information. For instance, in the next chapter evaluative research designs are considered. These all essentially involve comparative descriptions; in other words, they apply the types of methods outlined in this chapter to different samples or the same sample over time. The considerations in this chapter provide the first step for these relational or comparative elements of quantitative analysis.

Two types of descriptive study resource are focused on. The first type to be considered is information gathered as part of normal service delivery – which we call 'routine' data, in the sense that they are gathered by services as part of their everyday service delivery. The example of 'Adoption Scorecards' is used to illustrate the strengths and limitations of such an approach, and the ways in which an understanding of quantitative research can help provide a critical appreciation of such data. Questionnaires are then introduced. Key practical considerations in designing and developing questionnaires are outlined and illustrated. Ways of making them more robust are considered, including the return of reliability and validity; triangulation; and mixed methods. Panel surveys and other large-scale data collection approaches are introduced, but these are discussed further in Chapter 12.

'Research in practice' – Adoption Scorecards

Adoption Scorecards are a summary of quantitative data collected and released by the government in relation to adoption performance for different local authorities. They provide a good case study because they illustrate:

- the political and policy importance of routinely collected data in research;
- the contribution that an understanding of validity and reliability can make to critiquing and understanding such measures;
- the potential that such data may have for being a focus or starting point for research undertaken by students or academics.

Since 2010 the UK government has collated information provided by local authorities in England that relates to adoption and publicly presented it as a 'scorecard'. This is explicitly part of a broader programme of reforms aimed to increase the use of adoption and help support better outcomes for children and families where there is an adoption. A key aim is to reduce the time that it takes for children to be adopted. Here we unpick one relatively recent 'scorecard', namely that for 2011, because the findings made national headlines and proved very influential (Department for Education, 2011). The 'scorecard' presented information on the average for a local authority in relation to:

- the time from a child entering care to entering their adoptive placement;
- the time from a full Care Order to placement for adoption;
- the proportion taking longer than 21 months.

In addition, a number of other factors were presented, including the number of children awaiting adoption, the proportion from black or minority groups and the time it took for prospective adopters to be approved.

From a research point of view, how reliable and valid is this data? On the face of it, unless there are inaccuracies in data collection or recording, one would expect the data to be reliable: the numbers and timescales being reported on are relatively objective data, and reliability should therefore be comparatively easy to achieve. Validity is more complicated. Again, on the face of it the data may be 'valid' – in that they do report on the numbers of children adopted and the timescales they are experiencing. However, are these the outcomes that scorecards are ultimately interested in? The answer to this is 'no'. The ultimate focus of children's services is the welfare and safety of children. Swift adoption is argued to be a means to that end. Yet removing a baby at birth, placing the child for adoption and swiftly concluding care proceedings would not always be the best thing for that child. Often good practice would involve working with birth parents to help resolve issues and allow children to remain with or return to them. The 1989 Children Act identifies that birth families should always be the first choice in thinking about where a child should live. Even when birth parents cannot care for a child, members of the extended family may be the best option and should be the next option considered. In fact, child and family social workers have to balance a complex variety of considerations in making decisions about adoption. These include:

- What level of risk is unacceptable?

- How much effort should be put into helping children remain with parents – or with the wider family? And how long should such effort be sustained for?

- Is adoption the best choice for children? For instance, for an older child there may be a difficult decision to be made about whether to try for adoption or long-term fostering. For a sibling group, there may be a decision about whether to look for a placement for all the children together or whether to split them up to allow a swifter identification of families for them.

There are undoubtedly unacceptable reasons for adoption taking a long time. These can include drift in planning and a lack of decisiveness in decision making. The Adoption Scorecards attempt to influence local authority practice by making public potential problems such as these. However, a problem is that there may be legitimate reasons for adoptions taking longer on average. The Adoption Scorecard of 2011 provides a good example of this, and an excellent interactive resource on the results is provided by *The Guardian* (Rogers, 2011). The local authority with the highest average wait to adoption – of 33 months – was Hackney. Hackney had recently been identified as an example of good practice, pioneering the Reclaiming Social Work model of systemic practice in small teams (Munro, 2011). The then Director of Children's Services in Hackney, Alan Woods, provided a strong rebuttal of any accusations that Hackney children were experiencing unacceptable delay (BBC News, 2012). He argued that:

- far fewer children were adopted in Hackney than comparable local authorities in large part because the Reclaiming Social Work model had proved so successful in keeping children at home by helping families;

- where children could not be kept at home they often had a more challenging profile than in other authorities. For instance, there were very few babies placed for adoption;

- furthermore, he suggested that in Hackney they made an effort to find adoptive families for 'hard to place' children that other authorities might not even try to place for adoption. A high proportion of their adoptions were in fact older children or sibling groups.

These are all very important considerations in understanding the meaning of Adoption Scorecards; on the other hand the average wait between entering care and adoption in Hackney in 2011 was 33 months. That is almost three years – a huge chunk of a child's life.

Leaving aside the practice and policy issues over whether this is a valid measure, there is another consideration. The numbers involved in any year are very small, with most authorities placing fewer than 20 children. How might this suggest a problem for valid quantitative analysis? Given the small numbers one might expect any exceptional authority to 'regress to the mean'. This is a relatively simple statistical concept, discussed in detail later. Here it is sufficient to say it describes the tendency for outliers to move towards the average. That being the case, one would expect Hackney's results for subsequent years to reduce significantly. And that is exactly what one finds. In fact, to allow for the small numbers involved the scorecards cover three years. As a result the next scorecard actually covers two of the same three years as the previous one: and therefore the scope for reduction is significantly reduced. Nonetheless, what is seen in the next scorecard is a very substantial reduction in the time that children wait (Department for Education, 2012). Of course this may be the influence of the scorecard – and the public furore around it – or it could be a simple regression to the mean. How might you explore this, with the published data? (A suggestion is made at the end of the chapter.)

Basic concepts in routinely gathered data and questionnaires

Routinely gathered data

The example of Adoption Scorecards provides a good illustrative example of both the strengths and the limitations of routinely gathered data for research purposes. Strengths in routinely gathered data include:

- Somebody has already gathered them for you!
- They are usually freely or easily available from official sources.

- They can be reliable and valid – particularly when they relate to clear service-related measures, that is the counting of things that a service does. Services tend to be good at counting the number of assessments they have done or the number of adults or children they have provided different types of service for.

- They are often of considerable political or policy interest – if someone has asked for data on a particular issue to be collated and reported it is probably because they are of more general interest.

Yet there are considerable problems with routinely gathered data. First, there are rarely any data on the ultimate focus of the service, or indeed even a definition of the focus of the data collected. Most services are intended to improve welfare or meet needs or protect from harm, yet these are very difficult outcomes to collect data on. Instead, therefore, proxies relating to what the service actually did are often used. The Adoption Scorecard is a good example of this: the ultimate aim is presumably to protect children from harm and improve their well-being. There are good reasons for believing delays in adoption may tend to have poor outcomes for children. Yet it cannot be assumed that delay equals poor outcomes, still less that a speedy adoption is *always* good for a child. And this is a comparatively uncontroversial example – in that most people would agree that, all things taken into consideration, reducing the delay between identifying adoption as the plan and placing for adoption would be a good thing. Often data gathered may be far more difficult to interpret. For instance, how might one interpret an increase in the number of children in care or the provision of domiciliary services for adults? Or a reduction in child protection conferences or the use of compulsory sections under the Mental Health Act? Figures on these issues are important in their own right – but the complexity of the link to actual outcomes has to be recognised.

Second, when routinely collected data attempt to move beyond descriptions of what a service provided or what actions workers took, questions about the reliability and validity of the measures often need to be asked. For instance, in the government returns for children's services a categorisation by type of need is provided. When examined further there are multiple problems with this. In a nutshell, the categories do not seem to be valid or reliable. They are therefore likely to be useless for research – except for research about their lack of validity and reliability (Forrester et al., 2008a).

A third problem with routinely collected data is that data collected as a 'performance indicator' tend to be shaped by this fact. There is a long history of performance indicators being used by government, and therefore distorted by those who have to provide reports. A measure becomes a performance indicator when it is used as to make a judgement about the success or otherwise of a service. Unfortunately, as soon as this becomes the case it greatly increases the likelihood of misreporting – indeed, this has been formulated as 'Goodhart's Law', that 'When a measure becomes a target, it ceases to be a good measure' ('Goodhart's Law', 2016). An early example of such distortions was in Russian and Chinese production reports throughout the period of communism. Central government judged the success of factories, regions and sectors by their production performance against targets, and this led to mass over-reporting of actual production. Another example comes from the Vietnam War, in which the US army were not sure how to measure their performance against a guerilla army that rarely met them in open battles. They therefore introduced the number of enemy body bags as one in an array of performance measures. This certainly resulted in falsification of numbers killed (Graham, 2005) and was alleged to contribute to the killing of innocent civilians or surrendered enemy soldiers to boost the body bag count (Engelhardt, 2007).

These illustrations all point to the problem of indicators as measures. On a less dramatic scale the same problems can happen within child or adult social services. For instance, in the late 1990s when the government felt too many children were on the child protection register, the numbers were reduced across the country – but this was sometimes achieved by simply refusing to register some children who might be at risk. Similar processes can occur whenever a particular service response – from child protection investigations through to length of time on a child protection plan – is identified as a key performance indicator. The indicator will tend to shift, but the reasons for the shift may include procedural or bureaucratic manipulations of the figures. This makes the figures difficult to interpret for research purposes.

Finally, in pragmatic terms the routinely collected data on their own are rarely of sufficient interest to merit doing a piece of research on them. They tend to be of more interest when they are added to. One example of this is provided in Chapter 12, where the number of children in care for each local authority was compared to the indicators of deprivation in different local authorities. Using solely publicly available existing data, this allows for interesting and innovative research. A second way in which routine data may be useful is as a starting point: they may identify an issue (for instance how long adoption takes) or an area (for instance, a local authority that varies from others) that can be explored further. Third, sometimes the routine data provide contextual data. They help to explain the local situation for other types of data collection. These might include qualitative data, or further research using quantitative data. A key way of gathering such information would be using questionnaires – the next section considers this in greater depth.

Questionnaires

One of the most common ways of gathering specific quantitative information is through a questionnaire. Questionnaires provide a key way – perhaps the most common way – to gather data from medium or large samples. They could be used, for instance, to collect data from all the workers in a local authority or from all the students on a social work course.

A questionnaire is a research instrument using a series of questions for the purpose of gathering information from respondents. Questionnaires can be administered face to face, over the phone, online, by email or even by post. The questions within a questionnaire can include:

- Closed response questions – which provide a limited number of possible answers, for instance:
  - Yes/no questions
  - Ratings (often referred to as Likert questions, described further below)
  - Multiple-choice questions (MCQs)
  - Specific information questions, for example 'What is your name?'
- Open questions – participants are free to answer without being restricted by format. Common uses include:
  - Providing an opportunity for respondents to share their views freely
  - Offering a space for respondents to add anything not covered in the structured element

It should be obvious from this that not all the questions will necessarily be analysed quantitatively. Open questions in particular can be analysed qualitatively, though it is common for questionnaires to apply a thematic coding scheme that is then quantified (for instance, 40% of respondents said A, while 20% tended to mention B).

We now consider further some of these types of questions, before exploring issues around reliability and validity.

Issues in developing questions for questionnaires

There are advantages and disadvantages for each type of question. Open questions are particularly useful for capturing a range of opinions in an area that is being newly researched. However, open questions can fail to provide an indication of the strength of opinions.

A more fundamental problem is that in general it is not possible to present all the information provided in open questions. The responses therefore usually need to be simplified in some way. This is most commonly done by identifying common themes in responses and then applying the themes to code the open-ended data. Ultimately it is therefore usual for open-ended questions to be coded and as a result to be rather similar to pre-coded closed questions. This is a time-consuming process; it is far quicker – for respondents and researchers – to have an agreed set of answers for people to choose from than to code a set of open-ended questions to provide a set of themes. However, if one does not know the likely answers that one wishes to capture then this open-ended approach may be more appropriate.

Closed response questions are particularly useful for generating quantitatively analysable data. A simple approach is a dichotomous question, usually a yes/no response. For instance:

Do you think social work students should understand quantitative research?

Yes [ ]   No [ ]

The advantage of such a question is that it provides a very brief summary of data, and is quick and easy for respondents to complete (a key consideration in designing a questionnaire). Disadvantages include that many participants may be in a between position and a dichotomy may oversimplify a phenomenon.

A common response to this is to provide some sort of rating scale. These are commonly called Likert questions, named after Rensis Likert who is credited with first using them. They are widely used to investigate the strength of people's feelings on an issue. For instance, instead of the dichotomous question about quantitative research above it would be possible to ask the following Likert scale question probing how strongly respondents felt:

Social work students should understand quantitative research

I agree strongly	[ ]
I agree moderately	[ ]
I agree a little	[ ]
I neither agree nor disagree	[ ]
I disagree a little	[ ]
I disagree moderately	[ ]
I disagree strongly	[ ]

This can then easily be converted to a numerical score, for instance as follows:

Social work students should understand quantitative research

I agree strongly	[7]
I agree moderately	[6]
I agree a little	[5]
I neither agree nor disagree	[4]
I disagree a little	[3]
I disagree moderately	[2]
I disagree strongly	[1]

There are some obvious advantages to such an approach. Most obviously, Likert questions capture strength of opinions and can identify intermediate shades of opinion. Furthermore, subsequent analysis can combine numbers, allowing for the binary or other distributions to be also explored. For instance, the above Likert question could be converted to binary to identify what proportion of participants agreed that social work students should understand quantitative research (e.g. by combining 7–5 and 1–4).

Disadvantages of Likert scales include the fact that differences between points may be very subjective, and it can thus be difficult to interpret their meaning. In addition, some points are rarely used. A key practical point is that it is important to pilot Likert scales before using them. This takes us to the more general set of considerations around designing questions for questionnaires.

Considerations in designing a questionnaire

A questionnaire should be designed in order to allow a more fundamental research question to be answered. As such, questions should be designed to provide data that are likely to be helpful in understanding an area better. However, questionnaires are a form of self-report data; they are essentially accounts people provide about whatever it is that is being studied. Silverman (2010) provides an excellent critique of naïve approaches to self-report accounts in qualitative data. In essence, he argues that too often studies simply assume that people are telling 'the truth' but that in fact they are giving particular accounts through a socially structured situation (in his case the situation being the research interview). Essentially the same challenges apply to research questionnaires: they provide accounts provided by people and may or may not therefore be reliable sources of data. Specifically, the following may be questions to ask about a questionnaire:

- Is each question clear? In particular, will everyone answering the question understand it in the same way? If there are variations, what might these relate to?

- Are the meanings of the responses clear? Again, will everyone mean the same thing when they, for instance, strongly agree with a statement?

- Is the respondent likely to be able to provide accurate information in response to each question? Often questionnaires ask questions that people are quite poor at answering. An example would be asking people to estimate how they spend their time at work. In fact, there can be significant differences between how people say they spend their time and how they actually spend their time when observed.

- Is each question appropriate for the type of information being sought? For instance, is it appropriate to ask people how intelligent or attractive or good at social work they are? It is not reasonable to expect self-report to be a particularly good measure for any of these things. Even for some issues that we might think people were reliable witnesses on – for instance, whether a training course had made a difference to their practice – they are not particularly accurate in relation to. This may be because of the next point ...

- Self-report data are influenced by conscious or unconscious biases. We try to present ourselves – to others and even to ourselves – in positive ways. This may influence how we respond to questions. For instance, the vast majority of people in the UK today if asked in a questionnaire whether they are racist would say 'no'. This does not mean you would not find them talking or acting in ways that suggest they might be racist – at least in some ways and on some occasions. (For instance, the oft-quoted verbal indicator that someone is about to say something racist but does not want to be considered as racist is 'I'm not racist, but...' (Potter and Wetherell, 1987).)

Many of these considerations return to fundamental questions of reliability and validity. To put it simply: is the question measuring that which it is intended to measure?

There are some practical steps that can be taken to help minimise problems such as those noted above. Piloting questionnaires is an important way to identify questions that have poor clarity and are therefore open to misinterpretation. Often validated instruments will ask several questions that try to explore the same underlying issue. For instance, if interested in levels of stress they might ask about worry, impact on relationships, impact on sleep and so on. For this reason there are strong reasons to use or incorporate validated or standardised instruments either as part of a questionnaire or instead of a questionnaire. Standardised instruments have been tested so that the scores have been shown to be related to 'real-world' outcomes. As such, findings will have more validity. Furthermore, the questions within the instrument have been through a rigorous questionnaire development process. This includes identifying the degree to which questions that seek to explore the same area correlate with one another. Those that do not may be poor questions for examining a particular issue (see Chapter 4).

Unfortunately, it is not always possible to use a validated research instrument. Some instruments require a payment for use (though this is usually a comparatively small amount). A more common problem is that there is no instrument that is specific enough for the area you may wish to study. In such circumstances, it is worth thinking carefully about how you might improve the validity of the questionnaire you develop. One approach that is often used in research is 'triangulation'. In essence, this collects more than one type of data in the belief that this can lead to greater confidence in the data collected (see Chapter 10).

Box 5.1: 'Research in practice' – adoption

Read: Selwyn, J., Wijedasa, D. and Meakings, S. (2014). *Beyond the Adoption Order: Challenges, Interventions and Adoption Disruption*. Department for Education.

As discussed at the beginning of this chapter, there has been considerable political support for more use of adoption and a push to avoid delay in moving children into adoptive placements. Yet we know surprisingly little about outcomes for children adopted through the care system. In particular, there used to be no evidence on how many of the adoptive placements broke down, with estimates ranging as high as 30% and much vigorous disagreement based on different experiences. In particular, many social workers and managers who worked with children who had experienced more than once the breakdown of an adoptive placement and a child coming back into care felt that this terrible outcome was relatively common.

In this key study Selwyn and colleagues explored the rate of adoption disruption after an Adoption Order had been agreed by a court. There were a number of elements to the study – including a survey of agencies and qualitative data collection – but here we concentrate on probably the most important contribution of the study: the identification for the first time of the extent to which adoptions break down, using return to care as the definition of such breakdown.

To do this Selwyn and colleagues used Department for Education anonymised information on every child who entered care in the 12 years from 1 April 2000 to 31 March 2011. This data set allowed the researchers to identify all the children adopted during that period and then identify how many of those children had come back into care after adoption. A total of 37,335 children were adopted during this period. Data were missing for some children, but for 565 a disruption was identified. Statistical analysis for children found that over a 12-year period post-placement 3.2% of placements would result in a disruption and a child returning into the care system. While often when this happens it is a tragedy for the child and the family, it is a low figure overall and an important contribution to debates about adoption.

Selwyn and colleagues' use of a large data set allowed them to identify key factors that make a disruption more likely (including the age of the child and how long it had taken them from entry to care to adoption) and periods when disruption was most likely. It was supplemented by in-depth qualitative data that identified that often families were coping with significant difficulties and problems. It is a key social work study and well worth reading in full; here we only use it to demonstrate the importance of high-quality quantitative research in simply describing key issues in social work.

Exercise 5.1: Performance measurement

Most of the agencies that social workers work for have to collect and report on a variety of measures. For instance, children's services departments have to report to government on:

- The numbers of children in care at a specific point in time;

- The numbers of children entering and leaving care over time;

- The numbers of children adopted;

- The numbers of children subject to Child Protection Plans;

- The proportion of assessments carried out within certain timescales.

Are these reasonable things for the government to count?

What are their strengths or weaknesses?

What better things to measure can you suggest?

Critical Thinking Box

Read: Beckett, C. (2001). The great care proceedings explosion. *British Journal of Social Work*, 31(3), 493–501.

Chris Beckett's research (2001) could hardly be simpler. He obtained the number of care proceedings for each year from 1992 to 1999. Data are presented in a set of clear graphs. No statistical analysis is used, and indeed it is unnecessary: the trends are clear enough to make statistical analysis superfluous. Beckett identifies that the number of care proceedings grew steadily throughout the seven years after the 1989 Children Act was enacted in 1991.

What is worth noting is that what makes this worthy of an article – what in fact makes it research rather than simply a presentation of government figures – is that Beckett provides a scholarly context for understanding and interpreting the data. He does this by exploring the hopes and expectations of the 1989 Act, providing the data on the increased use of care proceedings, outlining that these seem directly against the ethos or expected impact of the Act and then suggesting some possible explanations. His conclusion is particularly noteworthy: 'To speak of heading in one direction while in reality heading precisely in the opposite way is surely no basis for sensible planning' (Beckett, 2001, p. 510).

Some questions to consider:

- How confident can we be from the data presented that the number of children entering care through care proceedings since the Act was put into place is increasing? Are there any other explanations for some or all of this change? How might you explore them?

- What can you *not* conclude from this increase? Can you think of any ways in which additional data might help shed more light on whether this increase is a good or bad outcome?

If you would like to have a more up-to-date picture you can find more recent data (see Cafcass, 2015). There is also a discussion of the recent situation in community care (Stevenson, 2015).

Summary

This chapter set out to introduce and explore the use of descriptive quantitative approaches in social work policy, practice and research. The specific learning outcomes were to ensure readers understood:

- Key elements and principles for descriptive quantitative research: that is, research that measures the extent or severity of an issue – this was illustrated through studies and measures that identify the extent of an issue (e.g. disruption in adoption) and approaches that attempt to measure severity (including Likert questions but also standardised instruments).

- What routine information gathered by agencies is and its strengths and limitations for research purposes – a particular focus of the chapter has been to turn a critical eye on routine information and its uses and misuses. This included Adoption Scorecards, numbers of children entering care and research on disruption in adoption.

- The contribution that questionnaires can make, and an understanding of some issues in questionnaire design – as illustrated through, first, a description of different types of question and then the application of some of these, for instance in the instruments accompanying the Assessment Framework.

- The contribution that repeat measures over time can make for improving our understanding of issues. This chapter introduced repeat measures, for instance by considering changes in Adoption Scorecards or changes in numbers of children entering care. This is picked up as a key feature in the next chapter.

The focus of this chapter has been on the use of numbers in describing important things, including how often events happen, how serious they may be and whether when repeatedly measured the numbers change. Often simple descriptive measures are the first part of a study; it is relatively rare for them to be sufficient in themselves. It is once they begin to be examined over time, or that the complex relationships between different variables are unpacked, that quantitative research can begin to say really interesting things. Such approaches are the focus of the next few chapters.

Further resources

Note on Adoption Scorecards: We asked the question of how we might examine whether the reduction in time waiting for care in Hackney was more due to the impact of the scorecards or 'regression to the mean'. One way of doing this might be to compare Hackney to some of the other local authorities (LAs) with particularly long waiting times (for instance the 10 with the longest waiting times). How does their reduction compare to that of others? Does it seem likely that the media coverage of Hackney had a particular impact? Then comparing the 10 with the longest waiting times to those with the shortest waiting times might be possible. For these, one might expect some 'regression to the mean'. The difference between the regression effects for the 10 LAs with the shortest waiting times compared to the 10 with the longest would allow us to be relatively confident that the scorecards were themselves having some effect.

6

HOW TO KNOW IF A SERVICE MAKES A DIFFERENCE

LEARNING OUTCOMES

By the end of this chapter you should be able to:

- Explain the rationale for a research study
- Name the basic components of research design
- Identify and describe the contribution and limitations of the following three research evaluative designs:
  - Before-and-after studies
  - Quasi-experimental designs
  - Experimental designs

Introduction

Research suggests that social workers want research to answer questions around what works (Stevens et al., 2009). This chapter explores the complexity involved in answering whether services or ways of working make a difference. It does this through a particular focus on three common evaluative designs. These designs provide a way of introducing broader debates about the nature of evidence around what works.

The chapter explores the key issue of how to establish whether services provided for people make a difference, including the debates around this topic within social work and the social sciences. The most popular evaluative designs are introduced, with a particular focus on before-after, quasi-experimental and experimental designs. The broader evaluative research tradition is considered, including logic models and realist approaches. Throughout, key critiques are considered in relation to each type of evaluative design. The overall argument is that each method has strengths and weaknesses, and is likely to be appropriate for particular purposes in specific contexts. In addition, the chapter provides an introduction to broader traditions and debates in evaluative research, including programme evaluation, logic models and realist evaluation.

The question, 'Does a particular service or innovation "work"?' is one that almost every policy maker or commissioner will ask regularly. It is one that social workers and other professionals also have to think about in making referrals for families or deciding how best to help people. Yet answering this question is fraught with complexities. The way in which policy makers or others judge different studies has considerable implications: resources flow or are stopped, jobs are lost and services funded, or not, based on findings from evaluations of what works. Perhaps in part as a result, the question of how such judgements may be made is one of the most contentious – perhaps *the* most contentious – in the social sciences. This chapter combines an introduction to how to do evaluative research with an exploration of some of these debates and their implications for reading and doing research.

Most approaches to evaluate a service (or an individual intervention or anything) tend to try to prove that *A causes B*,

where:

- *A* is the service being evaluated;

- *B* is the outcome measured (or more accurately the *change* in the outcome from before to after the service is provided – for this chapter we will call this change 'the outcome being evaluated');

- '*Cause*' is often taken to be unproblematic – but as discussed at length below is perhaps the most problematic element.

In fact, there are serious challenges in defining either 'service' or 'outcomes'. Chapter 4 considered many of the key issues in defining what may be measured. However, these are minor compared to the problem of establishing that the service *causes* the outcome; the issue of causality is fraught with both philosophical and practical problems.

The most common approach to establishing causality is associated with the scientific method. It is also an approach that appears to be 'common sense'. This is important – people making key decisions can readily understand the rationale for such an approach. In a nutshell, in this approach every effort is made to rule out other potential explanations for an outcome. It might be considered the Sherlock Holmes approach, after his comment: 'When you have eliminated the impossible, whatever remains, however improbable, must be the truth.' Thus, the more certainty that can be demonstrated that other explanations can be ruled out, the more one can be confident that it was A that caused B.

This relatively simple conception of causality can be illustrated by describing three progressively more robust research designs that exclude other explanations for findings. However, as we shall see later in the chapter, there are in fact problems even with this conception of causality.

The simplest way of evaluating an intervention is to measure the appropriate outcome prior to the service or intervention, and then to measure again after the service has been provided. For obvious reasons, this is often known as a before-after study design. This design is often used in research but can also be used in practice to see whether a programme of work is achieving a specified goal.

Yet for the researcher this is often a problematic design. Put simply, it is difficult to rule out other possible explanations for the findings. For instance, often people approach a service or are referred for help at a time of crisis. Things tend to get better after a crisis. This could be understood as people actively sorting out their lives, or it could be that when things are bad 'the only way is up' (statistically understood as 'regression to the mean' – see Chapter 5). On the other hand, social work services do not always exist to create positive change alone. In his book *The Essential Social Worker*, Martin Davies argues that often social work is about 'maintenance' – keeping things from actually getting worse, and thereby often keeping vulnerable people in their families and communities (Davies, 1994). This is certainly sometimes the goal of social work intervention. That being the case, things not changing may be a reasonable goal. As such a before-after study may see no change and yet the service may have been highly effective.

A problem for before-after studies is that we cannot know what might have happened if the service or intervention had *not* been provided. As such, we cannot be sure that A causes B. The scientific experimental method was developed explicitly to address this challenge. In particular a method called the randomised controlled trial (RCT) is particularly good at ruling out other explanations for findings, though, as discussed below, it has some very important limitations as a method. The RCT is the bedrock of medicine and many other areas of science. It is in essence a very simple research design. An RCT seeks to discover whether something – a service or a pill or a website – works better than an alternative (which might be no service, or service as usual, counselling or keeping the previous website). To find out whether the new service works better than the comparison people are randomly assigned to receive one or the other.

A key point to make here – and one that some people find instinctively hard to accept – is that because people are randomly assigned the only difference between the groups should be the impact of the service being evaluated. Of course, with small groups there is a danger that the groups may not be comparable. (There are a variety of research methods to explore this – and some complicated issues that are related to this which we discuss below.) Yet the best way of ensuring equivalence between groups in most circumstances is to have a relatively large number of people and then randomly divide them. The main reason for this is because random allocation means that not only the things that you know about but also the things you do *not* know about should be randomly divided between groups. In any case, most RCTs test for group equivalence prior to a service being provided. Where equivalence is not found, it is often an indication that randomisation has not happened (see the BetterEvaluation website for more information about the stages of an RCT (Ambroz et al., 2013)).

At its simplest an RCT randomly divides those receiving the new service or intervention being studied (the experimental group) and those receiving the comparison service (the comparison or control group). The equivalence of the groups is tested before and then after people receive the service. Crucially, because they were randomly chosen, any difference between the groups after they receive the service can reliably be ascribed to the service being studied. In an RCT other explanations for differences in outcomes can be ruled out. RCTs therefore rule out bias in findings. Furthermore, because other things that can influence the outcome should be equally distributed between the groups – things like people helping themselves, crises naturally resolving themselves – the specific impact of the service can be identified.

A good example of how helpful RCTs can be in this regard is Kratochwill and colleagues' study of Families and Schools Together (FAST) as an intervention in a Native American community (Kratochwill et al., 2004). FAST was provided for families and children at the age of 7. A follow-up found comparatively little impact on the behaviour or performance of children in school and it would have been easy to conclude that FAST did not work or had a very limited impact. However, this study was an RCT. And it was striking that in the control group the behaviour of children and their performance in school often got worse. This study is a useful example of why an RCT can be a helpful evaluative tool – but it also points out that RCTs do not hold all the answers. There are broader and more fundamental questions about why so many young children from Native American communities (or at least this community) were doing so poorly at school. To understand many of the issues we confront in social work requires an understanding of historical, sociological and political issues. RCTs are in essence only good at finding out whether specific services make a difference.

As noted above, RCTs are used extensively in medicine. They have also been used widely in psychology and psychiatry, in particular to evaluate different ways of helping people with specific problems. In social work, however, there have still been comparatively few RCTs. Bruce Thyer's team at Florida State University keeps a comprehensive record of RCTs in which any member of the team is a social worker (Thyer, 2015). However, it is striking on reading this that many of the studies are not of social work as such. Also, the vast majority have taken place in the USA and very few are directly applicable to social work in the UK (Dixon et al., 2014). Part of the reason for the lack of RCTs in social work is a reluctance to use them for theoretical or ideological reasons (Gibbs, 2001; Webb, 2001; Frost, 2002). The expense of RCTs is also often cited as another reason for their limited take up (see Oakley et al., 2003). There are sometimes ethical reasons why an RCT is not carried out, which may or may not be well founded (see Chapter 11). However, there are also legitimate practical reasons why it can be difficult to carry out an RCT:

- It is wrong to randomise some services because there are questions of justice and fairness (for instance, it would not generally be acceptable to take some children into care and leave others at home to find out the impact on their welfare – though see the practice example below).

- Some service innovations are so complex that it is not possible to randomise. For instance, it is almost impossible to do RCTs in relation to whole system reforms within local authorities.

- In practice, it is often not feasible to randomise unless demand significantly exceeds service capacity. For instance, if a project is set up to provide for families in an area, randomisation would often not be an evaluation option until there could be confidence that more referrals were being received than the service could provide for. (In other words, regardless of whether we know an intervention works or not, it is often simply not acceptable for workers not to be working.)

In these circumstances an RCT may not be feasible. In addition, there is often resistance to the idea of an RCT from those delivering or referring to a service. This can lead to problems in recruiting service users for studies, for example (see Rushton and Monk, 2010; Dixon et al., 2014). This resistance is often misplaced, as discussed in Chapter 11, but can in practice often make carrying out an RCT difficult.

In such circumstances a useful alternative design is to use a comparison group that is not achieved through randomisation. This might:

- compare outcomes for people before a service came into being;

- compare a similar area, for instance a neighbouring local authority;

- identify similar people who did not receive a specific service;

- look at people who are waiting for a service.

A study comparing outcomes for those receiving a service with a non-randomised comparison group is called a quasi-experimental study. In essence a quasi-experimental study tries to provide stronger evidence about whether a service or other intervention causes particular outcomes by including a comparison group in the study. This can be a far better study for evaluating the specific impact of a service than a before-after study. However, the strength of a quasi-experimental study rests almost entirely on how valid the comparison group is.

A challenge for quasi-experimental studies is that because there is a pre-existing difference between people in the experimental and comparison groups then there are also possible reasons why their outcomes may be different. For instance, if people live in a different area, they are likely to have different problems and access to different services. If the comparison is outcomes for people before a service came into play, then other elements of service provision or even public policy may influence findings (for instance levels of poverty or access to benefits may have changed). If one is looking at people who did not receive a service, then why did they not receive it? A comparison between people referred to a service who were refused it and those who were accepted can be particularly poor because there is very likely to be a clear difference between the two groups.

As a result, quasi-experimental studies almost invariably leave significant questions about whether the difference in outcomes might have occurred for other reasons. However, they can have important benefits. Obviously, having some sort of comparison group tends to strengthen the ability to ascribe outcomes to the service received. Furthermore, the more one can compare the samples prior to the service being received, the more confident one can be either that the samples are similar or – if that is not the case – that the differences are clearly understood and described.

However, the most important advantage of quasi-experimental studies is that they allow us to study changes in services that are not amenable to RCTs. In particular, complex systemic changes are almost impossible to study using RCTs. As discussed below, this can lead to RCTs trading their applicability to the real world of everyday practice for a purity of research design. Often quasi-experimental studies are strong in applicability to the real world, albeit allowing for potential bias in the interpretation of results.

Having provided an overview of these three approaches, we turn now to a practice example, or rather a few practice examples – namely a series of studies evaluating services to reduce the need for children to enter care. We then return to explore in greater depth the strengths and limitations of RCTs, before-after studies and quasi-experiments before introducing the broader field of evaluative research.

'Research in practice' – Intensive Family Preservation Services

In recent years there has been great interest in developing interventions aimed at preventing children from coming into care in the UK. For instance, a government paper commented that:

> We should concentrate our efforts on avoiding the need for care, except for those who truly need its support. We must identify problems earlier and respond quickly and effectively. And our responses must be driven by what we know are the key characteristics of effective interventions.

> (Department for Education and Skills, 2006, p. 21)

This seems on the face of it to be sensible. Yet what *are* 'the key characteristics of effective interventions'? This practice example considers the literature on a specific type of intervention, aimed at reducing the need for children to enter care, namely Intensive Family Preservation Services (IFPSs). It considers before-after, quasi-experimental and experimental studies.

Intensive in-home family interventions (which is what IFPSs are) to reduce placements in public care were first developed in the USA in the mid-1970s. They tend to use a 'crisis intervention' theory, with immediate, intensive support to help a family. They often combine therapeutic and practical elements. (See the Institute for Family Development website for a more detailed description of one model, Homebuilders.)

Such approaches attracted considerable attention when initial evaluations suggested that very high proportions of children 'at risk' of entering public care avoided doing so following such a service. For instance Kinney et al. (1977) found that of 80 families worked with, 97% of children did not enter care. Haapala and Kinney (1979) found 96% of children in a sample of 207 families remained at home. These were both before and after studies: the number of children receiving a service were analysed to see how many actually entered care. The outcome variable was whether they were in care (with none in care before the service).

Unsurprisingly, with results like these (and the possibility of the cost savings they might produce) IFPSs were widely rolled out in the US, and before-and-after studies continued to find that very high proportions of children referred to them remained at home. However, with widespread use of IFPSs more rigorous evaluations were also carried out, including several RCTs or robust quasi-experimental studies. These produced a very different picture.

For instance, Lindsey et al. (2002) carried out a review of the evidence on IFPSs. They identified 36 studies between 1970 and 2000 that evaluated IFPSs aimed at preventing the need for foster care. They found that of the four rigorous experimental studies, three found the *control* group had fewer placements than the intervention group, while for the fourth there was no significant difference. The remaining studies with comparison groups generally showed no difference between the groups and painted a discouraging picture of the ability of IFPSs to prevent children from entering care.

Following this the US government carried out a large-scale RCT of IFPSs in four states (DHHS, 2002). One of the largest RCTs of a social work service carried out to date, this study looked at 756 families receiving IFPS and 535 in control groups. Information was collected from multiple sources at start of service, at three months and at 12 months after service entry. Child welfare, family functioning and out-of-home placements were examined. Families reported positively about the interventions and there were some positive changes in individual intervention sites. However, the overwhelming finding was that were very few differences between the groups and no difference in out-of-home placement. Any differences at the end of the intervention (three months) had disappeared by the 12-month follow-up.

Undeterred by – and perhaps ignorant of – the findings from the US, variations of the IFPS model have been widely tried in the UK. There have been limited evaluations carried out, though Forrester et al. (2008a) carried out a quasi-experimental study looking at the impact on care entry, and therefore costs, of an IFPS. The IFPS was called Option 2, and was based on the Homebuilders model (Forrester et al. 2008a, p. 12). The study used the fact that, as a crisis intervention service, Option 2 did not have a waiting list. When a family was referred but there was not space to work with them, basic details were recorded and no service offered. The evaluation compared care entry data (including costs) for 278 children who received the service between 2000 and 2006 with the data for 89 children referred but refused the service because there was no space. The groups appeared broadly similar and differences were allowed for in the statistical analysis. Forrester et al. emphasise that the evaluation was an extremely challenging test of the impact of the service. The average follow-up period was 3.5 years – which is a very long period for a brief intervention. Furthermore the comparison group will have received a range of other services, many of which involve longer periods of professional involvement. There was no difference between the groups in the likelihood of children entering care (at 41% for Option 2 and 40% for the comparison group). However, Option 2 children spent considerably fewer days in care. This was in part because they took longer to enter care, but they were also much more likely to return to their family and to do so comparatively quickly. The cost implications were striking. When the cost of providing Option 2 was set against the savings in placement costs, it provided a saving of £1,178 per child worked with by the service.

This finding might seem at odds with the US literature – the RCT results might suggest that the IFPS does not work. However, the research literature is far more complex than that. Investigation of the interventions delivered in the RCTs found that the service being delivered varied very significantly from the original IFPS model. For instance, often the services ran quite long waiting lists (a practice completely at odds with a crisis intervention approach) or was not very intensive (for instance, consisting of weekly visits) (Forrester et al., 2008a, p. 24).

Additionally, two further conclusions can be drawn from the RCTs and other robust evaluations of IFPSs. The first is that often IFPSs did not actually have children who were genuinely at risk of entering care referred to them (Forrester et al., 2008a, p. 21). This may be in part because social workers who were actually worried about children took them into care rather than feeling they are leaving them at risk. It may also be because services lose their focus and work with 'easier' families. This tendency explains the apparent success of the initial studies and would also contribute to the low impact on care entry found in experimental studies. Secondly, there is a substantial body of evidence that the more robustly IFPSs stick to their description of good practice, the more effective they are. As a result, for instance, one review found that services applying the Homebuilders model are effective, but that IFPSs in general do not work (Washington State Institute for Public Policy, 2006).

The practice example of IFPSs suggests several issues that you may wish to consider. It illustrates the potential impact of research – both to support and to call into question the effectiveness of a service. Equally, the limitations of both before-after studies and experimental or quasi-experimental studies are demonstrated. This touches on issues of internal and external validity and implementation fidelity – all of which are discussed in the next section. However, the most important conclusion from this case study is this: a body of studies allows a deeper and more nuanced understanding of an area. It is the quantity and variety of studies of IFPSs that has allowed a better insight into the possibilities and limitations of such approaches and that therefore informs policy and practice in reducing the need for children to enter care.

Basic concepts/definitions/theoretical basis

The 'Research in practice' example illustrates two concepts that are central to evaluative research. These are external and internal validity. Internal validity is the confidence that can be placed in the causal attributions. In other words: to what degree can we be sure that in this study A caused B? External validity asks a different question: to what degree can we apply the findings from this study to other settings or situations?

There is often in practice a trade-off between internal and external validity. This is because internal validity is increased the more the circumstances of the study are controlled, as greater control allows us to be more confident that other explanations for findings can be ruled out. Yet the more variables a study controls the more difficult it can be to apply the findings to other settings.

This is not necessarily the case. There are some RCTs in which both the internal and external validity are high. This is usually when something very simple is being studied. For instance, without most people knowing, RCTs are quite often carried out by websites. Visitors are randomly provided with one of two different page set-ups. The use of the page is compared across the options. A comparatively famous example of this was carried out on Wikipedia (See Wikimedia Meta-Wiki, 2010). Visitors to a page were asked for a donation, but the style of banner, some including photos of the founder Jimmy Wales, was decided randomly. People shown banners with the photo gave far higher levels of donations.

The Wikipedia RCT is a beautiful example of the elegant simplicity of the RCT. It has very high internal validity. The only thing being compared was the photo, and the outcome – the level of donations – was straightforward to measure. It also had very high external validity – the reason you saw Jimmy Wales's photo asking for donations when you visited Wikipedia was because the study suggested that this makes a difference. The site has now evolved this testing further – at the time of writing it is using multiple-choice donation options. It can continue to evolve this owing to the simplicity of testing. Yet for most studies there are complexities that make the design far more difficult. In practice, increasing internal validity often means reducing external validity. (It is also perhaps worth thinking about the 'external validity' of the findings. The RCT identified that the photograph was more effective, but it cannot be concluded that this will remain the case for all time. One might expect reductions in effectiveness, for instance as people become used to ignoring the photograph. An RCT therefore provides a useful way of finding out something, but it always has a context).

Here are some common ways in which studies may increase internal validity, but may reduce external validity in doing so. RCTs will often:

- Carefully select the client group being studied so that the intervention is being used with the people it is intended to be used with. For instance, many studies in the alcohol misuse field exclude people with mental health problems, the homeless or older people.

- Carefully select the workers delivering the intervention. It is reasonable for a study to look at an intervention or a way of working that is being properly delivered, and therefore many (perhaps most) RCTs select good therapists to be trained to deliver it.

- Go to considerable lengths to ensure that interventions are delivered in the way they are meant to be delivered. This issue is an important one for evaluative research and is referred to as 'implementation fidelity', i.e. the degree to which the service being evaluated is being delivered as intended. Crucially, individuals or sites not delivering a service as intended are often excluded from studies.

At a more prosaic level, often those delivering a service in an RCT are provided with not just extensive training but also a great deal of enthusiastic interest by researchers who are determined that the service be delivered as it should be.

It is, of course, reasonable for researchers to expect services to be delivered as they are meant to be – to those who they are most likely to benefit, and by people well qualified and enthused about delivering them. Yet the more that these conditions are addressed, the more questions can be asked about the applicability of findings to the 'real world'.

In the studies of IFPSs there are several examples of these dilemmas. For instance, the US government evaluation of IFPSs (DHHS, 2002) appeared to value external validity over internal validity. There was very little quality control of the IFPS – the evaluation looked at the services actually being delivered rather than whether these services matched the original model. As such it found out something very important: IFPSs around the USA were probably having little or no impact on children or their families. On the other hand, this study was open to the criticism that perhaps when done well IFPSs did make a difference. The studies that have examined a tightly defined version of Homebuilders, and that have focused solely on children at genuinely high risk of entering care, have high internal validity. They have tended to find that Homebuilders works (see, for example, Washington State Institute for Public Policy, 2006). Yet a challenge is to what degree these findings can be applied to the real world. At the least they suggest very tight quality control is required for IFPSs to work.

The same kind of issues – whether the study has internal and external validity – should be considered in evaluating any research. For instance, what might be the implications of excluding certain groups from the evaluation of a particular intervention? If a high proportion of the actual people using alcohol and drug services also have mental health problems, then excluding such people from trials may lead to misleading conclusions about the effectiveness of different approaches. This is sometimes termed in the literature the difference between efficacy (the ability of an intervention or service to make a difference in ideal situations) and effectiveness (the impact that it has in real-world situations).

These types of considerations lead to a final key issue in evaluative research, namely 'implementation fidelity', or the degree to which specified services are delivered as they are meant to be delivered. There is a huge literature on this area, but a very simple summary would be that the more close attention that is paid to delivering a quality intervention the more likely it is to work. Conversely, when adaptations are made they tend to result in less effective services. As a result there has been a strong tendency for evidence-based practice to be increasingly based on tightly defined – sometimes copyrighted – interventions. These lend themselves to evaluation, and have evidence of working, but questions arise about how applicable they are to the more general world of everyday practice. There is perhaps a danger that this may result in a bifurcated world of, on the one hand, tightly focused and specified interventions and, on the other, all the other services, though this goes beyond the focus of this chapter.

Of course, researchers carrying out RCTs are aware of just these types of considerations and as a result they often differentiate between efficacy and effectiveness. Different types of RCTs are appropriate to measure each of these. A test of efficacy is called a scientific trial. A scientific trial tries to explore in principle whether – when delivered adequately to the intended group – an intervention works. If a scientific trial suggests an intervention may work, a pragmatic trial applies the intervention in a more real-world setting to test its effectiveness. A pragmatic trial researches whether an approach makes a difference when tried in practice, and often looks at wider-scale roll-out than a scientific trial. A large proportion of RCTs in social work have been pragmatic rather than scientific trials, and this is likely to have contributed to their relatively low levels of success in showing effectiveness.

It should be clear from the above discussion that no one study can ever show whether a service or intervention 'works'. Instead, a series of studies is required. This includes exploratory studies (such as before-after studies). If these prove encouraging perhaps scientific RCTs and then, if these in turn are positive, studies that explore the roll-out of services (here a pragmatic trial or a quasi-experimental study may be best).

Of course it is rare for this type of programme of research to be undertaken in social work. Furthermore many important innovations – such as complex whole system changes – cannot be evaluated using experimental methods. To address this, a different approach to evaluation has been developed and is widely used, particularly in North America. This is known as programme evaluation research, or sometimes 'theory-oriented evaluation'. There is not space to consider this approach in sufficient depth here, but some key points from one of the most important schools of evaluative research – realist evaluation – will be considered.

Realist evaluation has been developed by Pawson and Tilley, in particular in their book *Realistic Evaluation* (1997), as a philosophically coherent approach to evaluative research that is based on a very different set of assumptions than those that underlie the methods discussed thus far. As such, we introduce some of the key ideas of realist evaluation to support a critical and nuanced approach to the methodologies discussed thus far.

Pawson and Tilley are struck by the complexity of the findings of the evaluative literature and the partial and in many respects disappointing sets of results thus far identified in many evaluative fields (their particular focus is on criminology). They argue that this has been because of a failure to adequately conceptualise the causation that underlies the evaluative methods discussed above. Specifically, the evaluative tradition has tended to claim causality by using methods that minimise other explanations for findings. If other explanations are ruled out then it can be assumed that A causes B. Pawson and Tilley argue that this is based on a fundamentally flawed conceptualisation of causation in human affairs. In particular, people make decisions about their lives (albeit, as Marx said, not in circumstances of their own choosing). This they term the theory of 'generative causation'. In essence, realist evaluation is an attempt to understand how and why people change behaviour, make different choices: the reasons for different behaviours.

The failure to take human agency seriously – the fact that people make decisions, or what in social work we might call the concept of self-determination – has both theoretical and practical implications. In theory, Pawson and Tilley argue, evaluative research has a flawed conceptualisation of the human in society: outcomes are not caused by interventions, as if people were atoms or snooker balls, or other inanimate objects. In practice, it is a failure to embrace the agency of people and the complexity of the contexts in which they actively

Table 6.1 Definition of key terms

Term	Definition
Internal validity	The degree to which the findings or outcomes of a study can be attributed to the hypothesised cause (in evaluative research this is the service or intervention being studied)
External validity	The degree to which the findings or outcomes can be applied to other settings – and particularly applications in real-world settings
Efficacy	The extent to which an intervention or service produces an expected result under ideal circumstances
Effectiveness	The extent to which an intervention or service produces an expected result in a real-world situation
Implementation fidelity	The degree to which the intervention or service is implemented as intended

experience agency that results in the often disappointing nature of the evidence about 'what works'. In chasing the chimera of certainty by removing bias (i.e. other potential explanations) researchers fail to grasp that the question is not whether A causes B, but rather when and for whom and why does A result in B, and when and for whom and why is this not the case.

To address this complexity Pawson and Tilley argue that evaluative research should be focused on developing theories about patterns of findings. As such, a variety of study designs – in fact virtually any study design – can be used in order to answer questions as appropriate, with the goal that the research helps develop useful theories to understand patterns of relationships between services and outcomes. Pawson and Tilley enthusiastically embrace many key elements of the philosophy of science – such as the importance of falsification – but reject RCTs as the best way of exploring causation. Rather, they call for research and theory development to go hand in hand, with a variety of methods being helpful in this process.

If you are interested in these important research topics, then some further reading is provided at the end of the chapter. Pawson and Tilley provide highly readable and engaging outlines of the realist evaluation position, which anyone interested in developing a deeper understanding of research methods might benefit from reading. However, this chapter is intended to provide an introduction to some basic evaluative designs that are common in quantitative research. Table 6.3 provides a definition of some of these key terms.

Application to social work practice

What is the relevance of all this to social work practice? The discussion of the IFPS research started with a quote from the UK government suggesting we should use the best evidence available to develop services aimed at reducing the need for children to enter care (Department for Education and Skills, 2006). But what about the responsibilities of individual social workers? If you are working as a social worker with children and their families you may at some point have to consider whether a child needs to be removed from their family. In doing so, you would have to consider on the one hand what the risks were to the child (both of staying at home and of alternatives), but you might also need to think about what services might need to be provided to try to prevent the need for care.

In making such a judgement you need to be able to critically engage with the research literature. To do that you need to understand the different types of studies, including the strengths and limitations of different approaches to developing evidence about what works. Of course, it is not realistic to expect each practitioner to go out and undertake in-depth literature reviews before making key decisions. On the other hand, just as we would expect doctors or other health professions to make decisions based on an understanding of the best evidence, it is a reasonable expectation for social workers to do the same. As such, it is necessary to be aware of what research evidence says on key topics, but also to have a critical appreciation of the inevitable limitations of any particular type of research.

There is a second way in which some of the key ideas from this chapter can be applied into your own practice: you can try to evaluate your own work. Of course, comparative designs are likely to be impossible. However, before-after studies using freely available research instruments may well be possible. This chapter should have shown the limitations of simple before-and-after designs, but it is possible that the realist evaluation approach offers a particularly helpful way of approaching this. In this approach the evaluator is attempting to develop a theory about what is going on. Furthermore they are gathering data to test out their hypotheses and they are refining, or even scrapping, both their theory and the data they feel they need to gather in light of this. This is a relatively good overall description of an approach to assessment in social work, and suggests that workers might benefit from studying the strengths and limitations of different evaluative study designs.

Critical Thinking Box

Read: Blythe, B. and Jayaratne, S. (1999). *Michigan Families First Effectiveness Study: A Summary of Findings*. Michigan: State of Michigan Family Independence Agency.

Blythe and Jayaratne (1999) evaluated a service targeted at children at imminent risk of care entry. Children were randomly assigned either into foster care or IFPS following a decision by a court that foster care would be necessary if IFPS was not provided. At 12

▶

months, 93% of the IFPS children were living at home, compared to 43% of those who received foster care. Indicators of school performance and contact with police indicated little difference between the groups, suggesting that children were maintained at home without obvious harm to their welfare.

- A key first question is: do you feel this RCT is ethical? What might make you think it was or was not ethical?

- How would you judge this study in relation to:
  - Internal validity?
  - External validity?

- How applicable do you think it would therefore be to you if you were the manager tasked with setting up a new service for children at risk of entering care?

Summary

This chapter started by outlining three basic research designs for evaluative research. This was followed by extensive discussion of the limitations of each approach. It would be right to conclude that there are no simple answers in the complex world or evaluative research; however, it would be wrong to decide that there are no answers. Evidence-based practice does not mean the easy shift from 'unanswered questions to unquestioned answers'. Rather it involves a progressive identification of what seems to work, and an increasing appreciation of the complexities involved in understanding the complex factors that shape services that make a difference. We hope that this chapter has illustrated this complexity and left you able to have a critical appreciation of different types of evaluative study.

Further resources

W.K. Kellogg Foundation (2004). *Evaluation Handbook* [online]. Available at: www.wkkf. org/resource-directory/resource/2010/w-k-kellogg-foundation-evaluation -handbook (accessed 15 October).

7

HOW TO USE NUMBERS TO DESCRIBE A SAMPLE

LEARNING OUTCOMES

By the end of this chapter you should be able to:

- Identify and define a variable and the characteristics of variables in terms of level of measurement (nominal, ordinal, interval, ratio)
- Define and calculate descriptive statistics of frequency, percentage, measures of central tendency (mean, median, mode), range, standard deviation and variance
- Identify and critique the usefulness of descriptive statistics in describing a sample and in answering research questions based on a social work example

Introduction

In this chapter, we discuss how numbers can be used to describe a sample. In Chapter 3, we defined a sample as a subset of a population. For example, a population could be all 50 adults who live in a residential care home, and a sample could be 25 of those adults selected based on a specific sampling method (i.e. simple random, stratified, convenience). We would anticipate that an understanding of those 25 adults could provide an understanding and insight into the population as a whole; although, as Chapter 3 highlighted, the extent to which we can transfer knowledge of a sample to a population is contingent on the choice and rigour of our sampling methods. Through this chapter, we aim to demonstrate how a description of a sample, through the use of quantitative methods, can better assist in understanding the characteristics and needs of the sample and the population which the sample represents. This knowledge is relevant to your social work practice as such an understanding can enable you to better understand the characteristics of a particular group of service users, tailor social work services to service users' needs and begin to determine whether such services are effective. To begin, we must first revisit the concept of a variable.

A variable is something that varies in that it has more than one category and it can be measured. For example, sex is a variable where individuals could either be in the category of 'female', 'male' or 'intersexed'. Age is a variable where individuals have a chronological age assigned to them and this assigned age can vary from one person to the next. Level of satisfaction with a social work service is a variable in that some individuals will have a higher or lower level of satisfaction than others. In describing a sample, researchers often collect information (called data) on variables from the sample members. For example, a researcher may ask the sample members the following questions:

1   What is your sex? (please circle one below)
    a.   Female
    b.   Male
    c.   Intersexed

2   What is your age in years? _____

3   To what extent do you agree or disagree with the following statement?:

    The reablement programme enhanced my independence. (Circle one below)

1	2	3	4	5
Strongly disagree		Neither agree nor disagree		Strongly agree

In regard to the variable sex, the sample members will select one category that best describes their sex (e.g. female). The sample members will then input their age in years (e.g. 37), and finally, the members will circle a number that best depicts the extent to which they agreed that the reablement programme enhanced independence (e.g. 4). The questions capture information on specific variables (sex, age, level of agreement) of the sample members and the answers to the questions are referred to as data. The use of quantitative skills becomes important when the researcher needs to summarise all the answers to the questions. This is referred to as 'analysing the data', which is basically summarising all the responses to the questions and presenting a picture of the complete sample. For example, the total number of males, females and intersexed individuals among the sample members, the average age of the members and the average level of agreement from service users.

Data do not only come from asking specific questions directly from sample members, such as the examples above, but could also come from existing information. For example, many social service organisations keep information (data) on their service users, such as their sex, ethnicity, age, employment status, marital status, educational achievement or number of hours of contact with a social worker. Researchers will often gather data already held by social service organisations when available so that they do not need to gather the information directly from the sample members (see Chapter 11).

Variables, such as sex, age, and level of agreement, have characteristics that can be used to distinguish between 'types' of variables. This is often referred to as 'levels of measurement', which include nominal, ordinal, interval and ratio. In this chapter, we will define and examine the levels of measurement of variables and identify how the level of measurement of a variable can influence the type of data analysis to use that will best describe the variable among the sample. We will then look at the different types of data analyses, such as frequency, percentage, mean, median, mode, range, standard deviation and variance. Such types of data analysis are referred to as descriptive statistics as they merely describe the variables and the sample.

Descriptive statistics help to tell a story about the sample and can provide an overall picture of a phenomenon or situation. Throughout the chapter, we will define each type of data analysis and you will practise calculating them using example data. We will use a research example of the reablement programme – a programme for adults who need social care services on a short-term basis – to illustrate the levels of measurement of variables, and basic descriptive statistics of frequency, percentage, mean, median, mode, range and standard deviation.

'Research in practice' – reablement

To illustrate the key concepts within this chapter, we will use examples based on a piece of research that evaluates the effectiveness of the reablement programme. The reablement programme is a service provided by adult social service organisations, usually the local authority, to assist adults to live independently. The reablement programme is 'designed to help people learn or relearn the skills necessary for daily living which may have been lost through deterioration in health and/or increased support needs. A focus on regaining physical ability is central, as is active reassessment' (Francis et al., 2011, p. 1). Individuals are often referred to the programme through the community or via hospital discharge, particularly for individuals who are viewed as capable of regaining independence after a temporary loss, such as a hip fracture. Services could include assistance with relearning how to use the stairs, dressing, washing and preparing meals (Francis et al., 2011). The programme is designed to be time limited (usually 6–12 weeks), and after the end of the specified time the individual is either able to live independently or, if not, is referred to long-term adult social service support.

The reablement programme is considered a 'preventative' intervention in that the programme aims to assist individuals to regain independence so that they do not need to rely on adult social services. The aim of the programme is to 'reduce the number of care hours required to support a person at home or to develop their independence so that they can remain in their own home instead of being admitted to residential or nursing care' (Francis et al., 2011, p. 3). Social workers who refer to the reablement programme should have information regarding the extent to which the service actually enables independence and enhances quality of life. A basic question from social workers could be: 'What does the research say about the extent to which the reablement programme is able to achieve its aim of promoting independence and reducing a reliance on adult social care services?'

A piece of research conducted by Reidy et al. (2013) aimed to 'explore users' perceptions of the new reablement service and its impact on their lives, and evaluate short-term outcomes for users of reablement' (p. 3). They gathered data such as socio-demographics of the service users, referral data and other criteria. The data were collected before and after the reablement programme for each service user. The data analysis found that the service users' needs assessment were significantly lower after the reablement programme when compared to their needs assessment before the programme, there were significant reductions on the amount of money required for their care, yet there were no significant changes in terms of the scales that measured health and well-being. The results indicate that the reablement programme is successful in terms of reducing service users' needs and the financial costs of their care after reablement (Reidy, 2013). Thus, the results of this study could be useful to social workers when determining whether to refer a service user to the reablement programme as the research indicates that the programme is effective in the short term. In order to utilise this research in practice, social workers must be able to understand the key concepts of research and statistics to interpret the research, and determine its validity and applicability to their practice.

Based on this research in practice example, we will look at relevant research concepts and statistics by using factious 'reablement programme' data to answer the following research questions: (1) What are the characteristics of the adults using the reablement programme? (2) What is the primary reason for using the reablement programme? (3) Did the hours of care increase or decrease for the individuals from the start of the programme till their discharge? and (4) To what extent did the service users agree or disagree that the reablement programme enhanced independence?

Basic concepts: variables and descriptive statistics

In order to answer the research questions on the reablement programme, we must understand the key concepts needed to assist us. We will discuss the basic concepts by providing definitions and the rationale for their use. We will then provide examples of each by using example data on the reablement programme.

Variables, data and data sets

As discussed above, a variable is something that varies and can be measured. Information on variables is referred to as data. Within social work research, data often come from individuals, referred to as cases, and researchers will collect data from individuals across a number of variables. For example, researchers may collect data on several variables from individuals who use the reablement programme, such as sex, ethnicity, age, reason for being referred to the programme and number of hours of care at entry to and exit from the programme. All the data collected are then entered into a software package to enable data analysis, such as Excel or the Statistical Package for the Social Sciences (SPSS). When the data on the variables are entered into the package, this is referred to as the 'data set'. A typical data set will consist of all the cases (usually individuals) from which data were collected across all the variables.

For quantitative analysis, the data should be in numeric form. For example, our survey questions above will need to have a number assigned to each response to enable quantitative analysis. Age is already in numeric form (age in years) and our question about level of agreement assigns numbers to the level of agreement (1 = strongly disagree, 2 = disagree, 3 = neither agree nor disagree, 4 = agree, 5 = strongly agree). The variable 'sex' gives possible answers of 'female', 'male', and 'intersexed'. In order to enable data analysis, we will need to assign a number to each possible answer. We will then keep a 'codebook' to inform us of what each number represents. For example, 1 = female; 2 = male; and 3 = intersexed. Based

Table 7.1 Example data set – sample of 10 cases

Case number	Sex	Age	Reason for reablement	Hours of care at entry	Hours of care at exit	Level of agreement
1	1	73	1	10	5	4
2	1	65	1	7	0	4
3	2	89	2	5	0	3
4	2	89	1	15	7	4
5	1	78	3	5	0	5
6	2	69	1	6	0	5
7	1	80	2	7	0	2
8	1	66	3	10	7	5
9	2	58	2	4	0	4
10	1	72	1	7	4	3

Code: Sex (1 = female; 2 = male; 3 = intersexed); Reason for reablement (physical disability = 1; temporary illness = 2; mental health = 3); Level of agreement (1 = strongly disagree; 2 = disagree; 3 = neither agree nor disagree; 4 = agree; 5 = strongly agree).

on this information, Table 7.1 depicts our data set consisting of 10 cases. We have included additional variables required from the service users of the reablement programme in order to answer our research questions.

Levels of measurement

In order to analyse the data from the variables in Table 7.1, we must first determine the level of measurement of each variable. The level of measurement of the variable will inform us of which data analysis to use in describing the variable among the sample. Variables can be classified as categorical or continuous and can have different levels of measurement. We will first look at categorical and continuous variables and then move to levels of measurement of variables.

A categorical variable is one that is made up of categories or distinct entities (Field, 2009). For example, our variable of 'sex' above has three categories or distinct entities: 'female'; 'male'; and 'intersexed'. Other examples of categorical variables include ethnicity, religious affiliation, educational attainment, employment status, marital status or political affiliation. Continuous variables, on the other hand, provide a number (or score) and can take on any value on a measurement scale (Field, 2009). For example, age in years is a continuous variable in that the age can range from 0 to infinity! Height, weight, temperature and number of hours of care are examples of continuous variables. Continuous variables can also include discrete variables. Whereas a continuous variable can be measured to precision, such as a height and weight, a discrete variable is represented by certain values, which are usually whole numbers (Field, 2009). For example, level of agreement with the reablement service is a discrete variable in that the answers are whole numbers along a 5-point scale (1 = strongly disagree; 5 = strongly agree) and individuals are not given the option of selecting any other numbers, such as 4.25.

Before we go further, let's test your understanding of categorical and continuous variables by reviewing the questions in Exercise 7.1.

Exercise 7.1: Categorical and continuous variables

Identify whether the following variables are categorical or continuous:

1. Time in foster care
2. Number of drinks per day
3. Mental health diagnosis
4. Type of sentence for young people
5. Number of GCSEs at Grade C or above

Categorical and continuous variables can be further broken down into what we call levels of measurement, which include nominal, ordinal, interval and ratio level variables. Nominal level variables are categorical in that such variables are classified into categories. For example, sex is a nominal level variable where there are three categories (sometimes referred to as labels or names) from which to select: female; male; or intersexed. When we assign a number to each category (label or name) to enable data analysis (1 = female; 2 = male; 3 = intersexed), we are not assuming that one value (e.g. 3) is higher than another (e.g. 1), but rather we are merely assigning a number to the category to enable quantitative analysis. Because nominal level variables are categorical then the examples of categorical variables stated above are examples of nominal level variables, such as: sex, ethnicity, religious affiliation, educational attainment, employment status, marital status, political affiliation or a response of 'yes' or 'no'.

Whereas nominal level variables are categorical, in that the variable is a name, a label or a category, and the number assigned for data analysis does not imply value, ordinal level variables are also categorical yet can imply an order or rank. Ordinal level variables rank something according to a particular characteristic or criterion. Whereas the value assigned to the rank or order does matter, the difference between any two values does not. For example, after experiencing an injury you go to A&E and the nurse asks you to express the amount of pain that you are in on a scale from 1 to 10, where 1 means no pain at all and 10 means the worst pain you have ever experienced. You state an 8, which is clearly more pain than a 6, and a 6 is more pain than a 4. But what we do not know is whether the distance between an 8 and 6 is the same as the distance in pain experienced from a 6 to a 4. The value of pain experienced is simply a way in which to rank or order the pain experienced, but not to determine the distance between two values. Other examples of ordinal level variables can include degree classification (fail, third, lower second, upper second, first), order of preference (first, second, third, fourth), or rank order from tallest to shortest. Ordinal level variables can tell us more than nominal level variables because they can tell us not only what exists but also the order in which things happened. Despite this, ordinal level variables are unable to tell us the distance between two values on a scale (Field, 2009).

Interval level variables move us away from categorical variables into continuous variables. Interval level variables require the value associated with a variable to be ordered with equal units of measurement between them. For example, temperature as expressed in Celsius or Fahrenheit. The difference in terms of unit of measurement (degrees) between 22° Celsius and 24° Celsius (2°) is the same difference in terms of unit of measurement as between 20° and 22° (2°). Interval level variables also have an arbitrary zero, which means a score of zero does not mean that there is none of that variable, but rather it actually has meaning. Again, a temperature of 0° Celsius does not mean that there is no temperature, but rather 0° Celsius expresses how 'freezing' cold it is outside!

Ratio level variables are the same as interval level in that they have equal units of measurement between values, but there is a true zero. This means that when the value of the variable is a 0 then there is none of that variable. Examples include length, time, age or weight. For example, a value of 0 centimetres means there is no length, a value of 0 time means there is no time, a value of 0 age means that there is no age, and a value of 0 kilograms means there is no weight. Again, with equal units of measurement between values we can see that the difference between 36 years and 37 years is 12 months, which is the same as the difference between 37 years and 38 years.

Interval and ratio level variables only differ in terms of the meaning of the value 'zero'. Often, researchers will group interval level variables and ratio level variables together as one type of level of measurement, and the quantitative data analysis software package, SPSS, actually groups interval and ratio level variables together and refers to them as 'scale'. The use of scale merely means that the variable has numeric values that represent order and there is equal distance between the numeric values.

We must point out that there is some controversy within the social sciences about whether Likert scales are ordinal or interval. Likert scales are when researchers ask questions that require the respondent to select a number on a scale (usually listed in ascending order) and the number corresponds to a particular response. For example, the following question and Likert scale can be classified as ordinal or interval depending on the argument from the researcher.

Question 1: Overall, how satisfied are you with the reablement service? (Please circle one)

1	2	3	4	5
Very unsatisfied	Unsatisfied	Neutral	Satisfied	Very satisfied

Strictly speaking, we would classify this variable as having an ordinal level of measurement, because there is not an equal distance (in terms of unit of measurement) between a 3 (neither satisfied) and a 4 (satisfied). The argument for this variable being classified as an ordinal level of measurement is that the variable is measuring a person's experience, which is subjective where the meaning of a 4 to one person might actually be the meaning of a 5 to another. We are not actually able to measure the distance between the values using a standard unit of measurement. Despite this, other researchers argue that the responses to the question do enable equal unit of measurement between the responses. The difference between 1 (very unsatisfied) and 2 (unsatisfied) would be the same as the difference between 5 (very satisfied) and 4 (satisfied). Although we will refer to Likert scale variables as ordinal throughout this book, research on social work practice often includes variables that measure experiences and perspectives and researchers tend to treat such Likert scale responses as if they were interval to enable data analysis. We will discuss this in more detail when the issue arises throughout the book.

Before we move on, let's test your understanding of levels of measurement of variables. Exercise 7.2 provides some examples of variables.

Exercise 7.2: Levels of measurement

Look at the variables below and specify whether they are nominal, ordinal, interval or ratio.

1. Number of hours of care per week
2. Sexual orientation
3. Amount of alcohol consumed per week
4. Likelihood of using research in social work practice (on a scale of 1–5)
5. Postcode
6. Preference of hobbies (rank 5 listed hobbies in order of preference)
7. Household income
8. Confidence level of a social worker in conducting home visits (on a scale from 1–10)
9. Referral source
10. Risk assessment score (–10–+10)

We have defined a variable and examined the characteristics of variables in terms of whether they are categorical or continuous and their level of measurement – nominal, ordinal, interval or ratio. Now that we have explored the characteristics of variables, we will move to a discussion of how to analyse a group of variables, or otherwise stated, how to analyse data from a data set. We will first look at frequency and percentage and then move to measures of central tendency, which looks at the typical values or scores among a variable in a sample, and then conclude with range, standard deviation, and variance, which examines the variation between the data.

Frequency and percentage

The frequency is just one way of summarising (or aggregating) the data (or values) of variables within a data set. Frequency is defined as the count of the categories or values of a variable and is depicted by the symbol *f*. We calculate a frequency by combining like responses with like and counting the number within each category. For example, our nominal level variable of sex, which has three categories (female; male; intersexed), could be analysed by determining the number of people who responded as female, the number who responded as male and the number who responded as intersexed. The number of people who responded within each category is referred to as the frequency (*f*). Let's refer back to our reablement programme data set, with sex depicted below in Table 7.2.

We can see that there are 10 cases, which means our sample is 10. We now want to determine the frequency of the sample that is female, male or inter-sexed. We will count the number of cases that responded with 1, the number of cases that responded with 2 and the number of cases that responded with 3. From our calculations, we can conclude that the frequency of females in our sample is 6, the frequency of males is 4, and the frequency of intersexed is 0. We can report the results of our data analysis through written text as follows:

The sex of the sample of 10 service users of the reablement programme included 6 females, 4 males and 0 intersexed. Alternatively, we could report the results in table form through a frequency distribution. Table 7.3 illustrates the frequency distribution of the sex of our sample of 10 service users.

Table 7.2 Example data set – sex

Case number	Sex
1	1
2	1
3	2
4	2
5	1
6	2
7	1
8	1
9	2
10	1

Code: Sex (1 = female; 2 = male; 3 = intersexed)

Table 7.3 Frequency distribution of sex (*N* = 10)

Sex	f
Female	6
Male	4
Intersexed	0
Total *N* = 10	

We have looked at how to determine the frequency of responses, but we now want to calculate the percentage of the sample of service users that identified as female, male or intersexed. A percentage indicates the frequency as per 100 cases. The percentage is calculated by dividing the frequency by the total number of cases for that variable and then multiplying by 100. To calculate the percentage of cases identifying as female in our sample above, we would divide 6 by 10 and then multiply by 100. Let's take this step-by-step.

Step 1: Divide the frequency of females by the total number in the sample

6/10 = 0.6

Step 2: Multiply the value by 100

0.6 x 100 = 60%

The percentage of males within our sample is 40%:

Step 1: 4/10 = 0.4

Step 2: 0.4 x 100 = 40%

Finally, the percentage of intersexed within our sample is 0%:

Step 1: 0/10 = 0

Step 2: 0 x 100 = 0%

As with frequency, we can present the findings of our data analysis in written text as follows:

Out of a sample of 10 service users of the reablement programme, 60% identified as female, 40% identified as male and 0% identified as intersexed. Alternatively, we could present in table form as in Table 7.4.

Table 7.4 Percentage of sex (N = 10)

Sex	%
Female	60%
Male	40%
Intersexed	0%
Total = 100%	

The researcher has a choice as to the best way in which to present the data. One researcher may decide that the analysis of the data is best illustrated through frequencies, another researcher may decide that the findings are best depicted by percentages, and yet another researcher may provide a table with both frequencies and percentages. There is no one correct way in which to present findings, but rather the researcher should choose a presentation that gives the reader the most accurate and useful information about the sample. This takes us to another type of data analysis: measures of central tendency.

Measures of central tendency

'Measures of central tendency' refers to the typical value or score within a sample. This could be the average value among a sample, the middle point among the values of a sample or the most common value among a sample. Measures of central tendency help to describe our sample beyond just the frequency and percentage of values as they tell us the average value or where the majority of the values tend to centre (or lie) within the sample. There are three types of measures of central tendency, which are the mean, median and mode.

The mean is the sum of all values of a variable in a sample divided by the total number of cases for that variable. This is often referred to as the average. For example, let's refer back to our reablement data set with age depicted in Table 7.5.

To calculate the mean age among this sample, we would first sum all values of the variable age and then divide by the total number of cases. This would provide us with the mean age among the sample of 10. Let's calculate the mean of age of the service users:

Step 1: Sum all the values of the variable age

73 + 65 + 89 + 89 + 78 + 69 + 80 + 66 + 58 + 72 = 739

Step 2: Divide the value by the total number of cases

739/10 = 73.9

Table 7.5 Example data set – age

Case Number	Age
1	73
2	65
3	89
4	89
5	78
6	69
7	80
8	66
9	58
10	72

For our sample of service users of the reablement programme, we can report that the mean age is 73.9 years.

The median is the middlemost value in a list of values among a variable. In order to calculate the median, we must first put the values in ascending order. We will then count the number of values and divide by two. This will give us the position of the middlemost value, which means that there will be an equal number of values both above and below this value. Let's calculate the median of age using the data from Table 7.5.

Step 1: Arrange the values in lowest to highest

58   65   66   69   72   73   78   82   89   89

Step 2: Count the number of values and divide by two

10/2 = 5

Step 3: Determine the position of the middlemost value where there are 5 values above and 5 values below

58   65   66   69   72   73   78   82   89   89
                        ↑

The point would be between 72 and 73. Because the middlemost point is positioned between these two values, we must determine the value that is between these two values, or, otherwise stated, the average between these two values.

Step 4: Calculate the average between the values to determine the middlemost position

72 + 73 = 145

145/2 = 72.5

For our sample, we can report that the median age is 72.5 years.

Finally, the mode is the most frequent or common values in a list of values. For our example of age, we would need to look at all the values and the mode would be the most occurring value in the list of values.

Step 1: Examine the values and determine the most occurring value

58 65 66 69 72 73 78 82 89 89
                                    ↑   ↑
There is only one value that occurs more than once: 89.

For our sample, we can report that the most common age (mode) among the service users is 89 years.

Therefore, we can now report more information about our data set that more fully describes our sample. We can report that out of 10 service users of the reablement programme, there are 6 females representing 60% of our sample, 4 males representing 40% of our sample and 0 intersexed representing 0% of our sample. The mean age of service users is 73.9 years, the median age is 72.5 years and the most common age among the sample is 89 years. But how do we know what is the most appropriate statistic (or finding) to report?

The level of measurement of a variable (nominal, ordinal, interval, ratio) will determine the most appropriate measure of central tendency to report. As nominal level variables are categorical, it would not be logical to calculate the median or mean of the values that we assign for data analysis. The variable sex, from our example above, has three categories (female; male; intersexed) and we assigned values to each category in order to enter the data into the data set to enable quantitative data analysis (1 = female; 2 = male; 3 = intersexed). From the data, we can determine the frequency and percentage of females, males and intersexed as well as the most common value (mode) but it would not make sense to calculate the mean and median. Let's look at our data set in Table 7.6 to illustrate this point.

The mean of the variable sex is 1.4 (Step 1: 1 + 1 + 2 + 2 + 1 + 2 + 1 + 1 + 2 + 1 = 14; Step 2: 14/10 = 1.4), the median is 1 (Step 1: 1, 1, 1, 1, 1, 1, 2, 2, 2, 2; Step 2: 10/2 = 5; Step 3: 1 + 1 = 2 and 2/2 = 1) and the mode is 1. As this example illustrates, the mean of the variable sex would be 1.4 which would mean somewhere between female and male! Although the median does

Table 7.6 Example data set – sex

Case Number	Sex
1	1
2	1
3	2
4	2
5	1
6	2
7	1
8	1
9	2
10	1

Code: Sex (1 = female; 2 = male; 3 = intersexed)

point to a specific category (1 = female) it would have been different if there were one less female and one more male. In this situation, the median would have been 1.5, which again would mean between female and male. The mode is the only measure of central tendency that makes sense. The mode of sex is 1, which means female, and indicates that the most common response among the sample was a sex of female.

Whereas the mode is the only measure of central tendency that can be reported among nominal level variables, the mean, median and mode can be reported for ordinal, interval and ratio level variables. The researcher who is most familiar with the data set should report the statistic (or finding) that most accurately depicts the data. For example, our mean, median and mode for age yielded three different measures of central tendency (mean = 73.9; median = 72.5; mode = 89). Whereas the mean and median are only 1.4 units apart, the difference between the mode and the mean is 15.1 units and the difference between the mode and the median is 16.5 units. The researcher will need to look at the data to determine what is most logical in terms of best providing a picture of the sample. Let's look at our example data again:

58   65   66   69   72   73   78   82   89   89

Based on the data, we would argue that the mode does not accurately represent the age of the sample because 89 is at the highest end of the values and there are more individuals (7 in total) who are under age 80. The mean and median are more accurate in terms of describing the 'average' age of the sample.

The mean is the most commonly reported measure of central tendency as it fully takes into account every single value. But there are times when the mean is not the most appropriate to report, such as when 'outliers' are present. An outlier is an extreme value that does not naturally fit within a list of values. For example, if we were to add 18 to our values for age above, our new mean would be 68.8 and our median would be 72. The 18 would be considered an outlier because it does not naturally fall within the range of values as do the other values of age. In this situation, we would choose to report the median as it more accurately describes the age of the sample.

Reporting the range of values can be useful when reporting the measure of central tendency. The range is simply the lowest value in the list of values and the highest value in a list of values. For our variable of age, the range would be 58–89. Therefore, when describing the age of our sample, we would report the following: 'The mean age of the service users of the reablement programme is 73.9 years with a range from 58–89.' Test your ability to calculate the mean, median and mode of the values listed in Exercise 7.3 and determine which measure of central tendency you would report.

Exercise 7.3: Measures of central tendency

Calculate the mean, median and mode for each variable's list of values and determine which measure of central tendency you would report.

1. Level of satisfaction (1 = very unsatisfied to 5 = very satisfied)
   2 3 3 1 2 1 2 5 1 2 1

2. Assessment score
   72 45 56 38 74 65 74 59 60

3. Years in care
   7 5 4 5 6 2 1 3 1 5

4. Local authority (1 = North-east Somerset; 2 = Somerset; 3 = Bristol City Council; 4 = South Gloucestershire)
   2 3 3 3 1 1 2 4 3 3

5. Units of alcohol per week
   3 7 0 2 3 5 7 3 35

Standard deviation and variance

Finally, we would like to introduce you to two other concepts useful in describing a sample: standard deviation and variance. These two concepts will also form the basis of material presented in later chapters within this book. The range of values, as discussed above, tell us the difference in values from highest to lowest, but what the range doesn't tell us is the extent to which all the values vary in between the highest and lowest scores or the extent to which they vary from the mean score. We saw with our variable age that the variables ranged from 58 to 89, which is a difference of 31 units of measurement, and we know that the mean is 73.9, but we don't know the average distance of each value from the mean. For example, do all the values lie closely to the mean of 73.9 or do they lie further away and closer to the highest and lowest values of 89 and 58? To help describe a sample better, we might want to know the average (or mean) distance that the values lie from the mean of age (73.9). We are able to calculate the standard deviation, which is a measure of how much the values in the sample vary around the mean.

The standard deviation is often expressed as *SD* and is generally calculated by subtracting each value from the mean, adding the values together and dividing by the total number of values, which gives us the mean deviation. Although this would be the logical way in which to calculate the mean deviation (or the mean of the deviations of values from the mean), this does not work mathematically. This is due to the fact that the mean is generally the average value, where half of the values are above the mean and half of the values are below the mean. Therefore, summing the distances of the values above the mean and the values below the mean will cancel both out. Let's illustrate this point with numbers provided by Dancey and Reidy (2011, p. 76), which has a mean of 6:

$$1 \quad 4 \quad 5 \quad 6 \quad 9 \quad 11$$

Step 1: Subtract the mean from each of the values

$$11 - 6 = 5$$

$$9 - 6 = 3$$

$$6 - 6 = 0$$

$$5 - 6 = -1$$

$$4 - 6 = -2$$

$$1 - 6 = -5$$

Step 2: Add the values together and divide by the number of values

$$5 + 3 + 0 - 1 - 2 - 5 = 0$$

$$0/6 = 0$$

As the example illustrates, the sum of the distance of values above the mean is cancelled out by the sum of the distance of values below the mean (the value is 0!). In order to address this problem, we can square each of the deviations, which means multiplying a number by itself (e.g. 5 squared is 5 x 5 = 25; 3 squared is 3 x 3 = 9). This will result in all deviations being positive (remember that a negative (–) number multiplied by (x) a negative (–) number equals (=) a positive (+) number). At this point, we can then add all the squared deviations together and divide by the total number of values. The result is what is referred to as the variance. The variance is the mean deviation of values from the sample mean, yet this value is squared and is not expressed in the same unit as the values themselves (Dancey and Reidy, 2011). Therefore, we need to take the square root of the variance in order to obtain the standard deviation. Let's calculate the variance and standard deviation of age from our sample reablement data set, which has a mean of 73.9:

58 65 66 69 72 73 78 82 89 89

Step 1: Subtract the mean from each of the values

89 – 73.9 = 15.1

89 – 73.9 = 15.1

82 – 73.9 = 8.1

78 – 73.9 = 4.1

73 – 73.9 = –0.9

72 – 73.9 = –1.9

69 – 73.9 = –4.9

66 – 73.9 = –7.9

65 – 73.9 = –8.9

58 – 73.9 = –15.9

Step 2: Square each value and add together

228.01 + 228.01 + 65.61 + 16.81 + 0.81 + 3.61 + 24.01 + 62.41 + 79.21 + 252.81

= 961.30

Step 3: Divide by the total number of values in the sample to obtain the variance

961.30 / 10 = 96.13

Step 4: Take the square root of the variance to obtain the standard deviation.

$\sqrt{96.13} = 9.8$

The standard deviation is 9.8, which indicates that the ages within the sample vary around the mean age of 73.9 years by 9.8 years. Based on calculating the standard deviation of age, we can now describe the age of the service users of the reablement programme as follows:

> The mean age of the sample is 73.9 with a range from 58–89 and a standard devia-tion of 9.8. This means that although the ages range from 58–89, the majority of the sample members will have an age that is within 9.8 years above or below 73.9 years of age (64.1–83.7).

Let's now return to our 'Research in practice' example. Based on our findings, let's describe the sample of service users who use the reablement service.

'Research in practice' – reablement

We have looked at the key concepts and descriptive statistics that we need in order to answer our research questions of the reablement programme. We will now refer back to our example data set in Table 7.1 to answer the four questions using our knowledge of variables and data analysis.

What are the characteristics of the adults using the reablement programme?

We have already calculated the descriptive statistics for sex and age of the ser-vice users of the reablement programme, which will give us a picture of the characteristics of the adults using the programme. Our answer to the research question is: 'Out of 10 service users of the reablement programme, 6 (60%) are female and 4 (40%) are male. The mean age is 73.9 with a range from 58–89 and a standard deviation of 9.8 years.'

What is the primary reason for using the reablement programme?

Based on our data in Table 7.1, we can see data collected on the reason for using the reablement programme. The coding for the variable indicates that 1 = physical disability; 2 = temporary illness; and 3 = mental health. Because 'reason for using reablement programme' is a nominal level variable, we can calculate the percent-age and frequency as well as the mode. The answer to our research question is:

> Out of 10 service users of the reablement programme, 5 (50%) individuals were referred due to physical disability, 3 (30%) were referred due to temporary illness, and 2 (20%) were referred due to mental illness. The most common reasons for referral is physical disability.

Did the hours of care increase or decrease for the individuals from the start of the programme till their discharge?

We can see from Table 7.1 that there are two columns: (1) hours of care at entry; and (2) hours of care at exit. Both variables are ratio level variables. In order to answer our question, we will need to calculate the mean hours of care at entry and the mean of hours of care at exit to see if the mean has increased or decreased from the start of the programme till discharge. We might also want to report the median, mode, range and standard deviation for each variable to give a more complete picture of the data. Our answer to the research question is:

> The mean hours of care at entry was 7.6 hours and the mean hours of care at exit was 2.3 hours. The findings indicate a decrease in hours of care from the start of the programme till service users' discharge.

To what extent did the service users agree or disagree that the reablement programme enhanced independence?

Finally, we would like to know the extent to which the service users agreed or disagreed that the reablement programme enhanced independence. Table 7.1 provides the data for the variable 'level of agreement' with a code of 1 = strongly disagree; 2 = disagree; 3 = neither agree nor disagree; 4 = agree; and 5 = strongly agree. The variable is ordinal level. The data could be analysed in numerous ways, such as the frequency and percentage of service users who answered strongly disagree, disagree, neither agree nor disagree, agree and strongly agree. The data could also be analysed by calculating the overall mean of the responses. Our answer to the research question is:

> Out of 10 service users, 0 (0%) indicated they strongly disagreed that the reablement programme enhanced their independence, 1 (10%) indicated they disagreed, 2 (20%) indicated they neither agreed nor disagreed; 4 (40%) indicated they agreed; and 3 (30%) indicated they strongly agreed. The mean level of agreement was 3.9, indicating a level of agreement near 'agree'.

The data collected and presented in the data set have enabled us to answer the four research questions. We can conclude that the service users of the reablement programme are generally female and around age 73. They are often referred to the programme due to physical disabilities and their hours of care do decrease from entry to exit. The service users tend to agree that the reablement programme enables their independence. Although the results tend to be quite positive for the reablement programme, we cannot safely say that the results are illustrative of the reablement programme as a whole. Chapter 8 will give us more tools to explore the generalisability of the results and assist us in answering the question: are the results representative of the general population of people who use the reablement programme or are they only truly representative of the sample alone?

Test your understanding

Table 7.7 lists data on service users who attended a 10-week programme providing one-hour group peer support for people who experience depression. Funders of the group have asked you to provide them with a picture of the individuals who are currently attending the group. Based on the data set in Table 7.7, determine the level of measurement for each of the variables and analyse the data using descriptive statistics. Provide a summary of the overall picture of the service users.

Table 7.7 Service user data from group peer support

Case number	Sex	Age	Ethnicity	Depression assessment score
1	1	29	1	50
2	1	56	1	35
3	2	43	1	47
4	1	36	2	32
5	1	45	1	55
6	1	37	2	52
7	2	42	1	30
8	1	45	3	50
9	2	60	1	30

Code: Sex (1 = female; 2 = male; 3 = intersexed); Ethnicity (1 = White British; 2 = Black British; 3 = Asian British)

Critical Thinking Box

Butler, Baruch, Hickey and Fonagy (2011) sought to determine whether an intervention of Multisystemic Therapy (MST) was more effective in reducing youth offending and out-of-home placements among young people when compared to usual services delivered by youth offending teams (YOTs). They randomly assigned families to either the MST group or to the usual services of YOTs. The table below by Butler et al. (2011, p. 1223) provides a picture of the characteristics and demographics of the young people assigned to the MST group and to the YOT group. Examine the table and answer the following questions: (1) Provide an example of a frequency, percentage, mean and standard deviation (SD) and indicate what this tells you about the sample; (2) Create an argument for where and why the authors should have presented the median or mode when reporting; (3) Is the table clear and would you suggest any amendments to the presentation of the findings?; and (4) Provide an overall picture of the sample of young people assigned to MST and YOT.

TABLE 1 Pretreatment Demographic and Diognostic Data for the MUltisystemic Therapy (MST) and Youth Offending Teams (YOT) Samples

	MST		YOT	
	x̄ or n	SD or %	x̄ or n	SD or %
Demograpic Characteristic				
Number	56		52	
Mean age (months)	182.7	12.3	180.6	12.9
Female gender	9	16.4%	10	19.2%
Mean SES (range 0–6)	2.5	1.6	2.0	1.7
Ethnicity				
White British/European	24	49.1%	13	25.5%
Black African/Afro-Caribbean	15	27.3%	20	39.2%
Asian	2	3.6%	3	5.9%
Mixed/Other	11	20.0%	15	29.4%
Offenses in year before referral				
Total number	2.5	1.6%	2.4	1.8
Violent offenses	0.75	1.0	0.73	0.9
Nonviolent offenses	1.8	1.6	1.7	1.7
Number with custodial sentences	0	0	0	0
IPPA score	94.2	SD24.6	100.3	SD19.6

Note: PPA = Inventory of parent and Peer Attachment SES = Socioeconomic status.

Summary

In this chapter, we have reviewed the key concepts of variables, data and data sets, and the characteristics of variables in terms of levels of measurement. We also explored and practised calculating basic descriptive statistics of frequency, percentage, measures of central tendency, and variance and standard deviation. We used the example data from the reablement programme to illustrate how data and descriptive statistics can assist in providing a picture of service users and programmes delivered by social service organisations. Such tools are useful in better understanding who uses social work services, why, and the extent to which the service is effective and perceived as useful to the service user.

Further resources

Rosenthal, J. A. (2012). *Statistics and Data Interpretation for Social Work*. New York, NY: Springer Publishing Company. (See Chapter 3, 'Central Tendency', pp. 29–38.)

8

HOW TO MAKE A DECISION WITH CONFIDENCE

LEARNING OUTCOMES

By the end of this chapter you should be able to:

- Define probability and the characteristics of a probability distribution and normal curve
- Explain hypothesis testing and how to determine if findings are 'statistically significant'
- Define 'α-level' and 'p-value' and identify how to make a decision with confidence while considering Type I and Type II errors

Introduction

Social work research often relies on gathering and analysing data from a sample of subjects that represent a larger population. The aim of such research is to then generalise the findings from the subjects to the population. Yet how can we be confident that the findings from the research on a sample accurately reflects the true situation or condition of the population and that the findings are not due to chance? The use of specific statistical methods, referred to as inferential statistics, enable us to determine how probable it is that our findings from the research on a sample are not due to chance and, thus, are likely to reflect the situation among the population. In order to do so, we must understand the concept of probability. In this chapter, we will explore probability and a probability distribution, otherwise referred to as the standard normal distribution or normal curve. We will then move to discuss how we can use hypothesis testing to determine the probability that our research findings are not due to chance (or sampling error) and, thus, whether any research findings of differences between variables are 'statistically significant'. Finally, we will discuss α-level and p-level and the extent to which we might make a Type I or Type II error in interpreting the research results. Understanding the concepts of probability and statistical significance will enable you, as a social worker, to determine how applicable research findings are to real-life practice situations.

Before we explore an example piece of research, let's look at the concept of probability. Probability is the likelihood that a specific event will occur or how likely something is to happen. We often use the term probability in our everyday language and interchange it with terms such as 'likely' or 'chance'. For example, how likely is it that you will pass a research methods class? Or, what are the chances that you will use research to inform your social work practice? Or, what's the probability that a service user will remain abstinent from alcohol after treatment? You can answer each of these questions with some degree of precision – no chance, very likely, not likely at all, pretty good chance, probable, pretty sure, definite. Each of these responses indicates a different level of probability, from 'no chance' on one end of the spectrum to 'definite' on the other end. Probability is often expressed numerically with 0 indicating an improbable or impossible chance and 1.0 indicating certainty as depicted below.

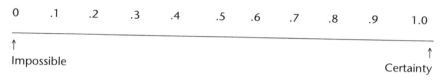

Probability, often simply expressed as 'P', can also be converted to and expressed as a percentage by merely multiplying the probability figure by 100. For example, if you state that the probability that you will pass your research methods course is .9, then you are stating that you are 90% sure you will pass the class (.9 x 100 = 90%). Based on this probability and percentage, you are then able to determine the chances of not passing the class by subtracting 1 from the probability. For example, 1 – .9 = .1. Thus, there is a .1 probability or 10% chance (.1 x 100 = 10%) that you will not pass the class. Alternatively, if you are not feeling very confident, you might state that the probability of passing the class is .4, which means there is a 40% chance that you will pass the class (.4 x 100 = 40%); thus a 60% chance that you will not pass the class (1 – .4 = .6 and .6 x 100 = 60%). As demonstrated, probability can be expressed as a decimal (.9) or as a percentage (90%).

In order to calculate probability, you need to determine the number of times the *specific event* can occur and the number of times *any event* can occur. Once you know these figures, then you would divide the number of times a *specific event* can occur by the number of time *any event* can occur. Therefore, the equation for P is as follows: P = number of times *a specific event* can occur ÷ number of times *any event* can occur. The result will provide you with the probability of the specific event occurring as expressed in a decimal (from 0–1.0). To convert the probability into a percentage, you would multiply the probability by 100.

For example, Box 8.1 consists of seven shapes: two stars, one circle, three triangles and one square. Let's imagine that without looking at the box you are to reach in and select one shape. What is the probability that you will select a circle? Based on the theory of probability, the first step is to determine the number of times a specific event (selecting a circle) can occur. As there is only one circle, the number of times you could select a circle is 1. The next step is to determine the number of times any event (selecting any shape) can occur. As there are seven shapes, the number of times you could select any shape is 7. Therefore, the probability of selecting a circle is 1 out of every 7 draws, or .14, or a 14% chance of selecting a circle (1/7 = .14; .14 x 100 = 14%). What is the probability of selecting a triangle? For this example, the number of times the specific event can occur is 3 (there are three triangles). The number of times any event can occur is 7 as there are seven shapes in total. Therefore, the probability of selecting a triangle is 3 times out of every 7 draws, or .43, or a 43% chance that you will select a triangle (3/7 = .43; .43 x 100 = 43%).

Box 8.1: Seven shapes

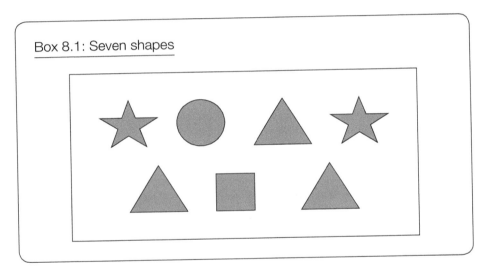

Test your understanding by answering the following exercise questions based on the box of shapes.

Exercise 8.1: What's the probability?

Answer the following questions based on the box of shapes in Box 8.1.

1. What is the probability of selecting a square from the box?
2. What is the probability of selecting a star from the box?
3. What is the probability of selecting any shape from the box?

Now that you have a basic understanding of probability, let's look at a research example that we will refer to throughout this chapter.

'Research in practice' – risk assessment

Social workers working in youth justice are required to assess youth via 'risk assessments' and make predictions about the likelihood, or probability, of future reoffending. The outcomes of risk assessments will assist the social worker in recommending the most appropriate interventions aimed to reduce reoffending. Yet, how accurate or precise are the risk assessment tools in predicting reoffending? Vaswani and Merone (2014) sought to establish the precision of a specific risk assessment tool, the Youth Level of Service-Case Management Inventory (YLS-CMI), used by youth justice social workers in Scotland, in predicting youth reoffending.

The YLS-CMI, developed in Canada, is a tool that assesses a youth's criminogenic risk and needs factors, but also assesses strengths and responsivity indicators, provides a case management plan and allows for the social worker's professional judgement, which means that the social worker can override the final risk classification identified by the assessment (Vaswani and Merone, 2014). Although the tool has been found to be effective in making accurate predictions of future reoffending, studies have found the tool's precision to vary based on the sample population and location of its use. Therefore, Vaswani and Merone (2014) examined data from 1,138 YLS-CMI assessments (883 young people) conducted in a local authority in Scotland between April 2008 and March 2010, as well as reoffending data from the police database, to answer the following research questions:

- Does the YLS-CMI predict future recidivism?

- Does the YLS-CMI predict future serious violence?

- Does the use of professional judgement increase the accuracy of the YLS-CMI?

The 1,138 assessments were on 920 males and 218 females, predominately from a white Scottish ethnic background (89%), with an age range of 8–20 and an average (mean) age of 15.8 years with a standard deviation of 1.6. The sample included both low-level and high-risk offenders. After social workers assess the youth against 42 risk/need items, the YLS-CMI provides a total score of between 0 and 42, which is classified into the following categories: low risk/need (0–8); moderate risk/need (9–22); high risk/need (23–34); and very high risk/need (35–42). Although the social worker cannot change the final numeric score, s/he can use her/his professional judgement to 'override' the final risk/need category and replace it with an alternative one from the list, which was done in 160 assessments from this study.

By analysing the results from the YLS-CMI and reoffending data, Vaswani and Merone found the average (mean) YLS-CMI total score was 15.2, indicating moderate risk/need. The standard deviation is 9.4. There was no statistically significant difference in YLS-CMI total scores between males and females, yet there was a statistically significant difference across the three age groups (under 15; 15–17 years; 18 years plus) with the 18 years plus group scoring the highest. A total of 838 young people were found to reoffend within 12 months of the initial YLS-CMI assessment; these young people also scored higher on the initial YLS-CMI assessment. In order to determine how precise the YLS-CMI tool is at predicting future recidivism, Vaswani and Merone used a summary statistic called the area under the curve (AUC) coefficient, which is considered both a sensitive and specific statistic. As Vaswani and Merone (2014) explain:

> Put simply, an AUC can be defined as the probability that a randomly selected individual who reoffended will score higher on the risk assessment in question than another randomly selected individual who did not reoffend (Catchpole and Greeton, 2003). The larger the AUC, the greater the accuracy of the tool, with an AUC of 1 representing perfect accuracy identifying both offenders and non-offenders and an AUC of 0.5 representing predictive accuracy that is no better than chance (Craig and Beech, 2010). Thus, an AUC of 0.75 suggests that a randomly selected individual who reoffended will score higher on the risk assessment than someone who did not reoffend, 75% of the time (p. 2166). (References within the quote are provided in the reference list.)

AUCs were calculated for (1) any recidivism; and (2) serious violent recidivism as a whole, but also by sex and age groups under each of these two categories. AUCs were also calculated based on using the YLS-CMI scores only, YLS-CMI risk/need category only, and YLS-CMI category resulting from a professional override only. Table 8.1 provides the AUCs for all the categories.

As Table 8.1 illustrates, the YLS-CMI total score, YLS-CMI risk/need category and YLS-CMI risk/need category professional override are all good predictors of any recidivism with scores of 0.72, 0.69 and 0.68 respectively. An AUC score of 0.72 for YLS-CMI total score means that the probability that a reoffender had a high score on the YLS-CMI assessment is .72; otherwise stated, there is a 72% chance that a young person who reoffends had a high score on the YLS-CMI assessment. Likewise, the YLS-CMI total score, YLS-CMI risk/need category and YLS-CMI risk/need category professional override are all good predictors of serious violent recidivism with scores of 0.68, 0.66, and 0.65 respectively. For both

Table 8.1 AUCs for YLS-CMI categories

	YLS-CMI total score AUC	YLS-CMI risk/need category AUC	YLS-CMI risk/need category professional override AUC
Any recidivism	0.72	0.69	0.68
Males	0.73	0.69	0.69
Females	0.72	0.69	0.68
Under 15	0.75	0.71	0.70
15–17 years	0.71	0.68	0.68
18 years plus	0.67	0.66	0.66
Serious violent recidivism	0.68	0.66	0.65
Males	0.68	0.66	0.64
Females	0.69	0.69	0.69
Under 15	0.70	0.66	0.65
15–17 years	0.68	0.66	0.65
18 years plus	0.74	0.67	0.62

Data from Vaswani and Merone (2014, p. 2174).

any recidivism and serious violent recidivism, the YLS-CMI total score is the best predictor of reoffending, followed by the YLS-CMI need/category and then the YLS-CMI need/category professional override. Such results illustrate to social workers that the YLS-CMI assessment is an accurate tool in assessing need and risk and in predicting reoffending among youth. But how confident are we that such results are a true reflection of the population of all young offenders in Scotland, or could the results have been due to chance (or sampling error), or, otherwise stated, based on a sample that does not reflect all young offenders in Scotland?

We will continue to use this piece of research throughout the remainder of this chapter to highlight further concepts and answer the above question. We will also refer to additional findings from Vaswani and Merone's (2014) study that will further illustrate the effectiveness of the YLS-CMI in predicting reoffending and the effectiveness of professional judgement in overriding the assessment outcomes.

Basic concepts: probability distribution, normal distribution and the normal curve, and hypothesis testing

Probability distribution

In order to interpret the results from social work research that uses quantitative methods and statistical tests, you must first understand the basic concepts and theories that underpin statistics. We have already discussed the concept of probability and calculated probability from an example involving seven shapes. Let's explore probability in more detail in terms of probability theory; or the underlying meaning of probability. Let's revisit our seven shapes.

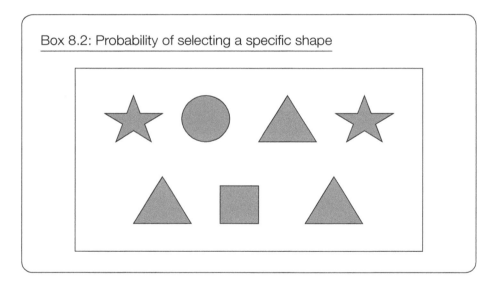

Box 8.2: Probability of selecting a specific shape

Probability is the likelihood that something will occur 'in a perfect world'. For example, looking at our shapes above, based on the theory of probability, we can say that the chances of drawing a star out of the box is .29 or 29% (2 times out of every 7 draws); the chances of drawing a circle is .14 or 14% (1 time out of every 7 draws); the chances of drawing a triangle is .43 or 43% (3 times out of every 7 draws); and the chances of drawing a square is .14 or 14% (1 time out of every 7 draws). If we were to put the possible outcomes, based on probability theory, into a frequency table called a probability distribution (refer back to Chapter 7 regarding frequencies and frequency tables), it would look like the following:

Table 8.2 Probability distribution of selecting shapes

Outcome	P (%)
Triangle	.43 (43%)
Star	.29 (29%)
Circle	.14 (14%)
Square	.14 (14%)
Total	1.0 (100%)

Such outcomes are merely theoretical as they are the results you would expect to receive in a perfect world. A probability distribution, therefore, tells us the probabilities associated with the occurrence of each event (randomly selecting each shape) in the distribution. But, as we know, we do not live in a perfect world and sometimes we might reach into the box 7 different times and select a triangle each of the 7 times despite probability telling us we only have a 43% chance of selecting a triangle each time we draw from the box. If we then conclude that there are only triangles in the box we are actually very wrong! In fact, we missed noticing that there are also two stars, one circle and one square in addition to the three triangles. So, probability is what would happen if all went according to plan. Let's try out this theory with an example. Take a piece of paper and cut out seven equally sized pieces. Then, write one shape on each piece of paper (star, star, circle, triangle, triangle, triangle, square) and fold them up. Put them into a bowl and randomly select a piece of paper and write down which shape is listed on the paper. Put the paper back in the bowl and select another piece of paper and write down the shape. Repeat this 10 times. Construct a frequency distribution based on your results. Our results are listed in the table below.

As Table 8.3 reveals, if we were to make a conclusion about what shapes are in the bowl, we would say that 60% of the shapes in the bowl are triangles, 30% are squares, 10% are stars and that there are no circles. But, we know this is inaccurate because we put all the shapes in the bowl and we know that 43% of

Table 8.3 Frequency distribution of selecting shapes 10 times

Outcome	f (%)
Triangle	6 (60%)
Square	3 (30%)
Star	1 (10%)
Circle	0 (0%)
Total	10 (100%)

the shapes in the bowl are triangles, 29% are stars, 14% are squares, and 14% are circles. What happened in our 'real-life' draw does not accurately reflect what is really within the bowl. Let's try drawing 1,000 times and see what happens. Okay, you actually don't have to draw 1,000 times, but we did (for fun!) and the results are listed in the table below.

After 1,000 draws from the bowl, we can see that the results in Table 8.4 more accurately reflect what is actually in the bowl. If we compare the results from our 1,000 draws (Table 8.4) with the probability distribution in Table 8.2, we can see that our results are now much closer to the probability of selecting each of the shapes. If we conclude (after our 1,000 draws) that 43.5% of the shapes in the bowl are triangles, 28% are stars, 14.2% are circles, and 14.3% are squares, we would only be inaccurate by a very small amount (we are only 0.5% off in terms of the triangles; 1% off for stars, 0.2% off for circles, and 0.3% off for squares). The point here is that probability tells us what should be in an ideal world. When we conduct research on a sample from a population and use statistics to analyse our data, we aim to generalise our findings from our sample to the population. Yet, because we are drawing a sample versus looking at the population as a whole, we are unsure as to how our sample accurately reflects the population.

The message from this exercise is that more draws, or a higher sample size, will result in the findings more accurately reflecting what is true in the population. This is important as statistics, particularly inferential statistics – which aim to generalise findings from sample data to a population – are based on probabilities. Therefore, you, as a social work practitioner applying research findings to your social work practice, need to be aware of the imperfection of statistical techniques. For example, referring back to our 'Research in practice' example, how certain can we be that a young person who scores high on the YLS-CMI assessment will reoffend? Although Vaswani and Merone (2014) found a 72% chance, is this accurate of the general population of young people in Scotland or only of the sample in the study? What is the degree of accuracy of the findings? More information in this chapter will help to assess the results and answer this question.

Table 8.4 Frequency distribution of selecting shapes 1,000 times

Outcome	f (%)
Triangle	435 (43.5%)
Star	280 (28%)
Circle	142 (14.2%)
Square	143 (14.3%)
Total	1,000 (100%)

Normal distribution and the normal curve

Inferential statistics require an assessment of how the sample data are distributed in order to determine which statistical test to use to analyse the data. Parametric tests are used for data that are normally distributed, whereas nonparametric tests are used for data that are not normally distributed (Chapter 9 explains parametric and nonparametric tests in more detail). A normal distribution is visually depicted as a 'normal' curve, often referred to as the bell curve, due to its shape as a curve with a peaked middle that then tails off on both sides. Figure 8.1 depicts a normal curve.

As the Figure shows, the normal curve peaks in the middle, which represents the mean, median and mode. A normal curve has a mean of 0 and a standard deviation of 1. The depiction of the normal curve can take many different shapes based on how the values are distributed around the mean. For example, it could be spread out so that the peak is not so tall, or more centred in the middle which will create a tall peak. Regardless of the shape, a normal distribution has the same value for the mean, median and mode (0), which is all exactly the middle value of the curve.

Just as a probability distribution is the theoretical ideal, the normal distribution, or normal curve, is the theoretical ideal of how the population data are distributed. We assume that if we were to take many different samples from the population, then the mean of sample means would equal the population mean, and the data would be distributed to depict a normal curve. This is referred to as the Central Limit Theorem, which states that as our sample size increases then the closer the mean of the sample means will be to the population mean and the closer the distribution of data will be to the normal curve. Therefore, we use the normal curve to understand patterns within a population, such as looking to see what is average (where the mean, median and mode lie) or what seems to be out of the ordinary (values that lie at the tails of the curve).

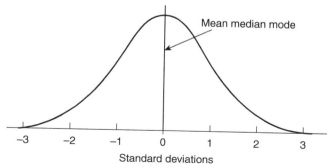

Figure 8.1 Normal curve

As illustrated through our example of the shapes, the more draws we took from the bowl the more likely our findings reflected the true results. In relation to the normal distribution and normal curve, the larger our sample size the more likely it is that our data will be normally distributed and depict the normal curve. Another assumption of the normal curve is that all social, psychological and physical data are normally distributed. Thus, the normal curve is used to help predict how likely it is that our sample data will accurately reflect the true population data.

Of course, we know that not all data will be normally distributed – especially due to sampling error, or general non-normality in the population, such as the distribution of wealth or the final grade results from a research methods class where all students except for one received an 80%. When plotting such data, we will not see a 'normal curve', but rather a skewed distribution – the peak of the distribution is not in the centre, but rather is shifted to the right or to the left of the centre. For example, the data of final grades from one research methods class are depicted in Figure 8.2, which illustrates a histogram (or bar chart) of all the scores from the research class.

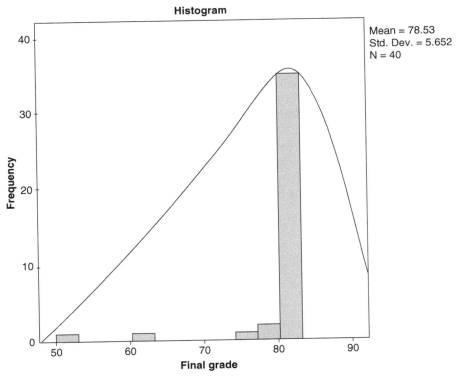

Figure 8.2 Negatively skewed distribution

As the histogram illustrates, the majority of the students received an 80%, the mean is 78.53 with a standard deviation of 5.65 and the curve does not depict a normal curve. In this situation, we can say that the sample data are negatively skewed as the peak of the curve is shifted to the right towards higher scores and the tail is pointing towards lower scores. Alternatively, Figure 8.3 depicts a positively skewed distribution where the peak of the curve is shifted to the left towards lower scores and the tail is pointing towards higher scores.

Figure 8.3 depicts the majority of the students receiving a 50% with a mean of 51.3% and a standard deviation of 4.96. Again, the curve does not depict a normal curve, but rather the data are positively skewed. You should always check the distribution of your sample data as any distribution that does not approximate a normal curve will require a nonparametric statistical test where a measure of central tendency other than the mean will be used (i.e. median or mode).

We discussed 'standard deviation' in Chapter 7, which is the mean deviation of a sample (i.e. the mean of the deviations of values from the mean). In regards to the normal distribution, you can plot the normal distribution when you have the mean and standard deviation from your sample data. Again, the larger your

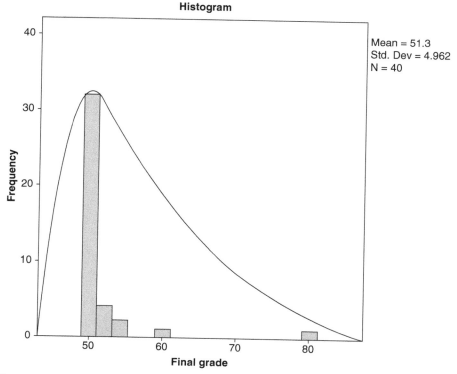

Figure 8.3 Positively skewed distribution

sample size the more likely the scores will resemble a normal distribution. If your sample data do not approximate a normal distribution, then this may be due to sampling error, or a general non-normality of the population as depicted in Figures 8.2 and 8.3. Thus it is always important to check the shape of the distribution of your data, which you can do through data analysis packages such as the Statistical Package for the Social Sciences (SPSS).

The area under the normal curve is important as it depicts the probability of obtaining a particular score within any specified standard deviation points. Figure 8.4 depicts the normal curve and highlights the area under the normal curve.

Again, the normal curve contains all the data from a sample or population and has a mean (median and mode) of 0 and a standard deviation of 1. The values on the horizontal line (x-axis) are the standard deviation units. As depicted in Figure 8.4, we can say that 68.26% of the scores in our sample will fall between –1 standard deviation and +1 standard deviation from the mean. This means that 68.26% of the time (probability of .6826), we will randomly obtain a score in our sample that lies somewhere between –1 standard deviation and +1 standard deviation from the mean. The probability of obtaining a score that lies between the mean and +1 standard deviation is 34.13% of the time (68.26%/2 = 34.13%). The probability of obtaining a score that lies between –2 standard deviations and +2 standard deviations is 95.44% of the time, and between –3 standard deviations and +3 standard deviations is 99.74% of the time. Therefore, we can safely say that the probability that any given data will fall between –2 standard deviations and +2 standard deviations is approximately 95 in 100. Test your understanding of the area under the normal curve by looking at Exercise 8.2.

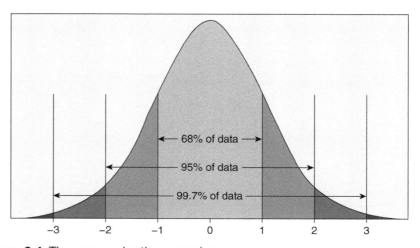

Figure 8.4 The area under the normal curve

Exercise 8.2: The area under the normal curve

Answer the following questions:

1. What percentage of data is likely to fall between the mean and +2 standard deviations?

2. What are the chances that a score will fall between the mean and –3 standard deviations?

3. What is the probability of obtaining a score between –1 and +1 standard deviations?

4. What percentage of data is likely to fall between –1 and +2 standard deviations?

Let's apply the theory of the normal curve and the area under the normal curve to our 'Research in practice' example. Vaswani and Merone (2014) reported the mean age of the young people to be 15.8 years with a standard deviation of 1.6 units and a range from 8–20 years. Given the principles of the normal curve, we could plot the ages along the standard deviations as follows:

Years	11	12.6	14.2	15.8	17.4	19	20.6
Standard deviations	–3	–2	–1	0	+1	+2	+3

We were able to calculate the values along each point by either adding one, two or three standard deviation units to the mean or subtracting one, two or three standard deviations units from the mean. For example, 15.8 (mean age) + 1.6 (1 standard deviation unit) = 17.4. Likewise, 15.8 (mean age) + 4.8 (3 standard deviation units [3 x 1.6 = 4.8]) = 20.6. To obtain the values to the left of the mean, we subtract standard deviation units. Therefore, based on such findings, we can say that 68.26% of the population of young people are likely to be between the ages of 14.2 and 17.4 years; 95.44% are likely to be between the ages of 12.6 and 19 years; and 99.74% are likely to be between 11 and 20.6 years.

As the information covered in this section is all based on theory or the ideal in 'real life', we are unable to determine the extent to which the values we obtain in statistics accurately reflect the true population. How confident are we that the sample mean age of 15.8 years is the population mean as well? Again, we can use statistical tests to determine how confident we are that the findings from the sample reflect the population and are not due to chance.

Hypothesis testing

We will now turn to applying the theoretical concepts discussed so far to the process of conducting research and interpreting findings. We will use the idea of 'hypothesis testing' to illustrate the points. A hypothesis is defined as a theory or a guess and is generally based on previous knowledge and research. In social work research, hypothesis testing is the process whereby the researcher analyses data to determine any relationship or difference between two or more variables where there can be two outcomes that occur: (1) there *is a relationship* (or difference) between two variables; or (2) there *is no relationship* (no difference) between two variables. For example, Vaswani and Merone (2014) tested the relationship between the YLS-CMI assessment tool and reoffending among young people. The two possible outcomes (a relationship; no relationship) are referred to as the research hypothesis and the null hypothesis. Hypothesis testing can be viewed as a competition between these two hypotheses. For example, the research hypothesis for Vaswani and Merone (2014) could be stated as: 'There is a relationship between the YLS-CMI assessment tool and reoffending among young people'; and the null hypothesis could be stated as: 'There is no relationship between the YLS-CMI assessment tool and reoffending among young people.' Table 8.5 provides examples of research hypotheses and null hypotheses.

As Table 8.5 highlights, the research hypothesis always assumes a relationship or a difference between two (or more) variables whereas the null hypothesis assumes no relationship or no differences between the variables. In our 'Research in practice' example, Vaswani and Merone (2014) predicted, or hypothesised, that there would be a relationship between the YLS-CMI assessment tool and reoffending and went out to test this hypothesis by collecting data (YLS-CMI assessment scores; rates of recidivism), and analysing the relationship between the variables using statistical tests. As Table 8.1 reported, there were fairly strong relationships between aspects of the YLS-CMI assessment tool and whether a young person reoffended as depicted through the

Table 8.5 Explanation and examples of research hypotheses and null hypotheses

	Research hypothesis	Null hypothesis
Explanation	There is a relationship or difference between two measured variables	There is no relationship or no difference between two measured variables
	A particular intervention makes a difference/has an effect	A particular intervention does not make a difference/does not have an effect
Examples	Smacking is an effective behavioural management tool	Smacking is not an effective behavioural management tool
	Children in kinship care have better outcomes than children with unrelated foster carers	There is no difference in outcomes based on whether children are in kinship care or with unrelated foster carers

AUC scores. Therefore, based on hypothesis testing, Vaswani and Merone (2014) should be able to reject their null hypothesis of: 'There is no relationship between the YLS-CMI assessment tool and reoffending among young people', and instead state that the relationship between the YLS-CMI assessment tool and rates of reoffending is not due to chance. In fact, they are even able to report the strength of the relationship between these two variables through the use of the AUC score. For example, the YLS-CMI assessment score is a better predictor of reoffending (0.72) than the YLS-CMI risk/need category (0.69). Despite being able to reject the null hypothesis of no difference, what is the probability that the results actually occurred by chance and the null hypothesis is actually true? How can we be sure that the results are not due to sampling error? How confident can we be, as social work practitioners, in applying the research findings to our 'real-life' practice?

Being able to reject the null hypothesis of no difference means that the probability of being wrong (the null hypothesis is actually true and there is no difference between the variables) is so small that it only makes sense to believe in the research hypothesis (there is a difference between the variables). Through statistical analyses, researchers are able to calculate the probability of obtaining a relationship between variables (supporting, although not proving, the research hypothesis) if, in fact, the null hypothesis were actually true (there really isn't a relationship between the variables). In order to support the research hypothesis, we would need to obtain a probability score that is so low that it would only make sense to *assume* the null hypothesis is actually false and the research hypothesis is true. A low probability score will indicate that the findings are unlikely to have come about by chance or sampling error and, therefore, most likely reflects the real situation in the population. This now turns us to the alpha level, probability value and statistical significance.

Alpha level, probability value and statistical significance

Researchers are able to set the probability value that they want to use as the cut-off point at which they would feel confident enough in rejecting the null hypothesis of no difference and, thus, assuming that any difference found in the sample is most likely to reflect a true difference in the population versus being due to chance (sampling error). For example, researchers might be confident in their findings with a 5% chance (5 times out of 100) that they are wrong and have found a difference or relationship between variables in the sample when, in fact, there is no difference in the population and thus any differences in the sample are due to chance. Another researcher might be confident in their findings with a 10% chance (10 times out of 100) s/he is wrong or a 10% chance that any findings are due to chance and not to an accurate reflection in the population. The process of setting the cut-off point at which the researcher is confident in rejecting the null hypothesis is called 'setting the alpha level'.

Alpha is represented by the Greek letter α. The α level is the level of probability where the null hypothesis (of no relationship or difference) can be rejected with confidence and, thus, the research hypothesis of a relationship or difference can be supported. For example, if a researcher sets $\alpha = .05$, then s/he decides to reject the null hypothesis only if the probability of falsely rejecting the null hypothesis (stating there is a difference when in fact there is not) is .05 or 5% or 5 times in 100. An $\alpha = .01$ means that the researcher is willing to take the chance that s/he falsely reject the null hypothesis 1% of the time or 1 time in 100; $\alpha = .10$ means the researcher is willing to falsely reject the null hypothesis 10% of the time or 10 times in 100. Researchers set the α level before conducting the research and data analysis. Convention in social science research is a 5% chance of falsely rejecting the null hypothesis, which means setting $\alpha = .05$. Again, another way of stating this is that there is a 5% chance that any findings of relationships or difference between variables in the sample is actually due to chance and not to any true differences in the population.

Whereas α is set by the researcher, the probability value, referred to as the p-value, is determined by the statistical test performed in data analysis. For example, if we set $\alpha = .05$, then we are saying that we will only reject the null hypothesis and accept that there is a relationship or difference between our variables if the p-value from our statistical test is at .05 or below. A p-value of .04 (expressed as $p = .04$) from our statistical test means that there is a 4% chance that we have falsely rejected the null hypothesis. Because we set $\alpha = .05$, we are saying that we are willing to take this 4% chance that our data are not a true reflection of the population data and that our conclusion of a relationship or difference between variables is inaccurate; most likely being due to sampling error.

Setting the α level and then reading the p-value generated from the statistical test you used will determine whether your findings are considered 'statistically significant' or 'not statistically significant'. In order for findings to be 'statistically significant' the p-value obtained from the statistical test must be lower than the α level set by the researcher. In this situation, for example obtaining a p-value of .01 ($p = .01$) when α was set to .05, we would say that the results are statistically significant, which means the relationship or difference observed in the sample is most likely an accurate reflection of any relationship or difference in the real population and is not due to chance. Otherwise stated, there is a 1% chance (1 time out of 100) that we have falsely rejected the null hypothesis and there is actually no relationship or difference between variables. If the p-value is higher than the α level, then the findings are deemed to be not statistically significant, which means we are not confident that any relationship or difference between variables is a true reflection of the population, but rather there is no relationship or difference between variables or any relationship or difference is likely to be due to chance.

It is important to note that the p-value tells us the probability of falsely rejecting the null hypothesis. It does not tell us the probability that our findings are true, or the probability that our research hypothesis is true. Some researchers make the inaccurate assumption that if α is set to .05 and their p-value is .01 ($p = .01$) that they are 99% confident that their findings or their research hypothesis (a relationship or differences between variables) is true. This is not the case. The p-value only tells us the probability that we have obtained our findings of a relationship or difference by chance – the probability that any observed relationship or difference between variables is actually false. Thus, when interpreting research findings, we can only be confident in *supporting* (not proving) our research hypothesis and although we cannot be confident in the extent to which our research hypothesis is correct, we can be confident in the probability of our findings being wrong. Before we go on, let's test your understanding of research and null hypotheses and statistical significance.

Exercise 8.3: Research and null hypotheses and statistical significance

Answer the following questions:

1. Write a null hypothesis for the following research hypothesis: 'There is a relationship between amount of supervision social workers receive and level of job satisfaction'.

2. Write a research hypothesis for the following null hypothesis: 'There is no difference in young people's reoffending based on whether they had custodial or noncustodial sentences'.

3. True or false – The p-value is set by the researcher and the α level is generated from a statistical test.

4. True or false – With $\alpha = .05$ and a p-value of .06 ($p = .06$), we would reject the null hypothesis of no difference and assume the relationship or differences observed between variables is not due to chance (sampling error).

5. With $\alpha = .05$, what are the chances the researcher is willing to take that any observed relationship or differences between variables is wrong – due to chance?

6. Are the following findings 'statistically significant' or 'not statistically significant'?

   a. $\alpha = .05; p = .03$

   b. $\alpha = .01; p < .001$

   c. $\alpha = .05; p = .50$

Type I and Type II errors

Because statistics are based on the probability, there is always a chance that our findings are wrong. For example, we already know that if we set $\alpha = .05$ there is a 5% chance (5 times out of 100) that we have falsely rejected the null hypothesis of no relationship or difference when in fact the null hypothesis of no relationship or difference is true. This type of error is referred to as a Type I error – falsely rejecting the null hypothesis when we should have accepted the null hypothesis. Otherwise stated, we said there was a relationship or difference between variables when, in fact, there is no relationship or difference between variables. The p-value obtained from the statistical test will tell you the likelihood that you have made a Type I error ($p = .01 = 1\%$ chance; $p = .03 = 3\%$ chance; $p = .05 = 5\%$ chance). The extent to which you are willing to make a Type I error should be considered when you are setting your α value. For example, the convention $\alpha = .05$ means you are willing to make a Type I error 5% of the time.

The reverse of a Type I error is a Type II error, which is accepting the null hypothesis when in fact you should have rejected it. In other words, you stated there was no relationship or difference between variables when, in fact, there is a relationship or difference between variables in the population. Again, the extent to which you are willing to make a Type I or Type II error should be considered when setting your α level. Setting your α level too high might prevent a Type II error, but will lead to a greater chance of a Type I error; likewise, setting your α level too low might prevent a Type I error, but will lead to a greater chance of a Type II error. The convention of $\alpha = .05$ seems to strike the right balance between the two types of errors. We will now revisit the 'Research in practice' example and determine the extent to which the findings are 'statistically significant' and the applicability of the findings to social work practice given our understanding of probability.

'Research in practice' – predicting reoffending

The research study reported by Vaswani and Merone (2014) sought to determine the precision of the YLS-CMI assessment tool in predicting future reoffending and future serious violence among young people in Scotland. They also aimed to determine the accuracy of the professional judgement aspect of the assessment tool in predicting reoffending and future serious violence. We will re-examine the findings from the study, presented in Table 8.6, which now also includes the approximate p-value against each AUC score. We should point out that Vaswani and Merone did not report the exact p-values from the statistical test, but instead reported whether p was less than .05, .01 or .001 or was greater than .05 ($p > .05$). Vaswani and Merone set $\alpha = .05$.

Table 8.6 AUCs for YLS-CMI categories with approximate *p*-values

	YLS-CMI total score AUC	YLS-CMI risk/need category AUC	YLS-CMI risk/need category professional override AUC
Any recidivism	0.72; *p* < .001	0.69; *p* < .001	0.68; *p* < .001
Males	0.73; *p* < .001	0.69; *p* < .001	0.69; *p* < .001
Females	0.72; *p* < .001	0.69; *p* < .001	0.68; *p* < .001
Under 15	0.75; *p* < .001	0.71; *p* < .001	0.70; *p* < .001
15–17 years	0.71; *p* < .001	0.68; *p* < .001	0.68; *p* < .001
18 years plus	0.67; *p* > .05	0.66; *p* > .05	0.66; *p* > .05
Serious violent recidivism	0.68; *p* < .001	0.66; *p* < .001	0.65; *p* < .001
Males	0.68; *p* < .001	0.66; *p* < .001	0.64; *p* < .001
Females	0.69; *p* < .01	0.69; *p* < .01	0.69; *p* < .01
Under 15	0.70; *p* < .001	0.66; *p* < .01	0.65; *p* < .01
15–17 years	0.68; *p* < .001	0.66; *p* < .001	0.65; *p* < .001
18 years plus	0.74; *p* < .05	0.67; *p* > .05	0.62; *p* > .05

Data from Vaswani and Merone (2014, p. 2174).

Based on Table 8.6, we can see that the three different categories of the YLS-CMI assessment are all good predictors of any recidivism and serious violent recidivism, which were found to be statistically significant – all with *p* < .001, indicating a 1 in 1,000 chance the findings are not a reflection of the true population. We could safely assume that the YLS-CMI assessment is precise in predicting future recidivism and future serious violence, with the total score being the strongest predictor, followed by the risk/need category and then finally the risk/need category with professional override. As we look over the table, we can see that not all the findings are statistically significant, thus indicating that such findings among this sample are likely to be due to chance and not a reflection of the larger population. For example, although the YLS-CMI assessment tool is a good predictor for future recidivism and future serious violence in the overall population, when examining by age group, the precision of the tool for young people 18 years and older is not statistically significant across any of the categories of the YLS-CMI assessment tool, except for predicting future serious violence using the YLS-CMI assessment total score only. Vaswani and Merone were not surprised by this finding as they reported the YLS-CMI tool was not intended for youth over 18 years.

From the findings of this study, social work practitioners working with young people in youth justice could conclude that the YLS-CMI assessment tool is a good predictor of future recidivism and future serious violence when being used with males and females up to the age of 18 years old. The most precise aspect of the tool is the YLS-CMI total score, followed by the risk/need category, and lastly the risk/need category with professional override. As the professional override category was the least precise, social work practitioners should be cautious in using their professional judgement and have more confidence in the predictive measure of the tool. Looking at the p-values across the table, there is between a .01% to 5% to chance that the findings are due to chance (sampling error) and do not reflect the real differences within the larger population; these are also the values for the chance of a Type I error.

Test your understanding

Chapter 7 used a 'Research in practice' example based on the reablement programme (review Chapter 7 for an explanation of this programme). Table 8.7 reports on the mean (M) number of hours of entry and exit for older adults from three different geographical areas across the UK. Each area consisted of 200 older adults ($N = 200$). The research hypothesis is: 'Older adults participating in the reablement programme will have a reduction in hours of care from entry to exit'; and the null hypothesis is: 'There is no difference in number of hours of care from entry to exit for older adults participating in the reablement programme'. The mean number of hours from entry to exit were statistically analysed to determine whether any differences between the hours from entry to exit were 'statistically significant' or whether any differences were due to chance. The researcher set $\alpha = .05$. The table reports the means at entry and exit, and the p-value from the statistical analysis (paired samples t-test – discussed in Chapter 9). Examine the table below and answer the following questions: (1) What does $\alpha = .05$ mean and why is it important in interpreting the results in the table?; (2) Which geographical areas produced a 'statistically significant' reduction in mean hours from entry to exit? How do you know?; (3) What are the chances that the difference between the 9.50 mean hours of entry and 7.00 mean hours of exit for Area C is due to chance and, therefore, most likely does not reflect a difference in the population?; and (4) From the research findings, what can you conclude about the reablement programmes in each of the three geographical areas? As a social worker, would you refer to the programme in each of the areas? Why or why not?

Table 8.7 Does the reablement programme work?

Geographical area	M hours at entry	M hours at exit	p-value
Area A (N = 200)	8.50	4.25	p = .01
Area B (N = 200)	10.25	10.00	p = .45
Area C (N = 200)	9.50	7.00	p = .03

Critical Thinking Box

Read: Charney, D. A., Zikos, E. and Gill, K. J. (2010). Early recovery from alcohol dependence: Factors that promote or impede abstinence. *Journal of Substance Abuse Treatment*, 38, 42–50.

You are a social worker working in a community mental health team. You are working with Adele (36 years old, White British) who has been diagnosed with a personality disorder and alcohol dependency. Adele is married, employed and has two children. Her recent alcohol misuse has greatly interfered with her employment and social life and her husband has threatened to leave her and take the two children with him if she does not address her alcohol use. Adele has also disclosed to you that she occasionally uses cocaine. Adele has volunteered to enter a 'total abstinence' 28-day treatment programme and you have supported her in entering the programme. You have also recently read the research article by Charney, Zikos and Gill (2010). The article addresses the probability of remaining abstinent following a four-week treatment programme and the factors that might impede abstinence. Based on Adele's personal characteristics and social situation and the findings of this study, answer the following questions:

● What would you say is the likelihood that Adele may 'slip' or 'relapse' during the first four weeks of treatment? What information and evidence from the article did you use to answer this question?

● What would you say is the likelihood that Adele will remain abstinent after treatment if she experiences a 'slip' or 'relapse' during treatment? How confident are you in your answer?

● As her social worker, based on the findings from this research, what resources and interventions could you put into place to increase her chances of remaining abstinent during and after treatment? How could you help to prepare Adele for the future?

Summary

Through this chapter, we have explored some of the key underlying theoretical concepts necessary in using, understanding and interpreting statistics. We first examined probability and how to calculate probability and a probability distribution. We then looked at the theory of the 'normal curve' and explored how knowledge of the mean and standard deviation of our data can help us to construct a normal curve and, thus, predict the likelihood of the probability (or percentages) of the population that will fall within a specific area under the normal curve. Both probability and the probability distribution/normal curve are theoretical ideals of what should be in a 'perfect world'. We then applied the theory of probability to hypothesis testing and looked at how quantitative research often seeks to determine, through statistical tests, the probability that a null hypothesis can be rejected. We discussed the importance of the α-level and p-value in determining whether the results from statistical tests are 'statistically significant' and, thus, whether we can reject the null hypothesis with some degree of confidence and assume that any relationship or differences between variables observed in our sample accurately reflects the population. Although the chances that we have made a mistake, Type I or Type II error, may be slim (e.g. 1% chance of falsely rejecting the null hypothesis when $p = .01$), we can never be certain that our research hypothesis is true.

Further resources

Weinbach, R. and Grinnell, R. (2014). *Statistics for Social Workers*, 9th ed. Upper Saddle River, NJ: Pearson.

9

HOW TO KNOW IF TWO VARIABLES ARE RELATED

Introduction

Quantitative social work research requires researchers to gather and analyse data in order to answer research questions or test hypotheses. The findings allow for researchers to tell a story about a sample, determine if social work interventions are effective or not and determine the extent to which the findings can be generalised to the larger population or across different situations. But, once we have collected our data, how do we know what statistical test to use to answer our research questions or test our hypotheses? How are we able to determine if variables in our data set are related, influence one another or cause one another?

In Chapter 7, we discussed a 'variable', the different levels of measurement of variables (nominal; ordinal; interval; ratio) and how to calculate descriptive statistics (frequency; percentage) and the measure of central tendency of variables (mean; median; mode) based on their level of measurement. Then, in Chapter 8, we looked at the theory of probability, probability distribution and the normal curve and how to determine if there is a 'statistically significant' relationship or difference between two variables based on the p-value from a statistical test and the set α level. The information from both chapters provides the foundational knowledge required to move to the content of this chapter, where we will analyse the relationships and associations between variables using specific statistical tests. In this chapter, we will explore how to look at our variables and the research question (or hypothesis) and determine the most appropriate statistical test to use. We will first look at the difference between parametric and nonparametric tests, and then move to the difference between correlation and causation. We will then look at a number of statistical tests that are commonly used in social work research. Having knowledge of a range of parametric and nonparametric tests will enable you as a social work practitioner to evaluate the validity of the social work research that you will use to inform your social work practice. This information will also give you a foundation for conducting your own research as a social work practitioner or future researcher!

Before we explore a social work research example, let's define and distinguish between parametric and nonparametric tests. Our decision to use parametric or nonparametric tests is based on the extent to which the data in our sample meet several criteria. Parametric tests require the following assumptions to be met:

1   The level of measurement of the dependent variable should be at least interval level, and when examining the extent to which two variables are correlated then both variables must have at least an interval level of measurement.

2   The sample should be from a population that is normally distributed (refer back to Chapter 8 for a discussion of normal distribution and the normal curve), thus our sample data should also be normally distributed.

3   Homogeneity of variances, meaning that the variances of the samples (or variables being tested) should be approximately equal. Dancey and Reidy (2011) report that convention for this assumption is that as long as the largest variance among the variables being tested is not more than three times the smallest variance among the variables being tested, then you can assume equal variances; and finally.

4   No extreme scores (outliers) as parametric tests use the mean as the measure of central tendency in the statistical test (Dancey and Reidy, 2011). Any extreme scores or outliers will influence the mean and often lead to an inaccurate indication of the measure of central tendency.

If the variables to be tested meet the above four assumptions, then you would select a parametric test; if the variables to be tested violate one or more of the assumptions, then you would select a nonparametric test. Often, if the fourth assumption is the only one that is violated and there are only a few extreme scores, researchers will remove the extreme scores in order to perform parametric tests. Parametric tests are often preferred over nonparametric as they contain more information about the variables being tested, such as the mean, standard deviation and error variance, and are therefore more powerful than nonparametric tests which often rely on rank or frequency of data because they use the median or mode. We will now explore a social work practice example that we will refer to throughout the remainder of this chapter.

'Research in practice' – stress among social workers and care managers

A study by Wilberforce et al. (2014) aimed to explore the cause of stress among social workers and care managers working in 'personalised' adult social care in England. The study was part of a larger national evaluation of the Individual Budget (IB) pilots where IBs were tested in 13 local authorities in England between 2005 and 2007. The IBs were being delivered through multidisciplinary teams to a range of adult social care service users such as older people, adults with physical disabilities, adults with learning disabilities and adults experiencing mental ill health. IBs, also referred to as Personal Budgets, were introduced in 2008 and were seen to bring 'new demands and new rewards for social workers in England' (p. 814). This new way of working included services that were more service user-led with the ability of service users to hold personal budgets which they would use to plan, manage and pay for services. In regard to the social work role, 'concern has also been expressed that Personal Budgets come with additional paperwork; may lead to greater risk for vulnerable adults; may be implemented as a cost-cutting measure; and may require skills and experience that are not commonplace amongst social workers' (p. 814). Therefore, Wilberforce et al. (2014) re-examined data from the national evaluation to establish the characteristics of social workers most at risk of stress by examining variables measuring job demands, control and support. We will only discuss certain aspects of their study and research findings throughout this chapter.

Data for this study were gathered through a self-administered questionnaire distributed to social workers and care managers. The questionnaire consisted of the Job Content Questionnaire (JCQ), which measures psychological demands, job control and social support (Karasek, 1979), a Likert-scale question regarding job satisfaction (1 = terrible; 7 = delighted), and personal, job and team characteristics. A total of 249 questionnaires were returned and used in the data analysis. Wilberforce et al. (2014) employed basic descriptive statistics, such as frequencies, percentages and measures of central tendency, to describe the characteristics of the sample; bivariate analyses, such as correlations and *t*-test, to determine the relationship between two variables; and multivariate analysis, such as multiple regression, to determine the factors that contributed to job satisfaction.

In regard to the descriptive statistics, the respondents of the questionnaire consisted of 75% female and 25% male, with a mean age of 43.5 years. Over 78% of the respondents worked full time, with 21.2% working part time. The majority of respondents were from a social care-only organisation (62%) with

the remaining 38% from a multi-agency team. 55% had a social work qualification with 19% having a nursing or occupational therapy qualification and 28%
having no professional qualification. The majority of respondents worked with
older people (51%), followed by learning disabled (37%), physically disabled
(35%), mental health (29%), and other client groups (9%). The average (mean)
number of team members was 16.3, and average (mean) active caseload size
was 22.5. 59% of respondents had IB holders on their caseload with 41% of
respondents having no IB holders on their caseload.

Before we present the remainder of the findings from this study, we will
review a sample of bivariate statistical tests in order to explore their purpose,
meaning and how to interpret the results. Multivariate tests will be explored in
Chapter 10.

Statistical tests: the difference between bivariate analysis and multivariate analysis

Bivariate analysis is simply looking at the relationship between two variables to
examine how they are related. For example, what is the relationship between
hours spent studying research methods and the results on a research methods
test? Are these two variables (hours spent studying; results of research methods
test) related? Does a student's test result increase/improve the more time s/he
spends studying? Multivariate analysis involves looking at the relationship
among more than two variables to see how they are related or influence one
another. For example, considering time spent on studying, hours accessing
additional learning resources, and number of homework assignments completed over the course of the semester, what predicts higher scores on a research
methods test? Do any of the variables (hours spent studying; hours accessing
additional learning resources; number of homework assignments completed)
predict a higher test result? Bivariate and multivariate statistical tests can help us
in answering these questions and help us to make sense of data and the relationship (and even influential power) between variables. We will review a sample
of bivariate analyses in this chapter.

Correlation and causation

Bivariate analysis explores the extent to which two variables are related. In
bivariate analysis, if two variables are related (or associated) then they are said
to be correlated – that is as one variable changes the other variable changes. For
example, we would assume that the more hours spent studying research methods the higher the score on the research methods test. Likewise, the less time
spent studying the lower the score on the test. Let's assume that we have the

number of hours each student in a research methods class spent studying over the course of the semester and we have the final test results for each student. We could plot the figures on a chart to see if there is any visual correlation between the two variables. The values for each variable are listed in Table 9.1.

Now, plot the numbers on a chart (such as the one depicted in Figure 9.1 – referred to as a scatterplot) where the bottom horizontal line (referred to as the x-axis) lists the possible values for one variable (we labelled this as hours spent studying) and the left-side vertical line (referred to as the y-axis) lists the possible values for the other variable (we labelled this as final test score). You can then plot each of the scores for each student on the x-axis and y-axis and visually examine the chart for any relationship between the variables. For example, Student 1 would have a point where the hours spent studying (value 50 on the x-axis) meets the final test score (value 85 on the y-axis). We have highlighted Student 1's location on the scatterplot.

Table 9.1 Hours spent studying and test results ($N = 20$)

Hours spent studying	Test results
50	85
55	90
60	97
55	92
54	92
65	95
70	100
40	60
50	80
30	50
0	25
10	35
15	45
50	80
55	90
60	95
65	100
50	80
65	95
60	95

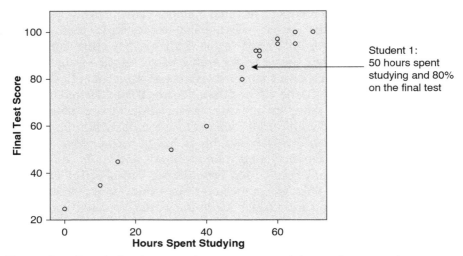

Figure 9.1 Correlation between hours spent studying and test results

A visual examination of the scores plotted in Figure 9.1 seems to indicate that the test scores increase as the number of hours spent studying increase. Although the results do not depict an exact straight line, you can see that there is a pattern of scores along an invisible line that goes from the bottom left-hand corner to the upper right-hand corner. For example, the student who spent 0 hours studying only received a score of 25 on the test whereas the student who studied 70 hours received a 100 on the test. From these results, we could assume that the two variables (hours spent studying and final test score) are correlated – as the number of hours spent studying change, the results on the final test change. What we cannot safely say from this example is that the hours spent studying *causes* the test results. This is because there is a difference between inferring correlation and inferring causation.

Although it would seem reasonable to assume that the number of hours spent studying caused the test results score, we cannot say this with certainty. This is because in order to infer causality (one variable *causes* the change in the other) the following three conditions must be met:

1 the two variables are related (correlated) in that as one variable changes the other variable changes;

2 the variable assumed to be the causal variable (also referred to as the independent variable) must have occurred prior to the outcome variable (also referred to as the dependent variable); and

3 the relationship between the two variables cannot be explained by any extraneous variables (other conditions outside of the two variables).

In our example above, we can meet the first assumption in that the two variables are correlated, and we can even say that hours of time spent studying came before the final test score, but we cannot safely say that the results are not explained by other extraneous variables. For example, what if we found out that the students who scored lower on the test were sitting in a test room where there were loud noises that greatly distracted them from understanding the test questions; this could mean that if there were better exam conditions for these students then they would have scored higher on the test regardless of the number of hours spent studying over the course of the semester. Therefore, for this example, we can infer that the two variables are correlated, but not that one caused the other.

The point of correlation and causation is important as you interpret the results from statistical tests. Researchers (and readers of social work research) should be cautious in inferring causality when, in fact, the three assumptions of causality cannot be fully met and the variables within the research can only safely be assumed to be correlated. It is only through experimental research designs, where the independent variable is manipulated to ensure it comes before the dependent variable, and the conditions of the study control for the influence of extraneous variables, that we can begin to infer causality (refer back to Chapter 6 for experimental designs).

Correlational analysis

We are able to use correlational analysis to determine whether two variables are correlated, the strength and direction of the correlation, and whether the results are statistically significant; that is, the probability (p-level) that the relationship between the two variables are due to chance is below our threshold (α-level). Assuming our data meet the requirements for a parametric test, then our correlational analysis will produce a statistic called Pearson's product moment correlation coefficient (r), which indicates the strength and direction of the correlation. If our data do not meet the assumptions for a parametric test, then our correlational analysis will use the nonparametric test, which produces the statistic called Spearman's rho. For this chapter, we will discuss Pearson's r.

Pearson's r will tell us the direction of the relationship – whether it is positive, negative, or no relationship – as well as the strength of the relationship. Pearson's r ranges from 0, indicating no relationship between variables, to 1, indicating a perfect relationship between variables, and can be both positive (0 to +) and negative (0 to –). An r of –1 means a perfect negative relationship and is as strong as a r of +1 which is a perfect positive relationship. In terms of the strength of relationship between two variables, it is generally agreed that a value of 0 is no relationship, 0.1–0.3 is a weak relationship, 0.4–0.6 is moderate, 0.7–0.9 is strong, and 1.0 is a perfect relationship. Again, a value of 0.7 is just as strong a relationship as

–0.7. The difference between these two values is that 0.7 indicates a strong positive relationship whereas –0.7 indicates a strong negative relationship.

A positive relationship is visually illustrated in Figure 9.2 where high scores
on one variable are associated with high scores on the other variable. As the
scatterplot illustrates, you could draw a straight line through the points on the
chart indicating a relationship between the two variables.

The Pearson's r for this relationship is 1.0, which indicates a perfect positive
relationship. Output 9.1 reports the results from the bivariate analysis run using
the Statistical Package for the Social Sciences (SPSS). The output provides several pieces of information. The first box in the first row provides the correlation
of variable 1 with itself, which, of course is a perfect relationship of 1! The second box in the first row provides the correlation of variable 1 with variable 2
(this is what we are most interested in). Here we see that the correlation, Pearson's r, is 1.000 (or merely 1.0). Under Pearson's r we will see the significance
level of the statistical test, which is the p-value, and below the p-value is the
sample size included in the analysis; that is, how many cases were paired
together. In Output 9.1, we see that the p-value is .000 and our sample size
(number of paired cases) is 10. Remember, when you come across a p-value of
.000, you must change the last zero to a 1 and report the value as $p < .001$.
Therefore, for our example, if we have set $\alpha = 0.05$, then we can say that there
is a statistically significant positive and perfect relationship ($r = 1.0$) between
variable 1 and variable 2. The probability that the relationship was due to chance
(sampling error) is less than 1 time in 1000. To report the results, you will want
to include the r value, sample size and p-value. Therefore, you would report the
results from this correlational analysis as follows: $r(10) = 1.0$, $p < .001$.

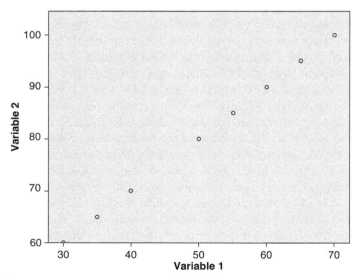

Figure 9.2 Positive relationship between two variables

Output 9.1 Pearson's product moment correlation coefficient (*r*):
positive relationship

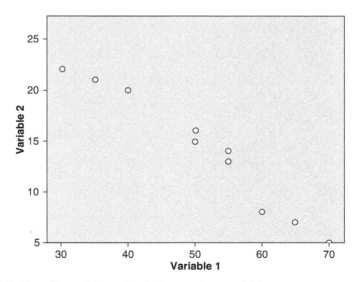

Correlations

		Variable 1	Variable 2
Variable 1	Pearson Correlation	1	1.000**
	Sig. (2-tailed)		.000
	N	10	10
Variable 2	Pearson Correlation	1.000**	1
	Sig. (2-tailed)	.000	
	N	10	10

** Correlation is significant at the 0.01 level (2-tailed).

Correlation of variable 1 with itself

Correlation of variable 1 with variable 2

Sample size

Statistical significance

The second row of the output is merely the inverse of the first row. Therefore, you only need to interpret the results of the correlation of variable 1 to variable 2 once.

Figure 9.3 indicates a negative relationship between two variables where high scores on one variable are associated with low scores on the other variable. Our visual interpretation of the data might be that there is a strong negative relationship between variable 1 and variable 2. We might assume a strong relationship because if we were to draw a straight line through the data, the data points would lie close to the straight line starting from between values 20 and 25 on the y-axis going down to value 70 on the x-axis.

Now, let's look at our output from SPSS (Output 9.2) that presents the results from the correlational analysis. The Pearson's *r* for this relationship is −.978 (or

Figure 9.3 Negative relationship between two variables

Output 9.2 Pearson's product moment correlation coefficient (*r*): negative relationship

Correlations

Correlation of variable 1 with variable 2

		Variable 1	Variable 2
Variable 1	Pearson Correlation	1	−.978**
	Sig. (2-tailed)		.000
	N	10	10
Variable 2	Pearson Correlation	−.978**	1
	Sig. (2-tailed)	.000	
	N	10	10

Statistical significance

** Correlation is significant at the 0.01 level (2-tailed).

−.98 when only reporting two decimal spaces), which indicates a strong negative relationship. Our findings are statistically significant (assuming $\alpha = .05$) as $p < .001$. We would report the results as follows: $r(10) = -.98$, p < .001.

Finally, Figure 9.4 reports a scatterplot indicating zero (or no) correlation. We can assume no correlation through visual interpretation as we are unable to draw a straight line through the data where all the data will generally lie around the straight line.

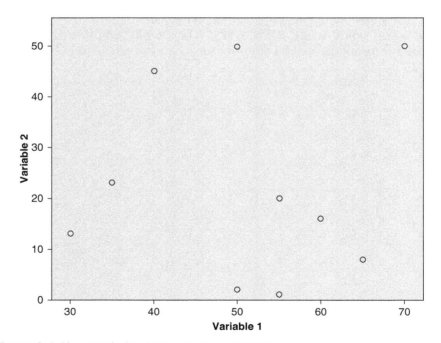

Figure 9.4 No correlation between two variables

Output 9.3 Pearson's product moment correlation coefficient (r): no correlation

Correlations

		Variable 1	Variable 2
Variable 1	Pearson Correlation	1	.046
	Sig. (2-tailed)		.899
	N	10	10
Variable 2	Pearson Correlation	.046	1
	Sig. (2-tailed)	.899	
	N	10	10

The output from SPSS (Output 9.3) confirms that there is a very weak (nearly zero correlation) between the two variables. As Output 9.3 reports, the Pearson's r for this relationship is .046 (or .05 when only reporting two decimal spaces), which indicates a very weak positive relationship. Assuming we set α = .05, we can interpret our findings as not as statistically significant as p = .90, which is greater than .05. Therefore, despite a very, *very* weak positive relationship, the finding of an association between variable 1 and variable 2 is not statistically significant, thus assumes no relationship between the two variables ($r(10)$ = .05, p = .90).

Before we move to the next parametric test, let's test your understanding of correlation and causation.

Exercise 9.1: Correlation and causation

Consider the following tasks and questions:

1. Using the values below, construct a scatterplot and visually interpret whether the scatterplot indicates a correlation between the two variables. Is there a positive, negative or zero correlation? Can we say that the more hours of peer mentoring will cause a reduction in risk assessment score? Why or why not?

	Risk assessment score	Hours of peer mentoring
Person 1:	5	10
Person 2:	19	7
Person 3:	42	1
Person 4:	30	3
Person 5:	24	6
Person 6:	35	2
Person 7:	21	5
Person 8:	15	8

2. You are reading a social work research article and come across the following finding (α = .05): 'Level of stress was found to be positively correlated with the amount of time spent writing social work reports $r(162)$ = .15, p = .06'. Identify what each value represents and interpret the findings.

3. Interpret the SPSS output of a correlational analysis:

Correlations

		Risk Assessment Score	Hours of Peer Mentoring
Risk Assessment Score	Pearson Correlation	1	−.822**
	Sig. (2-tailed)		.000
	N	15	15
Hours of Peer Mentoring	Pearson Correlation	−.822**	1
	Sig. (2-tailed)	.000	
	N	15	15

** Correlation is significant at the 0.01 level (2-tailed)

Finally, we want to point out exactly what r means, which is the ratio between the variance shared by the two variables and the measure of the variance that is unique to each of the two variables. For example, below we have two variables. You can see that they each have their own boundaries, as depicted by the lines that define each of them as circles. Although there are two variables (two circles), we can see that they overlap each other. The space that is overlapped is the 'shared variance'; the amount of space in one variable that is made up from space in another variable. So, although they are two separate variables, they actually are not completely independent of each other as they share similar space (variance).

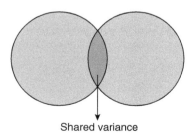

Shared variance

The test statistic, r, tells us how much variance two variables share by giving us a correlation coefficient that ranges from 0 to +1 and 0 to −1. If we want to know the amount of shared variance as expressed in a percentage, then we would square the value of r. For example, if r = .35, then the amount of shared variance between the two variables expressed as a percentage is r^2, which is .35 x .35 = .12 x 100 = 12%. Therefore, r^2 = 12 meaning that 12% of the variance of two variables is shared. 12% of the variance in variable 1 is explained by variable 2, and 12% of variable 2 is explained by variable 1. If 12% of the variance is shared between two variables, then we know that 88% of the variance is not shared and, thus, is the unique variance of the variables. An example of $r = -.86$ means that the amount of shared variance between two variables is $r^2 = .74$, or 74% (–.86 x –.86 = .74 x 100 = 74%). If 74% of the variance is shared between two variables, then we know that 26% of the variance is the unique variance of variables and is probably explained by other factors.

Testing the difference between means (*t*-test)

We will now turn to another bivariate analysis test that seeks to determine if there is any difference between the means of two groups, referred to as the *t*-test. The *t*-test is a parametric test in that the analysis uses the measure of central tendency of the mean and also assumes that the sample data and, thus, the population, is normally distributed. Let's use an example, based on the research content of our 'Research in practice' example, to illustrate the *t*-test and demonstrate how to interpret the results.

We are interested in the level of stress among social workers working in personalised adult social care in England and whether there is any difference in level of stress based on the sex of the social worker. Our research question is: 'Is there a difference in level of stress based on the sex of social workers working in personalised adult social care in England?' Alternatively, we could write a research hypothesis: 'There is a difference in level of stress by sex of social workers working in personalised adult social care in England' with a null hypothesis: 'There is no difference in level of stress by sex of social workers working in personalised adult social care in England'. The independent variable, or predictor variable, is sex of social worker, and the dependent variable, or outcome variable, is level of stress.

To answer our research question, we collected data on the level of stress among 50 social workers (25 males; 25 females) using a standardised measure of stress. The measure provides an overall score that indicates the level of stress and ranges from 0 (no stress) to 100 (extremely high level of stress). We also collected data on the sex of the social workers (female or male). We can see that the level of measurement for the dependent variable, 'level of stress', is ratio and the level of measurement for the independent variable, 'sex of social worker', is nominal. Therefore, assuming our dependent variable is normally distributed, we can conduct the parametric test, *t*-test, to see if there is a statistically significant difference in level of stress based on the sex of social worker.

The *t*-test uses the mean of the dependent variable, 'level of stress', across both categories of the independent variable, 'male' and 'female'. For example, the data we collected indicate that the mean level of stress for the whole sample (N = 50) was 36.02 with a standard deviation of 24.10. The mean by each sex of social worker is M = 43.28; SD = 22.16 for males and M = 28.76; SD = 24.17 for females. We can see that the mean score for level of stress is higher for the males (M = 43.28) than the females (M = 28.76). Does this mean that males are more likely to have higher levels of stress than females? In order to determine if this is the case, we will perform an independent samples t-test in SPSS. The t-test, which is performed by the computer, is a ratio between a measure of the between-groups variance (the variance of male and female scores) and the within-groups variance (the variance of scores within the male group and the variance of scores within female group) and produces a test statistic called t. The larger the t-value, the greater the variance between groups when compared to the variance within groups.

Before we move on, we should point out that an 'independent samples' t-test is where we look at the differences between means across two different 'independent' groups. For example, males and females, or those who received a service and those who did not receive a service. A 'paired samples' t-test is where we look at the differences between the means across the same group who provided data on two different variables or two different points in time. For example, the risk assessment scores for service users collected at the beginning and at the end of an intervention, or the hours of care at entry and hours of care at exit for individuals in the reablement programme, or the level of hope among social work students when thinking about research methods or thinking about taking a communication skills class. Now, let's go back to our example.

The independent samples t-test will provide us with the test statistic, t, as well as determine the probability that any observed differences between the means of the two groups within the sample (males; females) is due to chance and, thus, does not reflect a true difference within the population. The output from SPSS will report the results of the t-test and, therefore, allow us to answer our research question (or enable us to accept or reject the null hypothesis with a degree of confidence). Output 9.4 provides the results of the t-test for our data.

There are two outputs with the results of the t-test. The first output (Groups Statistics) box of the output provides the descriptive statistics of our sample by providing the sample size (N), mean (M), standard deviation (SD), and standard error of the mean for each of the two groups (males; females). The second output (Independent Samples Test) provides the results of the t-test. Remember that parametric tests assume homogeneity of variance, or equality of variances across groups or samples. The first part of the second output provides us with the results of 'Levene's test for equality of variances', which provide the test statistic, F, and the p-value for the test. Using the conventional α = .05, a statistically significant result of this test means that we cannot confidently assume

Output 9.4 Independent samples *t*-test

Group Statistics

	Sex of Social Worker	N	Mean	Std. Deviation	Std. Error Mean
Level of Stress	Male	25	43.28	22.163	4.433
	Female	25	28.76	24.173	4.835

Independent Samples Test

		Levene's Test for Equality of Variances		t-test for Equality of Means						
									95% Confidence Interval of the Difference	
		F	Sig.	t	df	Sig.(2-tailed)	Mean Difference	Std. Error Difference	Lower	Upper
Level of Stress	Equal variances assumed	.019	.892	2.214	48	.032	14.520	6.559	1.332	27.708
	Equal variances not assumed			2.214	47.643	.032	14.520	6.559	1.329	27.711

equal variances (there *is* inequality of variances) and we would need to interpret the second line of this output box. If the test is not statistically significant, then we can confidently assume equal variances (accept the null hypothesis of no difference in variances), as in our example (*p* = .89), and we would interpret the first line of this output box.

The output provides us with the *t*-statistic (*t* = 2.21), the degree of freedom, which is the sample size (50) – the number of tests (2) (*df* = 48), the significance of the test, which is the *p*-value (*p* = .03), the difference between the means of the two groups (14.52), the standard error (6.56) and the confidence interval (1.33–27.71). The confidence interval provides us with the upper limit of the mean difference between the two groups (27.71) and the lower limit of the mean difference between the two groups (1.33). This interval, comprising of the lower limit to the upper limit is providing us with an estimate of where the true mean difference between the two groups in the population is most likely to lie, with 95% confidence in assuming a normal distribution. It is often suggested to report the confidence intervals as this gives the reader a better picture as to where the true mean of the population might lie on the normal distribution. Assuming α = .05, based on our findings from the *t*-test we can say that the *t*-test reveals a statistically significant difference in the mean level of stress between males and females because our *p*-value of .03 is less than our set α = .05. Therefore, we can reject the null hypothesis of no difference in levels of stress between males and females as the probability of falsely rejecting the null hypothesis is 3 times in 100 (*p* = .03) and assume the research hypothesis of a difference in level of stress by sex of the social worker.

We would report our findings as follows:

Male social workers working in personalised adult social care in England were found to have higher levels of stress (M = 43.28; SD = 22.16) when compared to female social workers working in personalised adult social care in England (M = 28.76; SD = 24.17), $t(48)$ = 2.21, p = .03. The mean difference between males and females was 14.52 with a 95% confidence interval of 1.33–27.71.

Let's now briefly look at an example of a paired samples t-test. The research hypothesis is: 'Service users will have a higher level of satisfaction with adult social care services after receipt of Individual Budgets (IBs) when compared to level of satisfaction before receipt of IBs', and the null hypothesis is, 'There is no difference in level of satisfaction of service users with adult social care services before and after receipt of IBs'. The independent variable is 'receipt of IBs', which is a nominal level variable (not in receipt of IBs; in receipt of IBs), and the dependent variable is 'level of satisfaction'. The 'level of satisfaction' variable is measured through a seven-point Likert scale where service users were asked to indicate their level of satisfaction (1 = very dissatisfied and 7 = very satisfied) before and after receipt of IBs. As we indicated in Chapter 7, although Likert scales are technically ordinal level variables (because you cannot accurately measure the difference between the points on the scale) social science researchers often treat them as interval for the purposes of data analysis. This could be one occasion where you could treat 'level of satisfaction' as an interval level variable and, therefore, use a t-test to test the difference between the mean level of satisfaction of service users before and after receipt of IBs. (Note – do be cautious when treating ordinal level variables as interval level, particularly as some social science journals will not publish research results where this has been done (for example *Gerontology & Geriatrics Education*).)

The two satisfaction scores (satisfaction before IBs and satisfaction after IBs) have been entered into SPSS for 30 service users and a paired samples t-test run. The output is depicted in Output 9.5.

The first output indicates the descriptive statistics of the sample. From this output, we can see that the mean level of satisfaction before IBs (N = 30) was 3.23 with a standard deviation of 1.68, and the mean level of satisfaction after IBs (N = 30) was 5.53 with a standard deviation of 1.61; this indicates an increase in satisfaction with adult social care services from before IBs to after IBs. The second output provides the correlation of level of satisfaction before and level of satisfaction after. Although the findings of the correlational analysis indicate a weak positive relationship (r = .30), the correlation is not statistically significant (p = .11); we can accept the null hypothesis of no correlation between the two variables. Finally, the third output is the most important information in determining whether we can reject the null hypothesis of no difference in level of satisfaction with adult social care services. As the box indicates,

Output 9.5 Paired Samples *t*-test

Paired Samples Statistics

		Mean	N	Std. Deviation	Std. Error Mean
Pair 1	Level of Satisfaction Before IBs	3.23	30	1.675	.306
	Level of Satisfaction After	5.53	30	1.613	.295

Paired Samples Correlations

		N	Correlation	Sig.
Pair 1	Level of Satisfaction Before IBs & Level of Satisfaction After	30	.297	.111

Paired Samples Test

		Paired Differences							
					95% Confidence Interval of the Difference				
		Mean	Std. Deviation	Std. Error Mean	Lower	Upper	t	df	Sig. (2–tailed)
Pair 1	Level of Satisfaction Before IBs - Level of Satisfaction After	-2.300	1.950	.356	-3.028	-1.572	-6.460	29	.000

the mean difference between level of satisfaction from before to after is 2.30, with a standard deviation of 1.95. We can say with 95% confidence that the population mean difference between level of satisfaction before and level of satisfaction after will lie somewhere between −3.03 and −1.57. The *t*-value of −6.46 has a level of significance of $p < .001$, which indicates the results are statistically significant assuming $\alpha = .05$. Therefore, we can reject the null hypothesis of no difference and assume our results are highly unlikely (1 time out of 1,000) to be due to chance (sampling error). Therefore, we can report our findings as follows:

Service users had a higher level of satisfaction with adult social care services after receipt of IBs ($M = 3.23$; $SD = 1.68$) when compared to level of satisfaction before receipt of IBs ($M = 5.53$; $SD = 1.61$), $t(29) = −6.46$, $p < .001$. The mean difference between level of satisfaction before and after was 2.30 with a 95% confidence interval of −3.03−−1.57.

Test your understanding of the *t*-test by completing the exercise in Exercise 9.2.

Exercise 9.2: Is there a difference between the means?

Consider the following SPSS output from an Independent Samples t-test looking at the difference between number of days abstinent from alcohol (over 30 days following treatment) for service users from Treatment A and service users from Treatment B.

1. Construct a research hypothesis and null hypothesis. Construct a research question.

2. Identify the independent and dependent variables and their levels of measurement.

3. Interpret and report the findings from the output of the t-test.

Independent Samples Test

		Levene's Test for Equality of Variances		t-test for Equality of Means						
									95% Confidence Interval of the Difference	
		F	Sig.	t	df	Sig. (2-tailed)	Mean Difference	Std. Error Difference	Lower	Upper
Number of Days Abstinent	Equal variances assumed	7.543	.009	4.616	38	.000	15.950	3.456	8.954	22.946
	Equal variances not assumed			4.616	34.436	.000	15.950	3.456	8.930	22.970

Group Statistics

	Treatment A or Treatment B	N	Mean	Std. Deviation	Std. Error Mean
Number of Days Abstinent	Treatment A	20	26.50	9.000	2.012
	Treatment B	20	10.55	12.563	2.809

Testing the difference between three or more means (ANOVA)

We will now consider another parametric test that is used when comparing the difference between three or more means. Whereas the t-test is used to compare the means between two groups, analysis of variance (ANOVA) is used to compare the means of three or more groups. As a parametric test, ANOVA holds the assumptions that the test data are at least interval level, the data are normally distributed, the variances are equal, and there are no extreme scores. As is the case with the t-test, SPSS will also conduct a test for equal variances (homogeneity of variances). Although ANOVA will allow for small violations to the assumptions, if all of the assumptions cannot be met then you should use a nonparametric test.

Just as with the t-test, ANOVA aims to determine the likelihood that any difference between three or more means is due to chance (sampling error). A one-way

ANOVA can test for 'between-group' differences, where there is one dependent (or outcome) variable but different participants represented in each group or level of the dependent variable; or 'within-group' differences, where the same participants are represented in each level of the dependent (or outcome) variable, thus they have provided scores across each of the levels or over different points in time. An example of a 'between-group' difference may be the final score on a research methods test based on method of student instruction (in-class; online; or hybrid) where students are enrolled in one of the three types of classes. An example of a 'within-group' difference may be examining the final scores from three different classes (research methods; communication skills; and introduction to social work) for each student in the first year of the social work programme; every student is enrolled in each of the three classes. Both 'between-group' (also referred to as independent ANOVA) and 'within-group' (also referred to as related ANOVA) test for the difference between the means of the dependent (or outcome) variable by comparing each mean with the grand mean. Our example of 'between-group', or independent ANOVA, could be visually expressed as:

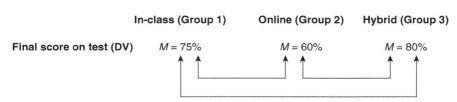

Method of instruction (IV)

	In-class (Group 1)	Online (Group 2)	Hybrid (Group 3)
Final score on test (DV)	$M = 75\%$	$M = 60\%$	$M = 80\%$

Here we are interested in whether the mean test scores differ based on the method of instruction. We are looking at the difference between Group 1 and Group 2, Group 2 and Group 3, and Group 1 and Group 3. If we find that there is a difference in mean test scores based on the method of instruction, we could then assume that one type of method of instruction will yield higher test scores than others and, thus, might be a more effective type of instruction. Our example of 'within-group', or related ANOVA, could be visually expressed as:

Final score (DV)

1st year social work class(IV)

Communication skills	$M = 68\%$
Introduction to social work	$M = 75\%$
Research methods	$M = 74\%$

Here we are interested in whether the mean final scores differ based on the type of class all the students took during their first year in the social work programme. We will compare the scores between communication skills and introduction to social work, introduction to social work and research methods, and communication skills and research methods. If we find that there is a difference in mean final scores based on the type of class, we could assume that students (in their first year) perform better in some subjects than others.

Both types of ANOVA tests consider the between-group variance and the within-group variance in order to produce a test statistic, 'F'. Based on our first example above, the test would consider the variance in scores *within* group 1, group 2 and group 3 and also the variance in scores *between* group 1, group 2 and group 3. Likewise, in the second example above, the test would consider the variance in scores *within* each type of class as well as the variance in scores *between* each type of class. Therefore, the F statistic represents a ratio between the between-groups variance and the within-groups variance. A larger F-value will be found when the between-group variance is larger than the within-group variance, which will decrease the probability that any differences are due to chance. Although we may be able to determine that there is a statistically significant difference in the group means, we will only be able to determine which means are statistically significant through the use of further tests (described below), referred to as post hoc tests.

Let's use an example based on the research content of our 'Research in practice' example to illustrate an ANOVA test and demonstrate how to interpret the results. We are interested in the level of stress among nurses, occupational therapists (OT) and social workers working in personalised adult social care in England. Our research hypothesis is: 'There is a difference in level of stress by profession among individuals working in personalised adult social care in England.' The null hypothesis is: 'There is no difference in level of stress by profession among individuals working in personalised adult social care in England.' The independent variable, or predictor variable, is profession (nursing; OT; social worker), and the dependent variable, or outcome variable, is level of stress.

We collected data on the level of stress among 75 professionals (25 nurses; 25 OTs; 25 social workers) using the standardised measure of stress as discussed in our t-test example. We also collected data on the profession of the workers (nurse; OT; social worker). We can see that the level of measurement for the dependent variable, 'level of stress', is ratio and the level of measurement for the independent variable, 'profession', is nominal consisting of three levels (nurses; OTs; social workers). Therefore, assuming our dependent variable is normally distributed, we can conduct the parametric test, ANOVA, to see if there is a statistically significant difference in level of stress based on profession of worker. The larger the F-value, the larger the between-group variance (across the three professions) in relation to the within-group variance (within each of the three professions). Output 9.6 provides the ANOVA results obtained through SPSS.

Output 9.6 Independent ANOVA

Descriptives

Level of Stress

	N	Mean	Std. Deviation	Std.Error	95% Confidence Interval for Mean		Minimum	Maximum
					Lower Bound	Upper Bound		
Nurse	25	41.80	16.641	3.328	34.93	48.67	10	70
OT	25	35.08	16.731	3.346	28.17	41.99	0	57
Social Worker	25	19.00	13.070	2.614	13.60	24.40	5	50
Total	75	31.96	18.131	2.094	27.79	36.13	0	70

Test of Homogeneity of Variances

Level of Stress

Levene Statistic	df1	df2	Sig.
1.106	2	72	.337

ANOVA

Level of Stress

	Sum of Squares	df	Mean Square	F	Sig.
Between Groups	6863.040	2	3431.520	14.147	.000
Within Groups	17463.840	72	242.553		
Total	24326.880	74			

The first output provides the descriptive statistics of the variables. As we can see, nurses have the highest mean level of stress ($M = 41.80$; $SD = 16.64$), followed by OTs ($M = 35.08$; $SD = 16.73$) and then social workers ($M = 19.00$; $SD = 13.07$). This box also provides descriptives in terms of the standard error and the confidence intervals. For example, we can be 95% confident that the true population mean for nurses will lie between the values 34.93 and 48.67. Finally, the box provides the minimum and maximum level of stress score for each group. The second output box provides 'Levene's test for equality of variance'. Remember, assuming $\alpha = .05$, we are looking for a non-statistically significant result so that we can accept the null hypothesis of no differences in variances between the three groups, thus assuming equal variances. The significance value of this test is $p = .34$, which is > than .05. Therefore, we can assume the null hypothesis of no difference in variances between the groups and go forward with our results. Finally, the third output box provides us with the main information for the differences between the groups. This box provides us with the F-ratio as well as the significance of the test. Here we see a F-ratio of 14.15, which is statistically significant at $p < .001$, which means we can reject the null hypothesis and assume that the observed differences in level of stress between the three groups is not due to chance.

As we stated above, ANOVA will tell us whether there is a difference between the groups, but we have to request additional statistical tests, referred to as post hoc tests, in order to determine exactly where the difference lies among the groups. We have requested, in SPSS, to conduct 'Tukey honestly significant difference (HSD)' to determine exactly where the difference between the groups lie. Output 9.7 provides the results.

Output 9.7 gives us the comparison of each of the three groups with each other, and provides the mean difference between each group, the standard error, significance level and the confidence interval. The confidence interval specifies with 95% confidence the two points between which the mean difference between the two groups would lie. From Output 9.7, we can see that there is a statistically significant difference in level of stress scores between nurses and social workers with a mean difference of 22.80 points, $p < .001$, and OTs and social workers with a mean difference of 16.08 points, p = .001. There is no statistically significant difference in level of stress between nurses and OTs. Therefore, we can write our final results as follows:

> There is a statistically significant difference in levels of stress based on profession, $F(2, 72) = 14.15$, $p < .001$. Post hoc comparisons using Tukey HSD test indicated that the mean score for social workers ($M = 19.00$; $SD = 13.07$) was significantly different from OTs ($M = 35.08$; $SD = 16.73$) ($p = .001$) and nurses ($M = 41.80$; $SD = 16.64$) ($p < .001$). There was no statistically significant difference in level of stress scores between nurses and OTs.

Test your understanding of ANOVA by interpreting the results of the SPSS output in Exercise 9.3. The research hypothesis is: 'There is a difference in social workers' perceived effectiveness of social work methods based on the type of method'; and the null hypothesis is: 'There is no difference in social workers'

Output 9.7 Independent ANOVA: post hoc test

Multiple Comparisons

Dependent Variable: Level of Stress
Tukey HSD

(I) Profession of Worker	(I) Profession of Worker	Mean Difference (I-J)	Std. Error	Sig.	95% Confidence Interval	
					Lower Bound	Upper Bound
Nurse	OT	6.720	4.405	.285		17.26
	Social Worker	22.800*	4.405	.000	12.26	33.34
OT	Nurse	−6.720	4.405	.285	−17.26	3.82
	Social Worker	16.080*	4.405	.001	5.54	26.62
Social Worker	Nurse	−22.800*	4.405	.000	−33.34	−12.26
	OT	−16.080*	4.405	.001	−26.62	−5.54

* The mean difference is significant at the 0.05 level.

Stastistically significant

Stastistically significant

perceived effectiveness of social work methods based on the type of method.' The independent variable is type of social work method (solution focused practice (SFP); cognitive behavioural therapy (CBT); psychoanalysis), which is nominal level, and the dependent variable is effectiveness score (1 = very ineffective; 10 = very effective), which although is ordinal level (strictly speaking) will be treated as interval level in the analysis.

Exercise 9.3: The perceived effectiveness of social work methods: ANOVA

Descriptives

Level of Stress

	N	Mean	Std. Deviation	Std. Error	Lower Bound	Upper Bound	Minimum	Maximum
					95% Condficence Interval for Mean			
SFP	25	7.96	5.224	1.045	5.80	10.12	1	30
CBT	25	4.72	2.525	.505	3.68	5.76	1	10
Psychoanalysis	25	3.40	2.723	.545	2.28	4.52	1	10
Total	75	5.36	4.128	.477	4.41	6.31	1	30

Test of Homogeneity of Variances

Level of Stress

Levene Statistic	df1	df2	Sig.
	2	72	.630

ANOVA

Level of Stress

	Sum of Squares	df	Mean Square	F	Sig.
Between Groups	275.280	2	137.640	10.051	.000
Within Groups	986.000	72	13.694		
Total	1261.280	74			

Multiple Comparisons

Dependent Variable: Level of Stress
Tukey HSD

(I) Profession of Worker	(I) Profession of Worker	Mean Difference (I-J)	Std. Error	Sig.	Lower Bound	Upper Bound
					95% Confidence Interval	
SFP	CBT	3.240	1.047	.008	.74	5.74
	Psychoanalysis	4.560	1.047	.000	2.06	7.06
CBT	SFP	−3.240	1.047	.008	−5.74	−.74
	Psychoanalysis	1.320	1.047	.422	−1.18	−3.74
Psychoanalysis	SFP	−4.560	1.047	.000	−7.06	−2.06
	CBT	−1.320	1.047	.422	−3.82	−1.18

*. The mean difference is significant at the 0.05 level.

Crosstabs and chi-square

The statistical tests we have discussed so far have been parametric tests, thus all assuming the level of measurement of the dependent variable to be at least interval level. But what test might you use when you want to explore the relationship between two variables where the dependent variable (or variable of influence) is nominal level and the independent variable (or outcome variable) is ordinal or nominal level? In this situation, you could use crosstabs and the nonparametric test of chi-square to determine any statistically significant difference between variables.

Crosstabs are merely crossing the levels of one variable with the levels of the other variable and determining the frequency of values that fall within each paired level. For example, let's look at sex of social workers (male; female) and the type of social work method they primarily use in their work (SFP or CBT). In this situation, we might explore whether there is a difference in type of method used (dependent or outcome variable) based on sex (independent or influential variable). We have collected the data listed in Table 9.2 on the sex of the social worker and her/his preferred method.

As both variables are nominal level, we can construct a crosstab, which will depict the frequency of males and females that prefer SFP or CBT. Generally speaking, you will construct the crosstab with the independent (or influential) variable in the columns and the dependent (or outcome) variable in the rows. Table 9.3 shows the crosstab for our data.

This crosstab is referred to as a 2x2 crosstab because there are two variables being compared with each variable consisting of two levels. The shaded part is

Table 9.2 Data of social worker sex and preferred method

Social worker	Sex	Preferred method
1	Male	SFP
2	Female	CBT
3	Female	SFP
4	Female	CBT
5	Female	SFP
6	Male	CBT
7	Male	CBT
8	Female	SFP
9	Female	SFP
10	Male	CBT

Table 9.3 Crosstab with frequencies of sex of social worker and preferred method

Preferred method	Sex of social worker		Total
	Male	Female	
SFP	1	4	6
CBT	3	2	4
Total	4	6	10

referred to as the cells within the 2x2 crosstab. As the table illustrates, there was one male who preferred SFP compared to four females who preferred SFP, and three males who preferred CBT compared to two females who preferred CBT. Although this information allows us to see which method was more preferred among males and females, we can also calculate the percentages within each cell, which gives us more information. Table 9.4 depicts both the frequency and percentage within each cell.

From the table, we can now see that of those that preferred SFP, 20% are males and 80% are females, and of those that preferred CBT, 60% were males and 40% were females. Although we can conclude that females prefer SFP whereas males prefer CBT, we are not able to say that the results are statistically significant with only the information provided above. Although constructing crosstabs can be useful in providing descriptive statistics of our sample data (frequencies, percentages), we need to perform additional statistical tests in order to determine if the observed frequencies in our crosstab is what would be expected in the population and, thus, whether we can infer any observed differences between two variables to be true among the larger population from which the sample was drawn.

We will now use an example based on the information from the 'Research in practice' topic to illustrate the chi-square statistic to test the difference between two categorical variables. We are interested in exploring whether there is a difference in whether someone receives IBs based on their reason for adult social

Table 9.4 Crosstab with frequencies and percentages of sex of social worker and preferred method

Preferred method	Sex of social worker		Total
	Male	Female	
SFP	1 (20%)	4 (80%)	5 (100%)
CBT	3 (60%)	2 (40%)	5 (100%)
Total	4	6	10

care services. Our research hypothesis is: 'There is a difference in receipt of IBs based on the reason for adult social care services' and the null hypothesis is: 'There is no difference in receipt of IBs based on the reason for adult social care services.' Our independent variable is 'reason for adult social care services' where there are three levels (learning disabled; physically disabled; mental health), which is nominal level. Our dependent variable is 'receipt of IBs' where there are two levels (yes – in receipt of IBs; and no – not in receipt of IBs). Our data on 100 service users are depicted below in the 2x3 (rows x columns) cross-tab produced by SPSS.

As the output depicts, of those individuals in receipt of IBs, 21 (47.7%) are receiving IBs due to a learning disability, 19 (43.2%) due to a physical disability and 4 (9.1%) due to mental health. Of those who do not receive IBs, 34 (60.7%) receive services due to a physical disability, 11 (19.6%) due to a learning disability, and 11 (19.6%) due to mental health. The frequencies we see within each cell are the 'observed' frequencies within our sample. We can assume, based on the observed frequencies, that people who receive adult social care services due to a learning disability are more likely to receive IBs than those receiving services due to a physical disability or mental health, but how can we determine if the results are statistically significant and not due to chance? How do we know that the observed frequencies from our sample would be the frequencies we would expect to see? A chi-square statistic, expressed as χ^2, will provide the answer to this question.

There are several assumptions to the χ^2 test. First, you must not have more than 25% of the cells with an expected frequency of less than 5; SPSS will report whether this assumption has been violated or not. If the assumption has been broken, and you are examining a 2x2 table, then SPSS will calculate the Fisher's Exact Probability test, which you will use to interpret the results over χ^2. Second, each cell should have a value of at least 1. If there is less than 1 value in a cell, then you might want to consider collapsing two cells into one to increase the frequency of values. Finally, χ^2 assumes

Output 9.8 Crosstab with frequencies and percentages of receipt of IB by reason for services

Receipt of IBs *Reason for Adult Social Care Services Crosstabulation

| | | Reason for Adult Social Care Services | | | |
		Learning Disabled	Physically Disabled	Mental Health	Total
Receipt of IBs	Yes Count	21	19	4	44
	% within Receipt of IBs	47.7%	43.2%	9.1%	100.0%
	No Count	11	34	11	56
	% within Receipt of IBs	19.6%	60.7%	19.6%	100.0%
Total	Count	32	53	15	100
	% within Receipt of IBs	32.0%	53.0%	15.0%	100.0%

the sample is drawn from a normal distribution. The χ^2 test calculates the expected frequencies in each cell, assuming there is no relationship between the two variables, and compares it to the actual observed frequencies in each cell. If there is no difference between what we observed and what we would expect to see, then the χ^2 value will be 0, and we can accept the null hypothesis of no difference. Output 9.9 reports the results from our χ^2 test of independence.

The first part of the output provides us with information on the observed frequencies within each cell as well as the expected count within each cell (these two values are needed to calculate the χ^2). We have also requested that SPSS produce the percentages by columns; if you prefer, you can request SPSS to give you the percentages by rows as well. The second part of the output provides us with the χ^2 test statistic and significance level. Here we see that $\chi^2 = 9.33$, with 2 degrees of freedom, and a significance value of $p = .01$. Assuming $\alpha = .05$, then we can reject the null hypothesis of no difference between reason for adult

Output 9.9 χ^2 test of independence 2x3

Observed count in sample

Receipt of IBs *Reason for Adult Social Care Services Crosstabulation

			Reason for Adult Social Care Services			
			Learning Disabled	Physically Disabled	Mental Health	Total
Receipt of IBs	Yes	Count	21	19	4	44.0
		Expected Count	14.1	23.3	6.6	44
		% within Receipt of IBs	47.7%	43.2%	9.1%	100.0%
	No	Count	11	34	11	56
		Expected Count	17.9	29.7	8.4	56.0
		% within Receipt of IBs	19.6%	60.7%	19.6%	100.0%
Total		Count	32	53	15	100
		Expected Count	32.0	53.0	15.0	100.0
		% within Receipt of IBs	32.0%	53.0%	15.0%	100.0%

What could be expected

Chi-Square Tests

	Value	df	Asymp.Sig. (2-sided)
Pearson Chi-Square	9.331[a]	2	.009
Likelihood Ratio	9.435	2	.009
Linear-by-Linear Association	8.255	1	.004
N of Valid Cases	100		

χ^2 test results

a. 0 Cells (0.0%) have expected count less than 5. The minimum expected count is 6.60.

social care services and receipt of IBs. The probability that we have obtained a χ^2 of 9.33 is 1 time in 100. The observed differences in our crosstab indicate an association between the two variables. We can report our findings as follows:

> Of those receipts of IBs, 47.7% receive services due to a learning disability, 43.2% due to a physical disability and 9.1% due to mental health, compared to 19.6%, 60.7% and 19.6% respectively. A chi-square test was preformed and indicated a statistically significant relationship between reason for receiving adult social care services and receipt of IBs, $\chi^2 (2, N = 100) = 9.33, p = .01$.

Test your understanding of χ^2 by interpreting the results of the SPSS output in Exercise 9.4. The research hypothesis is: 'There is a difference in type of stress relief based on profession'; and the null hypothesis is: 'There is no difference in type of stress relief based on profession.' The independent variable is profession (nurse; social worker), which is nominal level, and the dependent variable is type of stress relief, which is nominal (running; meditation).

Exercise 9.4: Difference in type of stress relief based on profession: chi-square

SPSS Output: chi-square test of independence 2x2

Type of Stress Relief * Profession Crosstabulation

			Profession		
			Nursing	Social Worker	Total
Type of Stress Relief	Running	Count	18	16	34
		Expected Count	17.0	17.0	34.0
		% within Type of Stress Relief	52.9%	47.1%	100.0%
	Meditation	Count	17	19	36
		Expected Count	18.0	18.0	36.0
		% within Type of Stress Relief	47.2%	52.8%	100.0%
Total		Count	35	35	35
		Expected Count	35.0	35.0	35.0
		% within Type of Stress Relief	50.0%	50.0%	100.0%

Chi-Square Tests

	Value	df	Asymp. Sig. (2-sided)	Exact Sig. (2-sided)	Exact Sig. (1-sided)
Pearson Chi-Square	.229[a]	1	.632		
Continuity Correction[b]	.057	1	.811		
Likelihood Ratio	.229	1	.632		
Firsher's Exact Test				.811	.406
Linear-by-Linear Association	.225	1	.635		
N of Valid Cases	70				

a. 0 cells (0.0%) have expected count less than 5. The minimum expected count is 17.00.
b. Computed only for a 2x2 table

'Research in practice' – stress among social workers and care managers

Let's now return to the findings from Wilberforce et al. (2014) in their study that aimed to explore the cause of stress among social workers and care managers working in 'personalised' adult social care in England, and examine the results from the bivariate analyses. The questionnaire used in data collection (JCQ) measured for job demands (psychological demand); control (decision latitude); and support (social support). In terms of individual-level differences across these three measures Wilberforce et al. reported the following results ($\alpha = .10$). There were no statistically significant correlations between age and psychological demands ($r = .02$), age and decision latitude ($r = .08$) or age and social support ($r = .03$). There were no statistically significant differences in psychological demand by sex ($M = 36.5$ for males; $M = 37.7$ for females), decision latitude by sex ($M = 69.7$ for males; $M = 69.2$ for females) or social support by sex ($M = 25.3$ for males; $M = 25.1$ for females). Full-time workers were not found to be statistically different than part-time workers on psychological demand ($M = 37.0$ for full-time; $M = 35.6$ for part-time), decision latitude ($M = 69.9$ for full-time; $M = 68.4$ for part-time) or social support ($M = 25.3$ for full-time; $M = 15.1$ for part-time). Finally, there was a statistically significant weak positive relationship between the hours: contact ratio and psychological demand ($r = .20$; $p < .01$), and hours: contract ratio and social support ($r = .15$; $p = .03$), but not between hours: contract ratio and decision latitude ($r = .00$). This finding indicates that the more hours worked over one's contract, the more psychological demand, but also the more social support, one will have.

In terms of characteristics related to the team, there was no statistically significant difference in type of team and psychological demand ($M = 36.6$ for social care only; $M = 36.9$ for multi-agency team), yet there was a statistically significant difference in type of team and decision latitude ($M = 68.8$ for social care only; $M = 70.9$ for multi-agency team, $p = .08$), and type of team and social support ($M = 25.6$ for social care only; $M = 24.7$ for multi-agency team, $p = .05$). This indicates that multi-agency teams have more decision latitude yet less social support when compared to social care-only teams. There was no statistically significant correlation between team size and psychological demand ($r = .07$) or decision latitude ($r = .07$), yet there was a statistically significant weak positive correlation between team size and social support ($r = .10$, $p = .01$) indicating the larger the team, the more social support. There was a statistically significant weak positive correlation between caseload size and psychological demand ($r = .21$, $p = .02$), indicating that as the caseload size increased, the psychological demand increased. There was no statistically significant correlation between caseload size and decision latitude ($r = .05$) or social support ($r = .07$). Finally, there was no statistically significant difference in having IBs on one's caseload and psychological demand ($M = 37.2$ for IBs; $M = 36.2$ for no

IBs), decision latitude (M = 69.5 for IBs; M = 69.8 for no IBs) or social support (M = 25.0 for IBs; M = 25.5 for no IBs).

Based on the findings from the bivariate analysis, we can conclude the following: (1) more hours worked over one's contracted hours is associated with higher psychological demand, yet also higher social support; (2) multi-agency teams have higher decision latitude, yet social care only teams have higher social support; (3) higher caseload size is associated with higher psychological distress; and (4) larger team sizes is associated with higher social supports. In terms of working with IBs, having IBs on one's caseload was not found to contribute to psychological distress, decision latitude or social supports.

Finally, we'd like to make a note about the reporting of research results. We highly advise you to report as much of your findings as possible in order to allow the reader to have all the necessary information to assess the quality of your research and the findings. In particular, we recommend always reporting the sample size included in each test, the mean and standard deviation (where calculated), and the exact p-value even for non-statistically significant findings. Unfortunately, Wilberforce at al. (2014) did not report all such findings – for example, they merely listed 'n.s.' under 'Significance level', versus reporting the p-value. The more information provided by the researcher the better for the reader.

Test your understanding

Based on the information covered in this chapter, answer the following questions:

1   List the assumptions for a parametric test.

2   What are the three requirements to be able to infer causality?

3   Which bivariate analysis should you use when you have the following variables with the specified level of measurement? (match each of the examples below to only one of the following: correlational analysis (r); t-test; ANOVA; or χ^2).

Independent variable Level of measurement	Dependent variable Level of measurement	Bivariate analysis
Nominal (2 levels)	Ratio	
Nominal (2 levels)	Nominal (2 levels)	
Ratio	Interval	
Nominal (3 levels)	Ratio	

Critical Thinking Box

Andrew (7 years old) was referred by his social worker to a domestic abuse intervention programme run by a local organisation. The social worker referred Andrew to the programme because he had witnessed domestic abuse between his mother and father and was presenting with behavioural and emotional difficulties. Andrew was described as 'withdrawn, easily tearful, and reluctant to engage with this fellow classmates at school'. The intervention programme consisted of 10 weeks of arts-based group work where 5–10 children (ages 6–11) met for 1.5 hours per week. The programme uses the Strengths and Difficulties Questionnaire (SDQ) to assess the participants on behavioural and emotional aspects. The social worker wishes to evaluate whether the programme is effective to determine whether to continue to use this service in the future. Based on the above scenario, you are tasked with designing an evaluation of the domestic abuse intervention programme. Start by exploring the Strengths and Difficulties Questionnaire by accessing the forms and scoring sheets on www.sdqinfo.com and then answer the following questions:

1. What is your hypothesis and null hypothesis?

2. Which form(s) will you use for the evaluation and why?

3. Who will fill out the form(s) and when?

4. How will you determine whether the intervention was successful? In particular, consider the type of statistical test(s) you will use and how you will interpret the results.

Summary

Through this chapter, we have explored four different types of bivariate analyses. We first looked at the difference between bivariate analysis, which looks at the relationship between two variables, and multivariate analysis, which looks at the relationship between more than two variables. We then examined the assumptions of parametric tests, and considered that any violation of the assumptions would require the use of nonparametric tests. We then explored the difference between correlation and causation and the three requirements for being able to infer causality. Bivariate analyses of correlational analysis, using Pearson's product moment correlation coefficient (r), t-test, ANOVA and chi-square (χ^2) were reviewed and outputs from SPSS were presented in order to discuss how to interpret the findings of the statistical tests. We relied on examples related to our 'Research in practice' topic of stress among social workers working in personalised adult social care in England. We anticipate that you now have a foundational understanding of a sample of bivariate analyses that will be useful in interpreting social work research findings that you will use to inform your social work practice.

Further resources

Acton, C. and Miller, R. (2009). *SPSS for Social Scientists*, 2nd ed. New York, NY: Palgrave Macmillan.

Dancey, C. P. and Reidy, J. (2011). *Statistics Without Maths for Psychology*, 5th ed. Harlow: Pearson Education.

Field, A. (2009). *Discovering Statistics Using SPSS*, 3rd ed. London: Sage.

Knapp, H. (2014). *Introductory Statistics Using SPSS*. Thousand Oaks, CA: Sage.

Salkind, N. J. (2014). *Statistics for People who (Think They) Hate Statistics*, 5th ed. London: Sage.

10

WHAT IS THE EFFECT OF ONE OR MORE VARIABLES ON ANOTHER VARIABLE?

LEARNING OUTCOMES

By the end of this chapter you should be able to:

- Define and explain linear regression analysis
- Distinguish between bivariate and multivariate linear regression analysis
- Interpret the results/output from the bivariate and multivariate linear regression analysis

Introduction

Quantitative research and statistics enable us to explore the relationship between several variables and determine the extent to which they are related or how one or more variables might influence another variable. Given this information, we are then able to see if a change in one or more variables is associated with a change in another variable and, thus, use this knowledge of those variables and their relationship to predict future situations. For example, through quantitative research and statistics we could determine the variables (or factors) that lead to receiving higher scores on a research methods test. This information will enable us to predict a student's research methods test results when we have information on the variables found to predict test results. Likewise, we may want to predict the number of days a service user will remain sober after completion of a substance misuse treatment programme when we have information about her/his demographic characteristics, substance misuse history and characteristics of the treatment programme. The statistical test we would use in both situations is called linear regression analysis. Whereas correlational analysis (discussed in Chapter 9) enabled us to determine the extent (strength and direction) to which two variables were related, linear regression analysis takes this one step further by specifying how much a variable will change when there is a change in one or more other variables.

In this chapter, we extend the discussion of how variables are related by exploring how to predict a change in a variable (dependent or outcome variable) when there is a change in one or more other variables (independent or predictor variable). In Chapter 9, we discussed the difference between bivariate analysis, which explores the relationship between two variables, and multivariate analysis, which explores the relationship between more than two variables. Whereas in Chapter 9 we covered several bivariate analysis examples, this chapter will extend into multivariate analyses. In order to do this, we will first explore one final bivariate analysis, bivariate linear regression analysis, which determines the extent to which the outcome (or dependent) variable will change with each change in the predictor (or independent) variable. We will then move the discussion to multivariate linear regression analysis where we will determine the extent to which the outcome (or dependent) variable will change given each change in more than one predictor (or independent) variable. As with the information from Chapter 9, the information from this chapter will enable you to evaluate the validity of social work research and its applicability to your social work practice. Understanding the results from linear regression analysis can be helpful in predicting future circumstances, situations or outcomes given knowledge of specific variables and can, therefore, be helpful in planning your social work practice interventions. We will now explore a social work practice example that we will refer to throughout the remainder of this chapter.

'Research in practice' – newly qualified social workers

In 2008, the newly qualified social worker (NQSW) programme was established in England to develop the workforce of social workers in children's services. The programme was piloted in 2008–2009 with 87 employers and was then made available to all local authorities and voluntary organisations in 2009. It was developed to address the need to smooth the transition from student social worker to qualified social worker where the responsibilities become more complex. The NQSW programme aimed to provide support for NQSWs in their first year of practice to enhance their skills, competence and confidence as social workers, and to promote the retention of social workers in children's services (Children's Workforce Development Council (CWDC), 2009). The programme involved additional funds for professional development, an allocated amount of time (10%) dedicated to training and development and portfolio preparation, two-weekly 'reflective supervision' sessions for the first three months and then monthly sessions after that, and a reduced caseload (CWDC, 2008).

Carpenter et al. (2015) report on their evaluation of the NQSW programme, which involved a longitudinal repeated measures design, by gathering information on three cohorts of the NQSW programme (2008–2009; 2009–2010;

2010–2011). The data collection instruments gathered information on self-efficacy, role clarity and role conflict, job satisfaction and stress. Self-efficacy was defined as 'an individual's assessment of his or her confidence in their ability (to) execute specific skills in a particular set of circumstances and thereby achieve a successful outcome' (Holden et al., 2001, p. 116 as cited by Carpenter et al., 2015, p. 155). A self-efficacy measure was developed that addressed the NQSW's confidence in their ability to accomplish tasks, which consisted of tasks related to direct work with children, young people, their families and carers, working with others to provide coordinated services, and professional development. A Likert scale was used to indicate the level of confidence (1 = not at all confident; 5 = moderately confident; 10 = extremely confident) and the final score could range from 12–120 with higher scores indicating higher self-efficacy.

Role clarity and role conflict were assessed by a Likert scale (1 = very false; 7 = very true) and intrinsic and extrinsic job satisfaction were measured through the Job Satisfaction Scale (Dyer and Hoffenberg, 1975). While intrinsic satisfaction relates to the job itself, tasks, accomplishments, opportunities to use own initiatives, having challenges to meet and relationships with co-workers, extrinsic job satisfaction relates to pay and working conditions, flexibility of hours of work, commute to work, management and supervision, job security and advancement opportunities (Carpenter et al., 2015). Finally, stress was measured using the General Health Questionnaire (GHQ) (Goldberg & Williams, 1988).

Carpenter et al. (2015) used a series of bivariate statistical tests, such as t-test and chi-square (χ^2 test), and a multivariate linear regression analysis to explore the predictors of self-efficacy. Basic descriptive statistics, such as frequencies and percentages were used to describe the demographic characteristics of the sample, such as age, gender, ethnic group, experience in child and family social work, degree level, and whether or not someone had a degree from outside the UK. Through the use of paired samples t-test, the findings indicated a statistically significant increase in mean total self-efficacy scores from beginning to the end of the NQSW programme for all three cohorts, thus indicating the NQSW was effective in enhancing self-efficacy. Additionally, through the use of paired samples t-test, the findings suggested that the respondents reported statistically significant lower scores when rating themselves retrospectively when compared to their actual ratings, indicating that they had overestimated their self-efficacy at Time 1. The NQSWs initially thought they were more confident, but after experiencing the actual job realised they were not as confident and should have rated themselves lower. The findings in relation to the factors that were found to predict self-efficacy will be discussed at the end of this chapter after we review the basic concepts of linear regression analysis and discuss how to conduct bivariate and multiple linear regression analyses and interpret the findings.

Statistical tests: linear regression analysis

In Chapter 9, we discussed correlational analysis which determines the relationship between two variables in terms of the strength of the relationship and the direction of the relationship. For example, using Pearson's product moment correlation coefficient (r) we are able to determine the strength and direction of any relationship between hours of time spent studying and final research methods test results. A Pearson's r of .93 indicates a strong positive relationship between the two variables. The time spent studying is correlated (or associated) with final test results with more time spent studying being associated with higher test results and less time spent studying being associated with lower test results. Although correlational analysis can tell us whether two variables are related, it cannot tell us exactly how much of a change will occur in final test results with each additional hour of study time. Linear regression analysis is an extension of correlational analysis in that it not only can tell us whether two variables are related, but also how much of a change will occur in a variable based on a change in one or more other variables.

Linear regression analysis is a useful tool for exploring the relationship between an outcome (or dependent) variable and one or more predictor (or independent) variables and can be used for either prediction or to infer causality between variables. For example, a bivariate linear regression analysis has indicated that for each additional hour of study time (predictor variable), the final test result (outcome variable) will increase by 2.74 percentage points. Therefore, if a student wants to get no less than a 95% on the test, s/he can determine the number of hours of study time needed to gain such results. Linear regression analysis is able to determine this through the use of a formula (or regression equation) where knowledge of the values or characteristics of the predictor variable(s) can be inputted into an equation that will result in an output value of the outcome variable. Such analysis is useful for social work practice as it can provide answers to questions such as: (1) 'What contributes to successful completion of an alcohol treatment programme?'; (2) 'What are the factors that contribute to psychiatric hospital readmission'; or (3) 'What contributes to higher self-efficacy among NQSWs in England?'

Remember, from Chapter 9, that in order to infer causality you must meet the following three requirements: (1) the two variables are correlated; (2) the independent (or predictor) variable(s) must have occurred prior to the outcome (or dependent) variable; and (3) the relationship between the variables cannot be explained by any extraneous variables. Therefore, in social work research unless you are able to meet the requirements for inferring causality, then the use of linear regression analysis is for predictive purposes only. We will first explore bivariate linear regression analysis and then move to multivariate linear regression analysis.

Bivariate linear regression analysis

Bivariate linear regression analysis examines the relationship between two variables and explores how a change in one variable (the predictor variable) leads to a change in another variable (the outcome variable). It is able to do this based on an equation that when presented graphically produces a straight line; thus the values of the two variables are predicted to fall around this line. The regression equation is:

$$y = a + bx$$

In this equation, y is the outcome (or dependent) variable and x is the predictor (or independent) variable. Both a and b represent numbers that are constant in the equation; meaning these two values do not change despite x and y changing. The letter a is the intercept (also referred to as the constant) or, otherwise stated, where the beginning of the line starts on the y-axis of the graph, or what the value of y is when x is 0. The letter b is the slope, or, otherwise stated, the actual amount of change in y we will see with every one change in x. Let's refer back to our example of hours of study time (x) and final research methods test results (y) to see if we are able to predict the final test results for students based on the number of hours they spend studying. The values for each variable are listed in Table 10.1.

Before we run a bivariate linear regression analysis, let's see if the two variables are correlated. Based on correlational analysis, using Pearson's product moment correlation coefficient (r), we are able to determine a strong positive relationship between hours of study time (x) and final test results (y), $r(20) = .93$, $p < .001$ as depicted by the scatterplot in Figure 10.1.

Although we are able to determine that the two variables are correlated, we have not been able to determine the extent to which y (final test results) will change given the value of x (hours spent studying). In order to determine this, we will need to conduct a bivariate linear regression analysis to give us the values of a and b so that when we plug in a value for x, we can determine the value of y. Once we have the values of a and b and have determined y given the value of x, we could graph the values of x and y, which would form a straight (linear) line. This line is called the 'line of best fit' because it is the line along which the majority of values is predicted to fall or, otherwise stated, no other line would fit as well through the data points! Of course, the extent to which this line is the best fit depends on whether our results are statistically significant, indicating that the likelihood that our prediction line is to have occurred by chance or sampling error is less than our threshold for error (set α level).

Although we can manually calculate the values of a and b using a formula, most researchers use a statistical software package, such as the Statistical Package for the Social Sciences (SPSS) to calculate the values for them. The output, or results, of the bivariate linear regression analysis will provide you with the

Table 10.1 Hours spent studying and final test results ($N = 20$)

Hours spent studying	Test results
15	90
20	95
5	70
0	40
2	65
18	95
15	94
12	85
10	85
20	100
0	50
7	75
10	95
22	100
5	0
0	40
13	85
14	90
2	45
1	40

values for *a* (the intercept, or the value of *y* when *x* is 0) and *b* (the slope, or the amount of change in *y* we will see with each unit change in *x*). This information will enable you to complete the regression equation and, thus, determine the extent to which *y* will change with each change in *x*.

We will not go through the steps of the analysis or the output from SPSS at this point, but rather, for illustrative purposes, we will merely tell you the results from the bivariate linear regression analysis. Our results indicated that $a = 48.83$ and $b = 2.74$. Given this information we are now able to predict the final test results for students if we know how many hours they spent studying. We are able to say that for every one extra hour that students study, their final test results will increase by 2.74 percentage points. The regression equation is as follows:

$$y = 48.83 + 2.74(x)$$

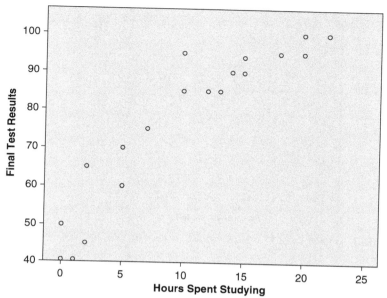

Figure 10.1 Correlation between hours of study time and final test results

For a student who spends five hours studying, we could predict her/his final test result to be a 62.53%, or 63% when rounding up, by plugging the values into the equation as follows:

$y = 48.83 + 2.74(5)$

$y = 48.83 + 13.7$

$y = 62.53\%$

A student who spends 0 hours studying is predicted to receive 48.83% [$y = 48.83 + 2.74(0)$], a student who spends 10 hours studying is predicted to receive 76% [$y = 48.83 + 2.74(10)$], a student who studies 18 hours is predicted to receive 98% [$y = 48.83 + 2.74(18)$], and a student who studies 20 hours is predicted to receive 103.6%! (Obviously, s/he can only receive the maximum score of 100%!) As stated above, the regression equation will be a straight (linear) line when graphically represented. We can then determine the extent to which our sample data fit around the 'line of best fit' (or the regression equation line). Let's look again at the correlational analysis scatterplot (Figure 10.2), which now has the regression equation line overlapping the actual data points.

As you can see the line approximately goes through the actual values from the sample but it clearly is not perfect. For example, our predictions indicated that studying for five hours resulted in a final test result of 63%, studying for 10

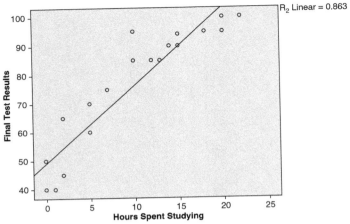

Figure 10.2 Line of best fit from bivariate linear regression analysis and actual data points

hours resulted in a final test result of 76% and studying for 18 hours resulted in a final test result of 98%. Based on this sample data the regression equation appears, visually, to be a good fit in terms of predicting future test scores when we have knowledge of the hours of time spent studying, but it is not perfect. For example, 10 hours of study time actually yielded a final test score of both 85% and 95% in our sample. This discrepancy (10 hours is predicted to yield a 76%) is referred to as an error in our prediction. In linear regression analysis, the error is calculated and referred to as residuals, which is the difference between the actual score and the predicted score. Residuals are reported in the output/ results of SPSS and are helpful in determining the accuracy of our regression analysis.

Therefore, knowing the values of a and b can help us 'predict' the final test results of students (y) when we know how many hours they spent studying (x), yet we should note that all predicted scores are merely that – predicted scores. As indicated above, you may actually find out that a student who studied 15 hours also received a 100% when s/he was predicted to receive a 90%. So the question remains, how confident are we that the results can be applied to other students outside of our sample or, in other words, how confident are we that the results reflect what happens in the true population and are not due to chance or sampling error? The results from SPSS will also provide you with an ANOVA summary table that indicates the probability that your line of best fit is due to chance or sampling error? It will also provide you with the probability that our values of b are statistically significant in influencing the outcome variable.

Let's use an example based on our 'Research in practice' topic to illustrate a complete bivariate linear regression analysis. Let's assume we are interested in whether there is a relationship between age of NQSWs and level of self-efficacy. Our research hypothesis is, 'There is a relationship between age of NQSWs and level of self-efficacy with self-efficacy scores increasing as age increases', and our null hypothesis is, 'There is no relationship between age of NQSWs and level of self-efficacy scores; there is no change in self-efficacy scores with a change in age.' The data for our sample of 20 NQSWs are presented in Table 10.2 (the data are fictitious, of course!). The self-efficacy scores (based on the measure discussed in the 'Research in practice' example) can range from 12–120. A score of 84–95 is interpreted as 'confident', 96 and above as 'highly confident', and a score of 60 or below would indicate an 'unconfident practitioner' (Carpenter et al., 2015). Our predictor variable (x) is age and our outcome variable (y) is self-efficacy score.

Table 10.2 Age and self-efficacy scores for NQSWs ($N = 20$)

Age in years	Self-efficacy score
25	80
50	96
32	85
28	81
42	89
37	86
35	85
27	82
55	98
45	91
48	93
26	81
30	93
43	90
36	86
52	94
49	93
58	97
24	79
30	84

Using SPSS, the output/results of the linear regression analysis are presented below. We will go through each output separately. For illustrative purposes, we have requested SPSS to provide correlational analyses as well. Therefore, the first part of the output provides us with the correlational analysis between age (x) and self-efficacy score (y). As Output 10.1 reveals, there is a strong positive correlation between age and self-efficacy scores, $r(20) = .92$, $p < .001$, which is statistically significant.

The next output is called the 'model summary', which is depicted in Output 10.2. Here Pearson's r is presented again in the first box and is expressed as 'R', which in regression analysis is known as 'Multiple R', or the extent to which the values cluster around the 'line of best fit'; higher values of R indicate better predictions. Here our R is .919, or as we did in the example above, we would report it as .92 (rounding to two decimal places). The next box, 'R Square' (often written as R^2), indicates the amount of variance that is shared between age and self-efficacy scores. Remember from Chapter 9 that if we want to determine the amount of variance in one variable that is shared by another, we would square the value of Pearson's r. Here, SPSS has provided us with the value of R^2 which is .845 (.919 x .919 = .845), or .85 when rounding to two decimal places. This high value indicates that 85% of the variance in self-efficacy scores can be explained by the age of the NQSW. The third box in 10.2 provides the 'Adjusted R Square', which gives a more realistic value of R^2 taking into account the sample size and number of variables; it is meant to more accurately represent the value of R^2 in the population. Finally, the fourth box provides the 'standard error of the estimate', which is the measure of accuracy of our estimation. This value means that for each value of x, the estimate of the variance of y is 2.44.

Output 10.1 Correlational analysis of age and self-efficacy scores

		Self-Efficacy Score of NQSW	Age of NQSW
Pearson Correlation	Self-Efficacy Score of NQSW	1.000	.919
	Age of NQSW	.919	1.000
Sig. (1-tailed)	Self-Efficacy Score of NQSW	–	.000
	Age of NQSW	.000	–
N	Self-Efficacy Score of NQSW	20	20
	Age of NQSW	20	20

Correlation between self-efficacy score and age

Correlations

Statistically significant

Sample size

Output 10.2 Model summary of age and self-efficacy scores

Model Summary

Model	R	R Square	Adjusted R Square	Std. Error of the Estimate
1	.919[a]	.845	.836	2.442

a. Predictors: (Constant), Age of NQSW

Output 10.3 provides the next output, which is the ANOVA table that determines whether our estimation (or 'line of best fit') is statistically significant; that is, the probability that the estimation occurred by chance (sampling error) and, thus, is not likely to represent the population. In our ANOVA table, we can see that the F-value is 97.82 and that this is statistically significant at $p < .001$ (assuming our set $\alpha = .05$). This means that our estimation ('line of best fit') is highly unlikely to be due to chance or sampling error, and we can reject the null hypothesis of no relationship between age and self-efficacy scores. Thus we can proceed to the next output that provides the information for our equation indicating the exact relationship between age and self-efficacy scores.

Output 10.4 provides the values for our regression equation (a and b) as well as a standardised value for b (referred to as Beta and expressed by 'b'), and a t-test value to determine whether the values are statistically significant. The value of a (intercept or constant) is listed in the first row, first box. Here the SPSS output refers to a as the 'constant' and we can see that the value is 68.46, which has a standard error of 2.07 (remember, the standard error is referred to as the residual). The second line of the output provides us with the value of b, which is .51 with a standard error (residual) of .05. This means that for each additional year of age, self-efficacy scores are predicted to increase by .51 points. The confidence intervals indicate that we are 95% confident that our value of b in the population will lie between .40 and .62. The output also provides us with the 'standardised coefficient of Beta' (β), which means that b has been adjusted (or standardised) so that we can determine when x changes by one standard deviation, how many standard deviations y will change, which is the value of

Output 10.3 ANOVA table for linear regression of age and self-efficacy

ANOVA[a]

Model		Sum of Squares	df	Mean Square	F	Sig.
1	Regression	583.232	1	583.232	97.823	.000[b]
	Residual	107.318	18	5.962		
	Total	690.550	19			

a. Dependent Variable: Self-Efficacy Score of NQSW
b. Predictors: (Constant), Age of NQSW

Output 10.4 Linear regression equation for age and self-efficacy

Value of *a*
(intercept)

Coefficients[a]

Model		B	Std. Error	Beta	t	Sig.	Lower Bound	Upper Bound
		Unstandardized Coefficients		Standardized Coefficients			95.0% Confidence Interval for B	
1	(Constant)	68.457	2.065	.919	33.158	.000	64.120	72.795
	Age of NQSW	.510	.052		9.891	.000	.402	.619

a. Dependent Variable: Self-Efficacy Score of NQSW

Value of *b*

the standardised coefficient of *b* (β). Here we can see that for each one standard deviation change of *x*, *y* will change by .92. (Note: the b values are more relevant in multiple linear regression analysis, which will be discussed later.) The *t*-value (9.89) and *p*-value ($p < .001$) indicate whether the predictor variable (*x*) of age is statistically significant. We can see that age is statistically significant in predicting a change in self-efficacy at $p < .001$.

Based on the information from the final output, we can now plug the values of *a* and *b* into our regression equation and use the equation to predict self-efficacy scores of NQSWs when we know their age. Our regression equation is as follows with the value of *a* (68.46) and *b* (.51) entered:

$$y = 68.46 + .51(x)$$
$$\quad\;\; a \qquad\; b$$

Based on the equation, if we have a NQSW who is 32 years of age, we can predict that her self-efficacy score will be 84.78 [84.78 = 68.46 + .51(32)], whereas a NQSW who is 55 years of age will have a predicted self-efficacy score of 96.51 [96.51 = 68.46 + .51(55)]. Thus, as age increases, self-efficacy scores are predicted to increase. The scatterplot in Figure 10.3 provides the actual data points from our sample of 20 NQSWs. The scatterplot also provides the 'line of best fit', which is the line in the middle that cuts through the data points. The upper and lower lines represent our confidence intervals; therefore, we are 95% confident that the 'line of best fit' in the true population will lie somewhere between the upper and lower lines.

We will report our final results by including the R^2 value (indicating the amount of variance in self-efficacy that is explained by age); the *F*-value from the ANOVA, the statistical significance of the ANOVA (indicating the likelihood that our regression equation has occurred due to chance or sampling error) and

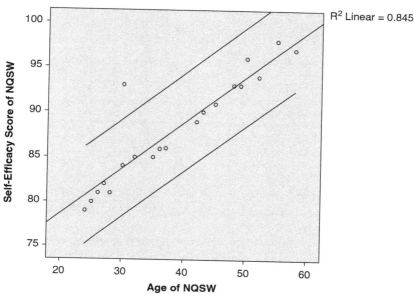

Figures 10.3 Line of best fit for age and self-efficacy of NQSWs ($N = 20$)

the degrees of freedom for the ANOVA; the value of the α (intercept or constant); the value of b; the standardised value of b (β); and the statistical significance of the t-test for the predictor variable. We could write our findings as follows:

> The results from a bivariate linear regression analysis indicates that age explains 85% of the variance in self-efficacy scores, $R^2 = .85$, $F(1,18) = 97.82$, $p < .001$. The results indicate that for every one additional year in age, self-efficacy scores increases by .51 points. Confidence intervals indicate that the population slope (b) is between .40 and .62 with 95% confidence.

In addition to the written findings, we could present a table that provides additional information (see Table 10.3), which we highly recommend!

We should also note that our examples have included relationships that are positive – as x increases, y increases. Regression equations can also result in negative relationships where with each change in x, there will be a decrease in y. We are able to determine the direction of the relationship through the correlational analysis, but also through the value of the slope (b). For example, using our regression equation above, our value of b may be $-.51$, which would

Table 10.3 Bivariate linear regression analysis results

Variable		B	SE B	β	t	p
Constant		68.46	2.07			
Age		.51	.05	.92	9.89	.000*
Adjusted R^2	.84					
F	97.82*					

*$p < .001$.

change our regression equation to $y = 68.46 - .51(x)$. This would indicate that with each additional year of age, the self-efficacy score for the NQSW would be predicted to decrease by .51 points.

Before we move to multivariate linear regression analysis, let's test your understanding of bivariate linear regression analysis by answering the questions in Exercise 10.1.

Exercise 10.1: Bivariate linear regression analysis

We are interested in whether there is a relationship between hours spent studying and final test results. Our hypothesis is, 'There is a relationship between hours spent studying and final test results; the more hours spent studying will predict higher test results.' Based on the SPSS output below, answer the following questions ($N = 20$):

1. Is there a correlation between hours spent studying and final test results? If, so present the correlation.

2. How much of the variance in final test results can be explained by hours spent studying?

3. What is the probability that the regression equation ('line of best fit') is likely to have occurred by chance (sampling error)? How do you know and what does this mean for the research?

4. Write the regression equation based on the output.

5. What would be the predicted final test result for a student who studied four hours? What about a student who studied 12 hours?

6. Write out the findings of the bivariate linear regression analysis and include a table of additional information.

Model Summary

Model	R	R Square	Adjusted R Square	Std. Error of the Estimate
1	.929[a]	.863	.855	8.328

a. Predictors: (Constant), Hours Spent Studying

ANOVA[a]

Model		Sum of Squares	df	Mean Square	F	Sig.
1	Regression	7862.446	1	7862.446	113.355	.000[b]
	Residual	1248.504	18	69.361		
	Total	9110.950	19			

a. Dependent Variable: Final Test Results
b. Predictors: (Constant), Hours Spent Studying

Coefficients[a]

Model		Unstandardized Coefficients		Standardized Coefficients	t	Sig.	95.0% Confidence Interval for B	
		B	Std.Error	Beta			Lower Bound	Upper Bound
1	(Constant)	48.829	3.080		15.853	.000	42.358	55.300
	Hours Spent Studying	2.735	.257	.929	10.647	.000	2.195	3.275

a. Dependent Variable: Final Test Results

Multivariate linear regression analysis

Multivariate linear regression analysis is an extension of bivariate linear regression analysis. Whereas bivariate linear regression analysis seeks to predict the change in one outcome variable (y) given a change in one predictor variable (x), multivariate linear regression analysis seeks to predict the change in one outcome variable (y) given a change in more than one predictor variable (for example, x_1, x_2, and x_3). It is able to do this by providing information about how all the predictor variables together contribute to a change in the outcome variable, but also the influence of each individual predictor variable on the outcome variable. Although the results from the analysis can be used to predict what might happen in the future, it is also commonly used to determine the extent to which each individual predictor variable contributes or influences the outcome variable.

The regression equation for multivariate linear regression analysis is an extension of the equation for bivariate linear regression analysis by simply adding each additional predictor variable to the equation. For example, if we have three predictor variables, our regression equation will be as follows:

$$y = a + b_1x_1 + b_2x_2 + b_3x_3$$

The regression equation for five predictor variables would be expressed as follows:

$$y = a + b_1x_1 + b_2x_2 + b_3x_3 + b_4x_4 + b_5x_5$$

As you can see, as with the bivariate linear regression equation, there is only one constant (or intercept) (*a*), but there is an additional slope (*b*) for each predictor variable (*x*). If you have more than five predictor variables, then you would continue to add the additional slope value which would be multiplied by the predictor variable (b_xx_x).

If we revisit our example of hours spent studying and final test results, we may hypothesise that it is not merely studying that contributes to final test results, but also the number of classes attended during the semester. While studying without attending class or attending class without studying might be better than nothing in terms of gaining a better final test result, we might hypothesise that both studying *and* attending class will result in higher scores. Therefore, we collect information on the hours each student spent studying and the total number of classes that they attended during the semester. We will employ a multiple linear regression analysis to not only determine the influence of hours spent studying on final test results and the influence of number of classes attended on final test results, but the extent to which the two of the variables together (hours spent studying; number of classes attended) contribute to final test results. Our multiple linear regression equation for this example is as follows:

$$y = a + b_1x_1 + b_2x_2 \qquad \text{or} \qquad y = a + b_1(\text{hours}) + b_2(\text{\# of classes})$$

We will refer to the first predictor variable (x_1) as hours spent studying and the second predictor variable (x_2) as number of classes attended. Table 10.4 has our values for hours spent studying and final test results with the additional values for number of classes attended (out of a possible 15) included. For this example, we will assume our sample size is 40 ($N = 40$) and will, simply, repeat the values in Table 10.4 when entering the values into SPSS.

Using SPSS, we have run a multiple linear regression analysis entering all the values above into the database twice to make a sample size of 40. Interpreting the outputs is very similar to interpreting outputs from a bivariate linear regression analysis, yet we will now have an additional predictor variable to consider in the regression equation. For this example, we will go through each output/result in turn.

Table 10.4 Hours spent studying, number of classes attended and final test results ($N = 40$)

Hours spent studying	Number of classes	Test results
15	15	90
20	15	95
5	10	70
0	0	40
2	15	65
18	15	95
15	14	94
12	13	85
10	12	85
20	15	100
0	0	50
7	12	75
10	13	95
22	15	100
5	9	0
0	2	40
13	12	85
14	15	90
2	3	45
1	2	40

In conducting our analysis, we have requested SPSS to provide descriptive statistics, such as the correlational analysis of the predictor variables with the outcome variable. Output 10.5 provides the correlational analysis of hours spent studying with final test results and number of classes attended with final test results. The first row of the output provides the Pearson's (r) for both correlational analyses, and the second row indicates whether the analysis is statistically significant. The third row provides the sample size, which indicates the number of values from each variable that were included in the analysis. From the output, we can see that there is a strong positive relationship between hours spent studying and final test results, $r(40) = .86$, $p < .001$, and a strong positive relationship between number of classes attended and final test results, $r(40) = .82$, $p < .001$.

Output 10.5 Correlational analysis for hours spent studying and classes attended with final test results

Correlations

		Final Test Results	Hours Spent Studying	Number of Classes Attended
Pearson Correlation	Final Test Results	1.000	.856	.824
	Hours Spent Studying	.856	1.000	.817
	Number of Classes Attended	.824	.817	1.000
Sig. (1–tailed)	Final Test Results	–	.000	.000
	Hours Spent Studying	.000	–	.000
	Number of Classes Attended	.000	.000	–
N	Final Test Results	40	40	40
	Hours Spent Studying	40	40	40
	Number of Classes Attended	40	40	40

Output 10.6 provides information on the entry method of variables in the multiple regression analysis. The information in Output 10.6 indicates that the 'variables entered' were the two predictor variables of 'number of classes attended' and 'hours spent studying' and the method of entry was 'enter', which means that both variables were entered into the analysis at the same time. The outcome variable is listed underneath the output box and indicates that the outcome (or dependent) variable is 'final test results'.

Output 10.7 provides us with the model summary. Whereas in bivariate linear regression analysis, 'R' was Pearson's product moment correlation coefficient (r) (because there were only two variables in the analysis), in multiple linear regression analysis 'R' is truly a 'Multiple R' as it is the correlation between the predictor variables (two or more variables) and the outcome variable. The value

Output 10.6 Entry method and variables of multiple regression analysis

Variables Entered / Removed[a]

Model	Variables Entered	Variables Removed	Method
1	Number of Classes Attended, Hours Spent Studying[b]	–	Enter

a. Dependent Variable: Final Test Results
b. All requested Variables entered.

Output 10.7 Multiple linear regression: model summary

Model Summary

Model	R	R Square	Adjusted R Square	Std. Error of the Estimate
1	.883[a]	.779	.768	11.841

a. Predictors: (Constant), Number of Classes Attended, Hours Spent Studying

of R in Output 10.7 indicates the correlation between hours of time spent study-ing, number of classes attended and final test results is .88. If we square R, then we can see how much of the variance in the outcome variable (final test results) is made up of the predictor variables (hours of time spent studying and number of classes attended). SPSS provides this value for us, and from Output 10.7 we can see $R^2 = .78$. Therefore, 78% of the variance of final test results can be explained by hours of time spent studying and number of classes attended. Remember that this means there is 22% (100–78) of the variance in final test results that is explained by other variables.

Output 10.7 also provides us with the Adjusted R^2, which takes into account our sample size and number of variables to make the R^2 more likely to be the true situation in the population. In our example, our Adjusted R^2 has been reduced to .77. Therefore, 77% of the variance in final test results is explained by hours of time spent studying and number of classes attended. Finally, the model summary provides our standard error of the estimate, which is 11.84.

Output 10.8 provides the ANOVA table, which indicates the likelihood that our predicted regression equation has occurred by chance (sampling error). Here we can see that the F-value is 65.40 and the test is statistically significant at $p < .001$. This indicates that the likelihood that our predicted regression equa-tion has occurred by chance (sampling error) is less than 1 time in 1,000. If we set $\alpha = .05$, then we can reject the null hypothesis that there is no relationship between predictor variables and outcome variable and assume that our pre-dicted regression equation has not occurred by chance. Therefore, we can accept the research hypothesis that our predictor variables influence our

Output 10.8 ANOVA for multiple regression analysis

ANOVA[a]

Model		Sum of Squares	df	Mean Square	F	Sig.
1	Regression	18338.322	2	9169.161	65.398	.000[b]
	Residual	5187.578	37	140.205		
	Total	23525.900	39			

a. Dependent Variable: Final Test Results

b. Predictors: (Constant), Number of Classes Attended, Hours Spent Studying

outcome variable. Thus, we will move forward with the next output to analysis of the regression equation.

The information for our multiple regression equation is provided in Output 10.9. The first line '(constant)' provides the value of a (constant or intercept), which is 38.69 with a standard error of 4.08. We can be 95% confident that a will fall between the values of 30.42 and 46.96.

The second line 'hours spent studying' provides us with the value of b_1 (1.85), the standard error of b_1 (.45), the standardised coefficient of b_1 ($\beta_1 = .55$), the t-value ($t = 4.12$) and the significance of the t-test ($p < .001$). Such results indicate that with one additional hour of time spent studying, final test results will increase by 1.85 points. We can be 95% confident that b_1 falls between the values of .94 and 2.75. The likelihood that our regression coefficient (b_1) is due to chance (sampling error) is less than 1 time in 1,000 (based on: $t = 4.12$; $p < .001$).

Finally, the third line 'number of classes attended' provides us with the value of b_2 (1.66), the standard error of b_2 (.60), the standardised coefficient of b_2 ($\beta_2 = .37$), the t-value ($t = 2.78$) and the significance of the t-test ($p < .01$). Such results indicate that with one additional day of class attended, final test results will increase by 1.66 points. We can be 95% confident that b_2 falls between the values of .45 and 2.86. The likelihood that our regression coefficient (b_2) is due to chance (sampling error) is less than 1 time in 100 (based on: $t = 2.78$; $p < .01$).

The standardised coefficients (β) are particularly important in multiple linear regression analysis. This is because we cannot actually compare the values of b for hours of time spent studying to the b of number of classes attended in terms of which one is more influential in predicting final test results as they are measured with different units. Hours of time spent studying is measured with 'hours' and number of classes attended is measured with a 'count variable' of 1–15 days. This is why the standardised coefficient of b (β) is provided, which standardises all the predictor variables according to standard deviations and, thus, makes them comparable in terms of which predictor variable is more or less

Output 10.9 Multiple linear regression analysis: regression equation

Coefficients[a]

Model		Unstandardized Coefficients		Standardized Coefficients	t	Sig.	95.0% Confidence Interval for B	
		B	Std.Error	Beta			Lower Bound	Upper Bound
1	(Constant)	38.693	4.082		9.480	.000	30.423	46.963
	Hours Spent Studying	1.846	.448	.552	4.119	.000	.938	2.754
	Number of Classes Attended	1.655	.595	.373	2.781	.000	.449	2.860

a. Dependent Variable: Final Test Results

a

b_1

b_2

likely to influence the outcome variables compared to other predictor variables. In our example we can see that β for hours of time spent studying is .55, indicating that for one standard deviation of hours of time spent studying the final test results will increase by .55 points, and β for number of classes attended is .37, indicating that for one standard deviation of number of classes attended the final test results will increase by .37 points. Therefore, hours of time spent studying is more influential in changing final test results than number of classes attended.

From Output 10.9, we can see that both b_1 and b_2 are statistically significant; therefore, they can both be included in the regression equation. Note that if one or more variables were not found to be statistically significant then they would not be included in the regression equation. Also, we need to pay attention to the sign of b as that would indicate whether we would add (+) $b_x x_x$ to the equation or whether we would subtract (–) $b_x x_x$ from the equation.

Based on the information provided in Output 10.9, we can write our regression equation as follows:

$$y = 38.69 + 1.85(x_1) + 1.66(x_2) \quad \text{or} \quad y = 38.69 + 1.85(\text{hours}) + 1.66(\text{\# of classes})$$

This information tells us two things. First, it indicates that both hours of time spent studying and number of classes attended account for a significant proportion of the variance in final test results (78% or 77% if using the Adjusted R^2); therefore, they both matter in predicting final test scores. Second, the information from Output 10.9 provides us with details of the extent to which hours of time spent studying and number of classes attended influence final test scores individually, and when using the standardised coefficient (β) we can determine which predictor variable influences the outcome variable more (or less) than others. In our example, we can see that time spent studying is more influential in increasing final test results than number of classes attended.

Again, if using the equation for predictive purposes, we could predict a final test result for a student when we know how many hours s/he spent studying and the number of classes attended. For example, a student who studied 10 hours and attended 13 classes is predicted to receive a 78.77 or a 78%.

$$y = 38.69 + 1.85(10) + 1.66(13)$$

$$y = 38.69 + 18.5 + 21.58$$

$$y = 78.77$$

A student who studied 20 hours and attended 15 classes is predicted to receive a 100.59% or the max of 100% [$y = 38.69 + 1.85(20) + 1.66(15)$; $y = 38.69 + 37 + 24.9$; $y = 100.59$].

We can report our results in both written and table form (which is recommended) and would include the following:

> The multiple linear regression analysis indicates that 78% of the variance in final test results can be explained by the hours of time spent studying and number of classes attended, $R^2 = .78$, $F(2,37) = 65.40$, $p < .001$. The results indicate that for every one additional hour of time spent studying, final test results will increase by 1.85 points, and for every one additional class attended, final test results will increase by 1.66 points. Standardised coefficients indicate that time spent studying ($\beta = .55$) is more influential in predicting final test results than number of classes attended ($\beta = .37$).

In addition to the written findings, we could present a table that provides additional information (see Table 10.5).

Before we return to the 'Research in practice' example, test your understanding of multivariate linear regression analysis by answering the questions in Exercise 10.2. For this example, we are interested in predicting the number of days an individual remains sober over the course of six months after leaving a 28-day alcohol treatment programme. We hypothesise that the higher the number of days remaining in the treatment programme (0–28 days), the higher the number of social supports the individual has, and the higher the individual's motivation score (25–100; higher scores indicate higher motivation) will predict more days of sobriety. We have collected information from 60 individuals 180 days after they have left the treatment programme, and analysed the results using multivariate linear regression. We have set α at .05.

Table 10.5 Multivariate linear regression analysis results

Variable		*B*	*SE B*	β	*t*	*p*
Constant		38.69	4.08			
Hours of						
study time		1.85	.45	.55	4.12	.000**
Number of classes attended		1.66	.60	.37	2.78	.008*
Adjusted R^2	.77					
F	65.40**					

$^{**}p < .001$; $^{*}p < .001$

Exercise 10.2: Multivariate linear regression analysis

Answer the following questions based on the output from the multivariate linear regression analysis:

1. What are the predictor variables and what is the outcome variable?

2. What percentage of the variance in number of sobriety days is explained by motivation score, number of social supports, and number of days in treatment?

3. Is the regression equation statistically significant? How do you know?

4. Which predictor variables significantly influence the outcome variable?

5. Report the results in written and table form.

Variables Entered / Removed[a]

Model	Variables Entered	Variables Removed	Method
1	Motivation Score, Number of Social Supports, Number of Days in Treatment[b]	−	Enter

a. Dependent Variable: Number of Sobriety Days
b. All requested variables entered.

Model Summary

Model	R	R Square	Adjusted R Square	Std. Error of the Estimate
1	.940[a]	.883	.876	28.169

a. Predictors: (Constant), Motivation Score, Number of Social Supports, Number of Days in Treatment

ANOVA[a]

Model		Sum of Squares	df	Mean Square	F	Sig.
1	Regression	334434.542	3	111478.181	140.493	.000[b]
	Residual	44434.708	56	793.477		
	Total	378869.250	59			

a. Dependent Variable: Number of Sobriety Days
b. Predictors: (Constant), Motivation Score, Number of Social Supports, Number of Days in Treatment

Coefficients[a]

Model		Unstandardised Coefficients		Standardised Coefficients	t	Sig.	95.0% Confidence Interval for B	
		B	Std. Error	Beta			Lower Bound	Upper Bound
1	(Constant)	−65.590	12.364		−5.305	−000	−90.358	−40.822
	Number of Days in Treatment	.729	1.181	.084	−618	−539	−1.636	3.094
	Number of Social Supports	17.506	4.425	.440	3.956	.000	8.642	26.370
	Motivation Score	1.358	.543	.442	2.499	.015	.269	2.446

a. Dependent Variable: Number of Sobriety Days

'Research in practice' – self-efficacy of newly qualified social workers

Let's now return to the findings from Carpenter et al. (2015) regarding the factors that predict self-efficacy among NQSWs in England. Carpenter et al. (2015) used a multivariate linear regression analysis with the following predictor variables: age; gender; ethnicity; level of qualification; previous experience of children's social care; type of organisation in which NQSWs were employed; region of organisation in which NQSWs were employed; role clarity; role conflict; job satisfaction; and stress. The researchers ran six multivariate linear regressions analyses: one each for Time 1 data and Time 3 data across the three cohorts (2008–2009; 2009–2010; 2010–2011). In their presentation of the findings, they only reported the predictor variables that were found to be statistically significant (across any of the six regression analyses) and only reported the b values; this is most likely due to the amount of space required to report all the values from six regression analyses. Let's examine the outcome for Time 1 and Time 3 data for the 2010–2011 cohort only, as presented in Table 10.6, to find out the predictors of self-efficacy among NQSWs.

As Table 10.6 reveals, at Time 1 the factors found to predict higher self-efficacy scores among NQSWs were age; pre-degree practice experience; post-degree temporary/agency childcare social work post; role clarity; role conflict; and intrinsic job satisfaction. At Time 3, the factors found to predict higher self-efficacy

Table 10.6 Results from multivariate linear regression analysis from Carpenter et al. (2015): NQSW cohort 2010–2011

Variable	Time 1 (N = 743)	Time 3 (N = 423)
(Significance of constant)	< .001	< .001
Age 31–40	−.012	.0002
Age 41 or over	.076*	.112*
Pre-degree practice experience for six months or longer	.237**	.018
Post-degree temporary/agency childcare social work post	.187**	.093
Role clarity score	.419**	.587**
Role conflict score	.081*	.210**
Intrinsic job satisfaction score	.168**	.144*
Extrinsic job satisfaction score	−.087	.014
Stress	−.002	−.011
R^2	.243	.388

$**p < .001; *p < .05$

scores among NQSWs were age; role clarity; role conflict; and intrinsic job satisfaction. The findings, among the 2010–2011 cohort, reveal that older NQSWs were found to have higher self-efficacy scores than younger NQSWs. Pre-degree practice experience and post-degree temporary/agency childcare experience was found to predict higher self-efficacy scores among NQSWs at Time 1, but this no longer significantly predicts self-efficacy scores at Time 3. Higher role clarity, higher role conflict and higher intrinsic job satisfaction were found to predict higher self-efficacy of NQSWs at both Time 1 and Time 3. Based on these findings, we can say that 24% of the variance in self-efficacy scores for NQSWs at Time 1 can be explained by age, pre-degree practice experience, post-degree temporary/agency childcare experience, role clarity, role conflict and intrinsic job satisfaction, and 39% of the variance in self-efficacy scores for NQSWs at Time 3 can be explained by age, role clarity, role conflict and intrinsic job satisfaction. Based on the values of b presented in the table, we can see that for Time 3, role clarity is the most influential in predicting self-efficacy scores ($\beta = .59$), followed by role conflict ($\beta = .21$), intrinsic job satisfaction ($\beta = .14$) and then age ($\beta = .11$).

The findings of this study reveal that the NQSW programme can increase self-efficacy from the beginning to the end of the programme (taking into consideration study limitations and generalisability). While the multivariate linear regression analysis revealed what contributed to changes in self-efficacy scores, it also indicated that gender, ethnicity, level of degree (undergraduate or postgraduate) or country of qualification did *not* predict a change in self-efficacy scores. The findings revealed that increasing the self-efficacy of NQSWs could occur by ensuring they have a clear understanding about their job (role clarity), ensuring job satisfaction in terms of the job itself, tasks, accomplishments, opportunities to use own initiatives, having challenges to meet, and relationships with co-workers (intrinsic job satisfaction), but also having more complex cases and increasing role conflict.

Test your understanding

Based on the information covered in this chapter, answer the following questions:

1 Write out a regression equation with one predictor variable and one outcome variable and explain the components of the equation.

2 Write out a regression equation with six predictor variables and one outcome variable and explain the components of the equation.

3 What is the difference between bivariate linear regression analysis and multivariate linear regression analysis?

4 What is the difference between R and R^2 and what do each mean?

5 What is the difference between b and β and what do each mean?

Critical Thinking Box

Welch, Hatton, Emerson, Collins, Robertson, Langer and Wells (2012) examined the characteristics, circumstances and experiences of 348 families (parents and carers) in England who use direct payments (DPs) to fund short breaks. Through a regression analysis, they found the predictor variables of the outcome variable (use of DPs) included:

> the presence of main carers who are female, more highly educated and from White British backgrounds, younger children, lower levels of area deprivation, greater access to service and social networks and use of more hours of short breaks. Characteristics not found to be significantly associated with use of DPs include various health and well-being indicators, impairment characteristics of children and service satisfaction (p. 900).

You are a social worker working with families with a disabled child and are being encouraged to increase the use of DPs, particularly for short breaks. Consider the following:

1. In what ways could this research be useful to you?

2. In what ways could it be problematic?

3. What are the benefits and disbenefits of generalising the findings from this research to your social work practice?

Summary

In this chapter we have explored how to determine the effect of one or more variables on another variable. We explored the idea of a linear regression equation – an extension of correlational analysis – which seeks to explain how a change in a predictor variable (x) will influence a change in an outcome variable (y). We first looked at bivariate linear regression analysis, which examines the influence of a change in one predictor variable on one outcome variable, and then moved to multivariate linear regression analysis, which examines the influence of a change in more than one predictor variable on one outcome variable. In discussing multivariate linear regression analysis, we discussed how the results could help us to determine the extent to which two or more predictor variables together influence an outcome variable, but also the individual influence of each predictor variable on an outcome variable. We examined both bivariate and multivariate linear regression analysis results/outputs using examples of predicting final test results and topics relevant to the 'Research in practice' example. We provide further resources below that we encourage you to use to extend your knowledge of statistical tests beyond multivariate linear regression analysis where the dependent (outcome) variable is ratio level.

Further resources

Acton, C. and Miller, R. (2009). *SPSS for Social Scientists*. 2nd ed. New York, NY: Palgrave Macmillan.

Dancey, C. P. and Reidy, J. (2014). *Statistics Without Maths for Psychology*. 6th ed. Harlow: Pearson Education.

Field, A. (2013). *Discovering Statistics Using SPSS*. 4th ed. London: Sage.

Knapp, H. (2014). *Introductory Statistics Using SPSS*. Thousand Oaks, CA: Sage.

Salkind, N. J. (2014). *Statistics for People who (Think They) Hate Statistics*. 5th ed. London: Sage.

11

WHAT ARE THE KEY ELEMENTS OF ETHICAL QUANTITATIVE RESEARCH?

LEARNING OUTCOMES

By the end of the chapter you should be able to:

* Explain some key underpinning principles for the ethical conduct of research
* Apply these principles to quantitative social work research scenarios

Introduction

Ethical principles are not limited to particular research designs or methods. Responsible research practice should be rooted in core principles which apply to all types of studies. The core concepts behind this chapter are therefore not only relevant to quantitative research. The chapter introduces the four principles of respect for autonomy, non-maleficence, beneficence and justice (Beauchamp and Childress, 2013) and outlines their application in social work research. In keeping with the rest of the book, the practical examples used will be taken from quantitative studies and there will be a focus on the particular ethical issues that arise for quantitative research. So, among other things, there will be discussion of the ethics of secondary analysis of survey data, using social services databases for research, following up participants in longitudinal studies and the ethics and politics of effectiveness research.

Ethical conduct should of course be kept in mind from the very start of a research study and not tagged on at the end. We do not want to imply in positioning this chapter in the last quarter of the book that ethics should not be considered throughout the research process. The reason for positioning the chapter after the main research designs and methods have been introduced is that some of this basic knowledge is needed before practical ethics can be properly understood. A good example of this is the 'Research in practice' illustration that follows. This illustration will make most sense for those who have already read Chapter 6.

'Research in practice' – evaluating parenting interventions

Some ethical issues will be discussed in relation to a specific example of a randomised controlled trial (RCT). This raises the ethics of experimenting with an intervention that service users and practitioners value and the practical enactment of ethical experimental research in a context where service delivery is already well established.

The study in question is the RCT of the Family Links Nurturing Programme (FLNP) (Simkiss et al., 2013). FLNP is a 10-session, group-based parenting programme which focuses on the emotional well-being of parents as well as on the management of children's behaviour. RCTs are very familiar in other fields, such as public health, but, as explained in Chapter 6, less used in social work and especially little in statutory services. The Simkiss et al. study was a trial of a parenting programme offered on a universal basis but in deprived communities. This was a pragmatic trial, where the programme was already established and other parenting programmes were available in the locality. The research team successfully recruited 286 families, which were allocated to receive FLNP straight away, or to be part of a waiting list control group. Outcomes were measured after three and nine months. The trial found that the programme did not have any significant effect on the specified outcomes, namely negative and supportive parenting and the well-being of parents and children. The experiment did not work out quite as would have been hoped. Only 47% of parents in the intervention group completed the course and 19% from the control group also attended a parenting programme before the nine-month follow-up. Ten per cent of parents in the control group went against the rules of the trial and attended FLNP. Even when a per-protocol comparison was made – that is, only comparing the families who attended six or more sessions with families in the control group who did not attend any FLNP sessions – there was no significant difference between groups in the specified outcomes. We will refer back to this example at various points during the chapter.

In the following section we outline the main principles to consider for responsible research conduct. We also introduce codes of ethics for social work research and explain the role and practice of institutional review boards.

Principles for ethical research

Four principles for ethical research are set out by the American philosophers Beauchamp and Childress (2013). Although this work was done in the context of medical research and is not free from criticism, it continues to be very heavily cited. The book is in its seventh edition, with 17,561 citations in

Google Scholar (as of 31 October 2015) and is often referenced by writers discussing social work research ethics (e.g. Butler, 2002; Peled and Leichentritt, 2002; Hayes and Devaney, 2004). As Peled and Leichentritt note, the principles outlined by Beauchamp and Childress underpin many social science codes of ethics and the practice of institutional review boards (of which more later).

Beauchamp and Childress's 'principlism' for health care argues that any ethical dilemma can be analysed by considering four principles: respect for autonomy, non-maleficence, beneficence and justice. Gillon (1994) has added to the four principles a concern with the scope of their application; that is how, to whom and in what circumstances the principles apply. The principles and their application in research ethics are outlined below, with beneficence and non-maleficence considered together.

Autonomy

Personal autonomy means that someone is free from the controlling interferences of others and has good enough understanding to facilitate meaningful choice. This highlights the importance of informed consent in research; that research participants are genuinely free to take part or not and that this decision is based on proper understanding of the implications of taking part (or not). It has to be acknowledged that some people may choose not to exercise autonomy; for example, they may sign consent without reading any information about a study. Researchers should make sure they maximise autonomy. To use the example of the Simkiss et al. (2013) RCT of FLNP, the process of recruiting trial participants would have needed to ensure the implications of taking part or not in the trial were understood as well as possible. In the area where the trial took place, there was alternative family support on offer, so not taking part in the trial, though it should have meant no access to FLNP (this was not in fact enforced), did not preclude participation in other kinds of family support, including alternative parenting programmes.

More generally, researchers need to ensure that potential research participants are informed about the purpose of a study and what exactly participation will mean for them. This will include making sure any written information is fully accessible to people with poor literacy in the language in which the information is presented. This could be to do with educational background or recent migration. Researchers should be cautioned against a box-ticking approach to defensible research practice. Informed consent is not a one-off process but needs to be seen as an ongoing process. This is especially pertinent to longitudinal quantitative research.

Non-maleficence and beneficence

We consider these two principles together, as they are closely linked, although Beauchamp and Childress (2013) argue that the requirement not to harm others (non-maleficence) is distinct from, and a greater moral obligation than, the need for taking positive action to benefit others (beneficence). So in any experimental or quasi-experimental study the most important principle is that the intervention should do no harm. This should not be taken for granted, as there are some well-known examples of RCTs showing that people receiving a social work intervention have had notably worse outcomes than people randomised to a control group – for example two approaches to preventing youth offending: the Cambridge-Somerville Study and 'Scared Straight' (McCord, 1978; Petrosino et al., 2013). It is important in a trial such as that by Simkiss et al. (2013) for the researchers not to give the idea that one arm of the trial is sure to be more therapeutic than the other. This stance of not assuming an intervention will be effective is termed 'equipoise'. Ultimately the aim of a study should be to benefit service users, for example by gaining information about whether or not a particular social work approach is effective in achieving what it claims to be achieving.

Confidentiality of research participants is also relevant to their autonomy, but there are considerations for avoiding harm. In social work practice, absolute confidentiality cannot be promised and this is also relevant to the research relationship, where protection from serious harm should in some situations override the need for confidentiality. This is an area of ethical debate and some controversy, as seen in the well-publicised case of Alice Goffman (see, for example, Lubet, 2015), who in ethnographic research with gangs in Philadelphia accompanied her research participants, and volunteered to be the driver, on what was set to be a revenge killing trip and did not inform the police. Limited confidentiality is an area which needs to be handled very carefully and a thorough risk-benefit analysis is needed. An example of where limiting confidentiality can restrict the knowledge gained about an important area of risk is the study by Lothen-Kline et al. (2003). These researchers compared adolescent reports of suicidal feelings when they were promised absolute confidentiality and when they were told that professionals and parents would have to be notified if their responses indicated suicide risk. The group promised absolute confidentiality disclosed a significantly higher level of suicidal thoughts. The more protectionist approach therefore led to an underestimate of the prevalence of suicidal ideation in these teenage children.

Justice

There are a number of different conceptualisations of justice. One is *distributive justice*, meaning the fair distribution of society's benefits. This might mean that an intervention that is not currently available should not be trialled if there is no prospect that it will become available – this might particularly apply in a low-income country but also in a more affluent one in a climate of austerity. Butler (2002) notes the idea of justice as fairness in the face of competing claims. This links to the idea of equipoise in an experimental or quasi-experimental study (see above). Butler also interprets justice in research ethics to mean not favouring one's own interests or those of one's own community over the interests of others, as well as equal treatment of competing rights.

We get into more controversial territory with an ethic of justice. Some would interpret this as the need to take the side of oppressed groups in research, to redress social injustice. Others would emphasise that the primary job of a researcher is to be as objective as possible. There will always be debates about what constitutes a just approach to research – for example, the question of what topics researchers should be choosing to focus on in the first place has potential implications for justice. We cannot offer simple prescriptions here, but can only note that when planning a quantitative social work study you consider what might be the implications for justice. These implications include the political context and what uses might be put to the research once it is completed and published. Again, researchers will not always agree about the correct approach here. Some would argue for being politically savvy. Others would argue that researchers should study what needs to be studied, regardless of the political context.

Codes of ethics

There are numerous attempts to codify ethical principles which are relevant to social work research and some of these are listed at the end of this chapter in the *Further resources* section. These codes are useful short summaries of the moral principles that are discussed in depth by authors such as Beauchamp and Childress (2013). One example is the US National Association of Social Workers' code of ethics for social work which includes a section on research (see Exercise 11.1). In the UK we do not have an equivalent, as practice codes address only practice. However, Butler's (2002) code of ethics for social work and social care research, although not officially representing any particular body, arose out of discussion with the academic social work community in the UK. Butler's code is predicated on the assumption that social work research is distinct from other fields of social science and its ethical basis should be close to that of social work practice. He therefore goes beyond the objective scientific tone of the National Association of Social Workers (NASW) code and sets out more ambitious goals of emancipation and empowerment. In Exercise 11.1 we set out the NASW code, not because we consider it superior, but because it is an official code agreed by a national membership organisation.

Exercise 11.1: US National Association of Social Workers code of ethics

Below is the entire section 5.02 of the code of ethics of the US National Association of Social Workers (2008).

Evaluation and Research

a) Social workers should monitor and evaluate policies, the implementation of programs, and practice interventions.

b) Social workers should promote and facilitate evaluation and research to contribute to the development of knowledge.

c) Social workers should critically examine and keep current with emerging knowledge relevant to social work and fully use evaluation and research evidence in their professional practice.

d) Social workers engaged in evaluation or research should carefully consider possible consequences and should follow guidelines developed for the protection of evaluation and research participants. Appropriate institutional review boards should be consulted.

e) Social workers engaged in evaluation or research should obtain voluntary and written informed consent from participants, when appropriate, without any implied or actual deprivation or penalty for refusal to participate; without undue inducement to participate; and with due regard for participants' well-being, privacy, and dignity. Informed consent should include information about the nature, extent, and duration of the participation requested and disclosure of the risks and benefits of participation in the research.

f) When evaluation or research participants are incapable of giving informed consent, social workers should provide an appropriate explanation to the participants, obtain the participants' assent to the extent they are able, and obtain written consent from an appropriate proxy.

g) Social workers should never design or conduct evaluation or research that does not use consent procedures, such as certain forms of naturalistic observation and archival research, unless rigorous and responsible review of the research has found it to be justified because of its prospective scientific, educational, or applied value and unless equally effective alternative procedures that do not involve waiver of consent are not feasible.

h) Social workers should inform participants of their right to withdraw from evaluation and research at any time without penalty.

i) Social workers should take appropriate steps to ensure that participants in evaluation and research have access to appropriate supportive services.

j) Social workers engaged in evaluation or research should protect participants from unwarranted physical or mental distress, harm, danger, or deprivation.

k) Social workers engaged in the evaluation of services should discuss collected information only for professional purposes and only with people professionally concerned with this information.

l) Social workers engaged in evaluation or research should ensure the anonymity or confidentiality of participants and of the data obtained from them. Social workers should inform participants of any limits of confidentiality, the measures that will be taken to ensure confidentiality, and when any records containing research data will be destroyed.

m) Social workers who report evaluation and research results should protect participants' confidentiality by omitting identifying information unless proper consent has been obtained authorizing disclosure.

n) Social workers should report evaluation and research findings accurately. They should not fabricate or falsify results and should take steps to correct any errors later found in published data using standard publication methods.

o) Social workers engaged in evaluation or research should be alert to and avoid conflicts of interest and dual relationships with participants, should inform participants when a real or potential conflict of interest arises, and should take steps to resolve the issue in a manner that makes participants' interests primary.

p) Social workers should educate themselves, their students, and their colleagues about responsible research practices.

Which aspects of the NASW code do you think would be especially relevant to a cross-sectional survey of adult service users about satisfaction with services received?

Institutional review boards

The Declaration of Helsinki (World Medical Association, 2013) represents an international consensus on the ethical framework of experimental research on human subjects. It included the requirement for independent ethical review of studies. Independent ethical review has only relatively recently extended fully to social science research in the UK and it has attracted some criticism (see, for example, Dingwall, 2008) for being an unnecessary and over-bureaucratic hammer to crack a nut. Whatever the rights and wrongs, and some of the criticism has been overstated, as Hedgecoe (2008) argues, independent ethical review via research ethics committees (RECs) or institutional review boards (IRBs) is here to stay and researchers have to learn to live with it.

Students and researchers applying to RECs or IRBs need to know what is expected of them. Most boards will have full information available to applicants, which might include examples of good practice from past applications. Committee or board members are likely to want to know about risks to the welfare

KEY ELEMENTS OF ETHICAL QUANTITATIVE RESEARCH

of research subjects and researchers and the dignity (and autonomy) of research subjects, in relation to confidentiality and informed consent, for example. They may also consider the validity of research, as there is an argument that research of poor quality, that is not likely to lead to findings of any importance or usefulness, is necessarily unethical. An example might be a quantitative survey with an unrepresentative convenience sample so small as to hold out no prospect of meaningful quantification. It can be argued that approaching people – especially those vulnerable in some way through complex needs, such as are many users of social work services – to take part in such a poor study is unethical. In the authors' experience, the most important thing in applying to a REC is to be explicit about research procedures – for example, exactly how research participants will be recruited and consent taken, how data will be kept confidential and secure.

Exercise 11.2: To what extent is it acceptable for researchers to chase non-response?

Where do researchers draw the line between assertive maximisation of response rate and harassment? Let's say you are returning to follow up research participants who are all children in foster care. The study is an evaluation of a mentoring project, based on pre- and post-intervention measurement of subjective well-being, so the follow-up data are crucial to the success of the study. Without an adequate response rate the study validity could be challenged. How many times is it reasonable to contact people? Is it acceptable to turn up at young people's houses if they have not responded to postal reminders?

'Research in practice' – evaluating parenting interventions

At this point, we return in more detail to the example outlined earlier – the trial of the Family Links Nurturing Programme (FLNP) (Simkiss et al., 2013). The most fundamental question, perhaps, and the one sometimes asked by practitioners, is whether it is ethical to withhold intervention from the control group. Is this compatible with beneficence and non-maleficence? This was after all a parenting course that was popular with local practitioners and had been found in various studies (short of an RCT) to show promise of likely effectiveness. Well, the answer to this question has to be 'yes', the trial was ethical if the effectiveness of the intervention was not definitively proven, as was the case here because FLNP had not previously been subject to an RCT. The trial results could be seen to have effectively vindicated the ethics of randomisation, as the intervention group did not in fact have significantly better outcomes than the control group, even when the analysis was restricted to 'per-protocol' comparison of only those who actually received the intervention and those in the control group who did not. We might speculate that local practitioners were not fully on board with the trial, perhaps because of misguided ethical qualms, hence 10% of the control group also attended FLNP.

Fundamental ethical qualms about RCTs could in fact be turned on their heads, by asking: how is it ethical social work practice to roll out an intervention for which there is no evidence of effectiveness? Of course in practice this happens routinely and we do not mean to suggest that a social work approach which has not been subject to RCT should never be used. This would be completely impractical when relatively few social work approaches have been tested in an experimental or even a quasi-experimental study. Our view is that more social work approaches should be subject to RCT. The reality of new interventions is that they are almost always rolled out gradually and there is often not enough staff capacity for everyone eligible to receive the service at once anyway. We would suggest making a virtue of the inevitable delay for some service users and distributing access to the service fairly by randomly allocating potential recipients to either have the service now or later – a waiting list design such as was used in the FLNP trial. This can be challenging of course, depending on the service context. Stewart-Brown et al. (2011) note, also in connection with the FLNP trial, that the existence of other parenting programmes in the area meant that some of the parents who were most motivated to change opted not to take part in the trial, because they knew that being in a waiting list control group would mean waiting up to a year to attend the course and they wanted some kind of parenting programme immediately. Qualitative interviews with parents who declined participation revealed this.

Even when there is very encouraging RCT evidence from another country, it can still be perfectly ethical to conduct a further trial in a new context. Sometimes the findings turn out to be quite different in the new context. For example, Robling et al. (2016) conducted a large RCT of the Family Nurse Partnership in England. This intervention had strong evidence of effectiveness from the US. However, the American trials were conducted in optimal (efficacy) conditions, whereas the English study was a 'pragmatic' trial on an intervention which was already being piloted on a large scale. The Robling et al. study found no additional short-term benefit for the intervention over usual care, for a range of primary outcomes to do with maternal and child health. One possible reason for these findings is that usual care is simply much better in the UK than the USA, with health care free at the point of use and a stronger welfare state.

Exercise 11.3: What are the ethical implications of secondary analysis?

Let's say you are a university student and the professor who is supervising your dissertation urges you to conduct secondary analysis of a data set she has from a previous study. This is a survey of social workers about their experiences of stress. The professor wants someone to examine the relationship between stress and academic background. There are data in the survey covering both these domains, but this specific analysis was not done in the original study and the respondents were not specifically told this would be done. The professor's hypothesis is that more highly qualified social workers will cope with stress better. Is the proposed secondary analysis ethical?

More examples of ethical conundrums

There are many more examples of ethical dilemmas facing quantitative researchers. Here we mention just a couple of them, namely the ethics of research with people who may lack capacity to give informed consent and the ethics of social media research.

When should people whose capacity to give informed consent is questionable be involved in research? There are potentially competing imperatives here. On the one hand there is a concern that people will be coerced into uninformed consent if they are enrolled in studies without properly understanding what is required of them and the implications of taking part. In the UK the Mental Capacity Act 2005 protects people (aged 16+) who lack capacity to give informed consent – for example through acute mental illness, dementia, learning disability, stroke or brain injury – from such coercion. Research that directly involves people who lack capacity to give informed consent should in the UK be approved by a National Health Service medical research ethics committee and not by a university research ethics committee, which is not considered sufficiently independent and disinterested. In order to be approved, such studies have to be directly related to the impairing condition or its treatment and the researchers have to satisfy a research ethics committee that the research could not be done without the participation of people lacking capacity.

The alternative imperative is the desire for people lacking capacity to have their voice heard, even when a study is not directly about their impairing condition or treatment. Boxall and Ralph (2009), for example, express concern that ethical regulation might result in people with learning disabilities being excluded from research. Interestingly, in the UK there is less regulation of research with very young children, for whom similar concerns about fully informed consent might apply. Research with young children who are not NHS patients can be approved by a university research ethics committee, whose approach tends to be lighter in touch, and the general view is that parents or carers can consent for young children to take part in studies. We do not propose there is any easy resolution of these tensions, but researchers need to be aware of the challenges of ensuring research participants' autonomy when they lack capacity for fully informed consent.

Social media data are increasingly used by researchers. It is possible for a researcher with some programming abilities to gather publicly available social media postings using the application programming interface (API). Examples of such studies relevant to social work are Guo and Saxton's (2014) research on how social media has affected advocacy by non-profit organisations and Colombo et al.'s (2016) study of the social networks of suicidal tweeters. Less high-tech options include the importing of tweets into N-vivo 10 software for analysis, which can include quantitative coding of content. This is ethically sensitive territory. The terms and conditions of social media platforms typically allow the downloading of content via APIs if the postings are public – that is, they are not subject to privacy settings such as most users of Facebook routinely use to restrict access to only the friends they have intentionally selected. However, although these terms and conditions exist, most users do not read them but simply select 'accept' and move on. So as a researcher you could legally be collecting data from social media users who are not aware this is happening. This may be legal but is it ethical?

Most researchers working in this field do in fact use public social media postings as raw data without seeking consent from every user, on the basis that users should understand that when something is posted it is publicly viewable. For a platform such as Twitter there is enough mass media coverage of tweet controversies that users should know the default setting is for accounts to be public. Private data accessible only to approved 'friends' cannot be accessed by researchers without explicit permission. However, there is still room for debate here and some internet privacy campaigners object to the use of their data by researchers and businesses. One important consideration is that directly quoting from a social media posting cannot be done without that post being searchable via an internet search engine such as Google.com. There can therefore be no direct quoting without explicit consent from the author of the post. Some would argue that you should not directly quote, even with consent, unless you identify the author of the post, as not to do so when the posting is published would constitute plagiarism.

Critical Thinking Box

Social work case records are often used for research purposes, including quantitative research. The basic question to think about here is: can the use of case records without service user consent be ethically justified?

Think about this with reference to a specific study. Gibbons, Conroy and Bell (1995) studied variations in the operation of the child protection register and what happened to children who were registered. They looked at case files and case conference minutes for children referred for child protection investigation in eight local authorities in England (1,888 cases) and quantitatively coded them in terms of outcomes. They found the startling result that only 15% of referrals ended up on the child protection register. Forty-nine per cent were not substantiated as abuse or neglect and 44% had no further action of any kind including any services provided. The families were disproportionately on welfare benefits and headed by lone parents. The picture painted was of vulnerable families who did not reach the threshold for child protection intervention but did not receive any help either. This study was very influential on the government of the time. It featured heavily in the much-cited *Messages from Research* summary (Dartington Social Research Unit, 1995) and resulted in the ultimately unsuccessful attempts to 'refocus' policy from child protection to family support in the mid-to-late 1990s in the UK.

This study was done without consent from parents or children to read the case files. Was this ethical? Could such a study have been done any other way? Could the importance of the study be said to outweigh any ethical concerns about lack of consent for access to records?

Summary

There can be no straightforward toolkit of research ethics. For the most part there are thorny moral debates, although some consensus and established practices do exist. We have tried in this chapter to outline some important principles for responsible research conduct, principles which are reflected in mainstream codes of ethical practice. These apply to all types of research designs and methods but there are some particular issues for quantitative research. There is sometimes debate in the social work field about whether randomised controlled trials are ethical. We think they are, but acknowledge there can be ethical challenges along the way. Hopefully this chapter has provided a useful starting point, but more detail can be found elsewhere, including in the items in the following list of further resources.

Further resources

Danchev, D. and Ross, A. (2013). *Research Ethics for Counsellors, Nurses and Social Workers.* London: Sage.

Iphofen, R. (2011). *Ethical Decision-Making in Social Research: A Practical Guide.* Basingstoke: Palgrave Macmillan.

Israel, M. (2014). *Research Ethics and Integrity for Social Scientists.* 2nd ed. London: Sage.

Mertens, D. M. and Ginsberg, P. E. (eds) (2008). *The Handbook of Social Research Ethics.* Thousand Oaks, CA: Sage.

Panter, A. T. and Sterba, S. K. (eds) (2011). *Handbook of Ethics in Quantitative Methodology.* New York: Routledge.

There are several codes of ethics agreed by disciplinary and professional associations which may be relevant. Here are some examples. All web links were accessed on 1 September 2016.

- American Psychological Association www.apa.org/ethics/code/
- British Psychological Association www.bps.org.uk/publications/policy-and-guidelines/research-guidelines-policy-documents/research-guidelines-poli
- American Sociological Association www.asanet.org/about/ethics.cfm
- Social Research Association (UK) http://the-sra.org.uk/research-ethics/ethics-guidelines/
- Economic and Social Research Council (UK) www.esrc.ac.uk/funding/guidance-for-applicants/research-ethics/

12

HOW TO DO QUANTITATIVE RESEARCH WITHOUT COLLECTING NEW DATA

LEARNING OUTCOMES

By the end of the chapter you should be able to:

- Access some publicly available data sets for quantitative research on social work
- Describe the pros and cons of using social work databases and case files for quantitative research
- Explain the advantages and disadvantages of secondary analysis

Introduction

Generating original quantitative data can sometimes be very challenging for many different reasons. For many students, time is limited. For example, they may need to do some of their dissertation research while also working full time on placement. It may be difficult or impossible in practice to identify a robust sample. You may have a brilliant idea but a gatekeeper refuses you access to approach potential respondents. Or you may get as far as carrying out a quantitative study – for example a survey – but you get a terrible response rate which risks invalidating your study. You may find it impossible to contact service users for follow-up interviews because they have moved or changed their phone numbers. Life can get in the way of good quantitative research.

However, you should not be pessimistic after this downbeat chapter opening, because the good news is that students and other researchers *do not necessarily need to collect their own original data*. There are some excellent existing data sets out there and you can take these data sets and carry out quantitative *secondary analysis*. Some of these data sets are in fact much more detailed and have been conducted with far better standards of validity than you as a lone researcher could possibly achieve on your own. Other sources of data are more problematic but nonetheless usable – for example to build up a picture of service use. This chapter therefore reviews some of the methodological and practical issues associated with using publicly available data and social work databases or case files for quantitative research.

'Research in practice' – social inequalities

Social inequalities are fundamental to social work. You could say that social work only exists because of them. Social work has never been a universal service but has always been targeted on social need. However, social deprivation is so much a 'bread-and-butter' issue in social work that often we do not actively consider it, but instead take it for granted. Paul Bywaters is highlighting the importance of social inequalities for child welfare interventions in the UK and making links with work already done on health inequalities. He began this programme of research with a paper which illustrates the issues by examining publicly available data on child welfare interventions (rates of children in care and children on child protection plans) and their relationship with area-level deprivation (Bywaters, 2015). For this small study, unlike most of the research projects referred to in the current chapter, he did not get hold of a database which included multiple variables. His approach was really quite simple and as such it is a useful example here. The research he carried out for his paper would be eminently possible for a Masters dissertation by a student with only a basic understanding of inferential statistics. Bywaters got hold of publicly available government aggregate statistics on the rates per head of population of children 'looked after' (UK term for 'in public care', including foster care and residential homes) and children on child protection plans for each English local authority (i.e. the local government geographical area). He then found online the publicly available spreadsheet of data on multiple deprivation by local authority. He put these variables (i.e. rates of child welfare interventions and deprivation rates) together in a statistical package and correlated the variables.

What is secondary analysis?

In a nutshell, secondary analysis takes place where the researcher has not collected the data him- or herself but analyses data collected by someone else. The distinction is made from 'primary' data collection which is your own original data collection. Secondary analysis can be qualitative as well as quantitative but it is much more often quantitative. The main reason for this is that quantitative data lend themselves more easily to manipulation by someone else. The effect of the primary researcher should not be a major issue, whereas with qualitative data generated through observation or interviews it is not possible to separate out the impact of the researcher. Their own personal style will have been integral to the process of data generation and it is therefore more of a challenge for someone else who was not involved in the data collection to make sense of their data.

The advantages of secondary analysis

There are several strong arguments in favour of doing secondary analysis if you can, which we will discuss below.

Most studies have already been done somewhere

In the end you usually find that someone has done your research project before you. This can be difficult to find out about and it takes a lot of careful searching of databases – crucially using a creative range of search terms. But unless their topic is *very* specific – and in our experience social work students' topics sometimes are – for example what is the impact on practice of a brand new policy that has only come into effect in the last month? – then you will eventually find an existing study that is rather like your idea. Most of these studies are not available for secondary analysis, it should be said. But the general approach to any new research should be humility and the assumption that work has already been done that at the very least you need to read about, these studies, rather than charging off to collect new data – and often not doing it very well – when better data may already exist.

Quality and quantity of sample

There are broadly two types of data set for secondary analysis covered in this chapter – previously funded studies and social work agency data. Both of these are likely to have better samples than you could possibly achieve as a lone researcher. Previously funded studies will vary but many of them will be surveys which are the product of major government funding. These surveys will have proper probability samples and will use standardised measures. Many tens of people will have worked on design, sampling and data collection, meaning that way more expertise and person power will have been expended on them than a lone researcher could possibly muster. Our advice would be that as long as an existing study is compatible with your research questions it makes a lot of sense to work with what is already out there rather than trying to pull off an inevitably flawed survey of your own.

Saving time

What we have here is swings and roundabouts, as the saying goes. So you potentially save a considerable amount of time on data collection because you do not have to negotiate access, first with the director of social services and then with the team manager and every individual social worker; neither do you have to spend many hours chasing down potential respondents only for them to ignore your approach. And you do not have to input data from a paper questionnaire into a statistical software package. But you do have to invest time on data analysis. This might involve very time-consuming aspects such as cleaning data sets and learning about statistics! Not having to collect data allows you to focus your time and effort on analysis. As long as your data set is good enough and big enough, this will be time well spent. You will be free to spend time checking out what is the very best statistical approach for the type of data you have – advice from an academic supervisor should help here – and producing the best tables and charts that you can.

Exercise 12.1: Locating existing studies

Locate existing studies with some social work content via the UK Data Service variable and question bank. Go to http://discover.ukdataservice.ac.uk/variables and try out a search. For starters, try typing 'child abuse'. Use inverted commas. Explore the data sets for a while – see what potential they would have for social work research.

The disadvantages of secondary analysis

Lack of input into design

This is an important limitation. It is probably helpful to divide it in two. Firstly, we have the fabulous data set whose questions are just not quite right for your ideas. For example, the Millennium Cohort Study from the UK is a wonderful study with very detailed data on pretty much everything you can think of – socio-economic background, parenting, health, education, you name it. But there is only one question specifically about social work, addressed to parents: 'I'd like you to think about the kinds of advice you've had for yourself, your child or your family since [one year ago]. Have you turned to any of these for help or advice in the last 12 months?' They are given a list of options which includes 'social worker' alongside a number of other health and social care services. So there is nothing to tell us why they have had a social worker and what kind of social worker (child and family, adult social care, local authority, voluntary sector). There is also no clarity on who the social work was for. It could have been the parent, child or family. And the question collapses together help and advice which can be quite different things. Also, this question is only asked when the child is 3 and 5 and not in other waves of the study.

Secondly, we have the scenario where what you are really interested in is something quite specific – a particular policy or intervention. It is unlikely you will find existing data (that you are allowed to reanalyse) on anything so specific. This may mean that you have to find some way of conducting an original primary study.

Quality of data

In noting the poor quality of data, we are especially thinking about the limitations of client databases. This type of research is addressed more fully below. If your data are routine records from a social work agency, they are subject to all kinds of real-life contingencies. Staff will forget to complete records or be seriously delayed. They might write up something that looks good, regardless of its relationship to the truth of what they did. The agency may have no system for quantitatively coding anything, so that all you have is entirely qualitative data in case files which are full of highly personal information and ethically difficult to access.

Area-level and individual-level data

There is an important distinction to be made between data at area level and data at individual level. In some large survey data sets you may have both and, just to be confusing, there can be both individual-level and area-level data for each individual in the data set. It is important to make the distinction because often there are socio-economic data of both types.

It is easiest to explain with examples. Individual-level socio-economic data would be such things as whether or not the respondent him- or herself is employed and what their income level is. Slater et al.'s (2015) study of social work contact with suicidal people is just one example of a study which includes such variables in its multivariate model. Having data at area level means having information about the place in which an individual lives. Winter and Connolly (2005), for example, studied the relationship between child welfare referrals (as reported in social services records) and levels of deprivation in local areas in Northern Ireland, in the same way as the Bywaters (2015) 'Research in practice' example introduced earlier and returned to later in the chapter.

Analysis of data from social work records

Social work records can be a very useful source of quantitative data if permission is given for their use. In the most optimistic scenario, properly anonymised databases can be produced for research purposes, with any identifying features removed – for example dates of birth can be changed to ages and addresses generalised to a postcode or a larger geographical area. Such data sets can allow for valuable study of the population using social work services, perhaps looking at the presence or absence of specific problems, if these are routinely noted, and category of service (e.g. how many child protection cases involve parental alcohol problems?).

There are many limitations, however. As noted above, the quality of record-keeping can be extremely variable. In some countries, including the UK, there is very little information which is routinely gathered on all cases using quantitative coding, in contrast to health records. Files may not include any standardised measures which allow comparison with other populations, unlike many archived survey data sets. A social work service user data set is just that – data on people who use services – therefore it is very difficult to contextualise this group by comparing them with other people in the same community, some of whom may be facing similar issues but just may not be known to social services. In our experience in the UK, most data in social work case files are solely qualitative and can be challenging to operationalise as quantitative data. (Later in the chapter, examples are given of where qualitative data from social work records have been quantified.)

Unlike health records which patients expect to be routinely used for research, there can be ethical concerns from social work organisations about researchers accessing records without specific permission from individuals. Some argue that people who are the subject of social work records should always have a say over who reads these records. On the face of it this seems to be natural justice. However, there is an ethical argument about public interest sometimes overriding this individual right to privacy. For example, social work records might arguably be necessary for research on the causes of child abuse and the effectiveness of interventions to protect children. This public interest argument is widely accepted in relation to health records. In some respects these concerns exist about social work records because there is little culture of research in social work organisations. In fact there is legal support in the UK for records to be used by researchers. There is an exemption to the Data Protection Act in relation to the use of personal data only for research purposes. These ethical tensions are discussed in more depth in Chapter 11 (see p.201 and p.255).

Using archived survey data

Major surveys, including those which have been generously invested in by research councils or government departments, tend to have data and accompanying documentation deposited in a data archive. The UK Data Archive, for example, is accessible to all university students and staff and data can be downloaded for research purposes (see Exercise 12.1). There are two main designs to be aware of: (1) cross-sectional studies, some of which are repeated regularly; and (2) longitudinal studies. Cross-sectional studies include, for example, public attitude surveys such as the British Social Attitudes Survey and crime surveys such as the Crime Survey for England and Wales (formerly British Crime Survey). Both of these British examples are surveys repeated annually, although there is a fresh sample taken each year so they do not involve the same respondents being followed up each time, unlike with longitudinal studies.

Both cohort and panel studies are longitudinal, following individuals over time and conducting repeated surveys with these same respondents. The only difference between these two types is that cohort studies typically recruit and follow-up study members of the same age or stage (e.g. parents of new born babies, teenagers or newly adopted children) whereas panel studies recruit study participants from the whole population. There are two types of longitudinal survey with great potential for social work research. Firstly, there are studies with explicitly social work-related variables. In the UK, these include major cohort studies such as the 1958 National Child Development Study and the Millennium Cohort Study (see Maxwell et al., 2012). We return to these at the end of the chapter in Table 12.1. Longitudinal studies lend themselves to research on outcomes of social work (see, for example, Henderson et al., 2016), although it is very challenging to take account of the extreme vulnerability of most social work service users in relation to the rest of the population when comparing outcomes. Secondly, there are longitudinal studies which, while they do not include direct data on use of social work services, nonetheless include data on topics which are highly relevant for social work and have potential for social work dissertation research. An example would be Understanding Society, a British panel study, which includes a wide range of variables relevant to social work. One example is its data on social participation, featured in this chapter's Critical Thinking Box.

Exercise 12.2: Exploring the Longitudinal Study of Young People in England

Go to http://nesstar.ukdataservice.ac.uk/webview/. There is free access unless you want to do cross-tabulations and basic analysis, in which case you need to register using a UK university ID http://esds.ac.uk/newRegistration/newLogin.asp.

First select 'Teaching Datasets' – these are simplified versions of the full data sets. Select 'Longitudinal Study of Young People in England'. Open this up and select 'Wave 1'. Open up 'Variable Description' and then 'Main Parent Section'. Open up 'Relationship with Young Person and Contact with Services'. Select 'Whether YP currently in care'. What do you think about the frequencies reported here?

'Research in practice' – social inequalities

At this point we return to the example introduced at the start of the chapter. Bywaters (2015) produced a Pearson's correlation coefficient (Pearson's r – see Chapter 9) to examine the relationship between area-based deprivation and child welfare interventions (children in out-of-home care and on child protection plans). This analysis showed there was evidence of a strong, positive correlation and therefore a gradient of deprivation and intervention (i.e. the more deprived the local authority, the higher the intervention rate). For 'looked-after' children he found $r = 0.73$ ($p < .001$) and for child protection plans he found $r = 0.53$ ($p < .001$). As noted earlier, this analysis is based on publicly available data and it is the kind of research that could be done by a student who is reasonably confident with quantitative data. But what does it tell us and what does it not tell us?

One obvious limitation is that this is only a relationship at the level of aggregate data. We do not know from this study whether or not deprived individual children are more likely to be in care or on child protection plans. Bywaters et al. (2016) have gone on to use individual-level data on children (from children's services departments) in their subsequent research. These data are more difficult for students to access but it may be possible with ethical protocols in place. However, there are no data available on the socio-economic backgrounds of individual children, so the best the researchers can do is use data on the small-scale local area that the children were living in when they came into care or were put on a child protection plan. So this subsequent study uses a mixture of individual-level data (e.g. child who is in care) and area-level data (e.g. level of deprivation in area where child lives/lived). An older study on the backgrounds of children in care, by Bebbington and Miles (1989) took a different approach by comparing data on individual children provided by social workers with an aggregate picture on the general population from the General Household Survey.

It is difficult to know what exactly the policy implications of the Bywaters studies are. The over-representation of children from poorer areas in out-of-home care may be cause for concern if it means poorer families are being unfairly targeted, but we cannot know that from Bywaters et al.'s (2016) data. Since there are also socio-economic inequalities in relation to child development and some forms of child harm, perhaps we should expect that poor children are more likely to be in care. However, it does raise the question of whether or not more and better preventative services could have improved the parenting environment to allow children to stay with their birth families. The practice and policy implications also depend on whether or not you think out-of-home care works. Certainly, children in care have worse outcomes than the general population, but some studies suggest this is more to do with the adverse circumstances they were in before their care placement and that in fact children in care do better than maltreated children who stay at home (Forrester et al., 2008b). So, this is a complicated issue and there are no easy lessons to take away.

More examples of social work studies using existing data

In this section there are some other examples of studies using existing data. We have chosen a range, to cover various different kinds of data.

Quantification from qualitative data in social work files

An example of this approach is the Canadian study by Strega et al. (2008). These researchers looked at 282 child welfare case files, limiting the sample to those cases where the mother was aged 19 or under at the birth of at least one child. This further limited the sample to 116 child protection service files. The authors present only descriptive statistics, but these were revealing. For example, they found that 50% of all fathers were considered irrelevant to both mothers and children, while 20% were viewed as a risk and 20% were considered an asset to both mothers and children. Baynes and Holland's (2010) study is an example of research on the same topic. This was a very small-scale study, but it is worth noting here as it is an example of how research done for a Master's degree can result in a publication in a peer-reviewed journal. This study involved just 40 case files and presented descriptive statistics only. Descriptive statistics can be powerful, however. In this case, it was observed that the mean number of points in child protection plans relating to mothers was 5.72, whereas the mean number of points in child protection plans relating to fathers (in the broad sense of that term) was 2.1, further illustrating the tendency of child welfare services to focus on mothering, even in cases where the main risk to children is presented by fathers.

Using archived data to contextualise a qualitative study

The paper by Slater, Scourfield and Greenland (2015) was mentioned briefly above. This is an example of secondary analysis of a publicly available, cross-sectional data set to contextualise a primarily qualitative study. The work was done as part of a primarily qualitative PhD by a social worker, on the topic of social workers' role in preventing suicide. Tom Slater set out to find an existing data set that would describe the population of suicidal people that social workers encounter. The first thing he did was search the UK Data Archive (see Exercise 12.1). He located a psychiatric morbidity study with data on suicide attempts and social work contact. The timeframes were not ideal. In order to identify a large enough sample of suicidal people who had social work contact, he had to use lifetime suicide attempt and social work contact over the previous year. This part of the PhD did not require any access negotiations or application for ethical approval. However, there were limitations to what insights could be gained from a survey that was not set up for the purposes of social work research and the subsequent qualitative research was very necessary for a proper exploration of this topic.

Research on research

This is entirely desk-based research using readily available data and it does not necessarily require high-level statistical competence, as descriptive statistics alone can be very revealing. Some authors have in fact used inferential statistics to study relationships between, for example, some kind of study characteristic (e.g. method, author) and a metric of some kind (e.g. number of publications or number of citations). An example of research on research is Hodge et al.'s (2012) study, which used Google Scholar to identify the 100 most-cited papers published in 79 social work journals. This study has been followed up by others using this list of 100 to take the analysis further. Slater et al. (2012) looked up author affiliations to identify country location. When considering the UK and US, the location of most authors of these 100 articles, they found a very strong tendency for within-country citation. Kreisberg and Marsh (2016) compared the content of the European and US articles and demonstrated a difference which is readily evident if you attend research conferences both sides of the Atlantic, namely that European articles are mostly not empirical but are focused on the profession of social work or on theory while US articles are more likely to be empirical, typically reporting on service user populations and on intervention effectiveness.

Test your understanding

Neighbourhood statistics are very useful for social work research and also on a personal level very interesting as you can, for example, find statistics to describe the area you currently live in or the place where you grew up. This link takes you to a site for England and Wales: www.neighbourhood.statistics.gov.uk

Have a play around. You can select from a range of variables from the 2011 census and other data sources and you can break down locality to a population of 1,000. Within the UK there are equivalent sites for Scotland and Northern Ireland.

Critical Thinking Box

Emerson et al. (2014) used the panel study Understanding Society to look at the self-rated health of adults with learning difficulties ('intellectual disability' is the term used in the paper) and the extent to which this is associated with their perceptions of their neighbourhoods and their social and civic participation. This is an open access article, so is readable by anyone regardless of university affiliation. The study contained 279 people with intellectual disability and 22,297 without. The researchers used bivariate comparisons between individuals with and without intellectual disability and multivariate logistic regression with self-reported health as the outcome. Respondents with intellectual disability were identified using cognitive test results plus the lack of any educational qualifications. The study found that favourable perceptions of neighbourhood and higher levels of social and civic participation were associated with better self-rated health for both groups of adults but that self-rated health was worse in the adults with intellectual disabilities.

1. What does this study tell us and what does it not tell us?

2. What are the benefits and disadvantages of this kind of secondary analysis?

3. What are likely to be the implications of using a general population sample for coverage of people with intellectual disabilities?

Summary

What we hope this chapter has done is to illustrate the potential of using existing data for quantitative research as well as note some of the challenges. There are quantitative or quantifiable data available in social services records, in archived surveys and in research databases. Each data source has its potential and its limitations. The fact that some great data sets exist is not a reason to never collect any more data. There are all kinds of reasons why we might need to collect new data. But before embarking on data collection it is really important to explore what is already out there. You should be driven by important and interesting research questions, of course, but it is also quite sensible to adapt your research questions in the light of what excellent data may already be available. There are advantages and disadvantages to all forms of research and it is important to understand these before you start your study.

Further resources

Maxwell et al. (2012) explored the major UK cohort and panel studies in order to identify those with social work variables and large enough samples of social work service users to allow for multivariate analysis. They located seven such studies and these are summarised in Table 12.1.

Table 12.1 Seven UK cohort or panel studies with data on social work

Study name	Study population	Social work variables
Avon Longitudinal Study of Parents and Children	Over 14,000 pregnant women recruited in 1991–1992 and followed up since. Also data from children and mothers' partners	Question about contact with social services and/or social workers when child aged 21 months and 73 months. Some questions asked separately of mothers and their partners
1970 British Cohort Study	The families of around 17,000 babies born in 1970	Questions about social work contact when child aged 5, 10 and 15. Also data on care, adoption and statutory orders
British Household Panel Survey (BHPS)	5,500 households recruited in 1991 and followed up annually. Now part of the expanded panel study Understanding Society	Questions about 'use of' a social worker at each of the 17 waves of BHPS but no social work questions in Understanding Society
Edinburgh Study of Youth Transitions and Crime	4,000 young people recruited in 1998	Social work records of all study members are available as data. Includes case history, involvement of other agencies and child protection status
Longitudinal Study of Young People in England	Began in 2004 with 13 year olds in over 15,000 households. Three initial waves and now the study has been re-initiated as 'Next Steps' with study members in their 20s	Questions about the young person having contact with social worker because of their behaviour. Also 'in-care' variables
Millennium Cohort Study	Parents of around 18,000 babies born soon after the turn of the Millennium and followed up every few years	Question about advice for parent, child or family when child aged 3 and 5
1958 National Child Development Study	Around 17,000 people born in 1958. Study is ongoing with a ninth sweep in 2012	Questions in early waves about children's departments and social services. Also questions about being in care

Adapted from Maxwell et al. (2012), pp. 169–174.

The Centre for Longitudinal Studies, based at the University College London Institute of Education, hosts four of the studies in Table 12.1 – the 1958 National Child Development Study, the 1970 British Cohort Study, the Longitudinal Study of Young People in

England (now 'Next Steps') and the Millennium Cohort Study. Its home page is www. cls.ioe.ac.uk.

In the USA, the Inter-university Consortium for Social and Political Research, based at the University of Michigan, is the world's largest data archive. It has 16 specialist collections on ageing, criminal justice and substance misuse, to name just a few. www.icpsr.umich.edu/icpsrweb/

13

USING MIXED QUANTITATIVE AND QUALITATIVE METHODS IN SOCIAL WORK RESEARCH

LEARNING OUTCOMES

By the end of the chapter, readers should be able to:

- Recognise the limitations of quantitative research methods in social work research
- Appreciate the advantages of using mixed methods to answer many research questions
- Define mixed-methods research and describe the varieties of mixed-method designs
- Select an appropriate mixed-method design for a research study

Introduction

In a book which advocates the value and importance of quantitative research for social work, it may seem strange to begin a chapter with some comments about the limitations of these methods. Certainly, quantitative social work research can tell us a great deal about such matters as the extent of social problems, the outcomes of services and the effectiveness of interventions. But sometimes the numbers do not tell us enough. For example:

1   A survey of a 'new' population (e.g. young people with a life-limiting condition living unexpectedly into adulthood because of advances in medicine and surgery) may not ask the most pertinent questions; existing instruments may miss the mark.

2   Statistical analysis based on average scores may fail to attend to, or actually mask, the 'outliers', those cases whose results are markedly different from the rest of the study population (e.g. children who are exceptionally resilient in the face of extraordinary life circumstances such as migration alone across continents).

3 The findings of an evaluation may identify a counter-intuitive result but, despite the use of the best multivariate statistical methods, we can only speculate why this might have happened (e.g. round the clock 'assertive outreach' services for people with severe mental illness designed to prevent psychiatric admissions are actually more likely to admit service users than those services working 8 to 5).

These instances are all examples of situations where qualitative research methods could add greatly to our understanding. Thus (example 1), pre-survey focus groups with a sample of young people living with the condition could help identify their particular concerns and issues which could then be incorporated in the planned survey. The survey could then identify how many young people in a much larger sample experienced these issues.

In example 2, a sample of children with exceptional resilience scores identified by a survey could be invited to take part in a group or individual interview to explore *how* they had coped and thrived.

In example 3, a researcher could join both a 24-hour outreach team and then an 8 to 5 team and observe how the team members made decisions about admissions. Ethnographic observation could be supplemented by interviews with team members to explore their understandings, together with interviews with staff elsewhere providing out-of-hours services to these service users.

These would all be examples of mixed-methods research – research which uses both quantitative and qualitative methods in combination to investigate social issues. In this chapter we shall explore the variety of mixed methods which can be used in social work research. In some of these examples, qualitative research methods are used to supplement quantitative methods, which are seen as the more important in answering the research questions. In others, in-depth qualitative research is thought more important, but having identified the issues or processes the researchers may be asked: 'Yes, that's really fascinating, but how many people think this? Are they representative? Are the apparent differences between the groups studied statistically significant?' Of course, questions like these can only be answered by quantitative research methods.

In yet other cases, quantitative and qualitative research methods are given equal weight. In research on social work practice, we generally want to know not just what works (outcomes) but also how and why it works, as well as why it often does not work (processes and mechanisms) and finally, in what context (Pawson and Tilley, 1997). The answers to the questions are likely to require *both* quantitative and qualitative social research methods.

'Research in practice' – Home-Start

We start with an interesting evaluation study of the outcomes of Home-Start, an established programme of family support in the UK and Northern Ireland. Home-Start is a charity. In its own words:

> Home-Start helps families with young children deal with whatever life throws at them. We support parents as they learn to cope, improve their confidence and build better lives for their children. We provide one-to-one support for parents. Our volunteers visit the family's home for a couple of hours every week. They tailor-make their support to the needs of the parents and children. Volunteers are very committed and will keep visiting until the youngest child turns five or starts school, or until the parents feel they can stand on their own two feet. Parents and volunteers often develop a deeply trusting relationship which can lead to *powerful change within the family* (emphasis added). (www.home-start.org.uk, accessed 6 August 2015)

This sounds good. But what is the evidence to support the claims made in this statement? Does Home-Start help parents learn to cope, improve their confidence and build better lives for their children? To what extent do parents and volunteers develop deeply trusting relationships and is there evidence that Home-Start can lead to 'powerful change in the family'?

In Chapter 6 we considered how quantitative methods can be used to evaluate social work and social care services using experimental and quasi-experimental designs. These research designs, incorporating carefully chosen measures (e.g. validated scales) and appropriate statistical analyses, can help us answer questions about effectiveness. McAuley and her colleagues (2004) secured funding from the Joseph Rowntree Foundation to conduct an independent evaluation of Home-Start schemes in Northern Ireland and south-east England. The researchers employed a quasi-experimental design to compare the outcomes for 80 families receiving Home-Start services to a comparison group of 82 families in areas without a Home-Start scheme. The Home-Start families (the intervention group) had all been referred to their local scheme and had agreed to take part in the evaluation. The comparison group families had been referred to the research team by local health visitors; they would all have accepted home support if a service had been available.

In order to assess the claim that Home-Start can lead to change in the families, the researchers had first to identify suitable outcome measures. They would subsequently compare scores on these measures between a baseline and scores at some point in the future when a change might be evident. Considering the reasons why families were being referred to Home-Start is a sensible place to start identifying potential outcomes. The main reasons were the mother's mental and physical health and her isolation and loneliness; in addition, some of the children had 'special needs' arising from delayed development and physical and cognitive impairments. Consequently the researchers decided to focus on maternal and child well-being and sought agreement with Home-Start that these outcomes reflected the organisation's priorities.

The outcomes selected for the evaluation were 'parenting stress', maternal mental health, maternal self-esteem, maternal social support and child development. These were all measured using a set of validated scales (see Chapter 4). (The scales are summarised in McAuley et al., 2004, Table 1, p. 3.) Given that the focus was on mothers and that their children were under 5 years old, it is perhaps not surprising that the researchers only interviewed the mothers. An interview schedule was drawn up and they were asked to respond to the various statements indicating the extent to which they agreed or disagreed with them using a typical Likert scale (see Chapter 7). The researchers decided to compare the outcomes in the intervention group with those in the comparison group over a 12-month period.

Exercise 13.1: Evaluating Home-Start

At this point, go back and have another look at the extract from the Home-Start website reproduced above. Then consider the following questions:

1. To what extent do you consider that the claims made by the charity about its effectiveness could be addressed by this research project? (You may find it helpful to refer to Chapter 6 for this and the next three questions.)

2. Do you agree with that the outcomes chosen could reflect 'change in the family'? What other members of the family might have been included?

3. Why is it important to have a comparison group in the evaluation? What is the weakness of this quasi-experimental design?

4. Do you think there are any significant ethical issues raised by this design? (See Chapter 11.)

5. Can you suggest a research hypothesis and a null hypothesis concerning the relationship between the intervention status (Home-Start vs. comparison group) and the outcome 'maternal stress'? (See Chapter 8.)

We will come back to the findings about the outcomes later in this chapter. First, let's consider the following question:

What could the research tell us about the families' experiences, including their experiences of Home-Start and other services which they may have used?

Aside from the quantitatively measured outcomes of the scheme (positive or negative), you might be very interested in the answer to this question to help you decide whether or not you would recommend this service to a family on your caseload. But, as we have presented the study so far, it is not obvious that it would be useful in this regard; there is, for example, no mention of a user satisfaction measure in the extensive list of instruments used in the evaluation. Even if there was such a measure, how much would it tell you about what the service users thought about the scheme? Furthermore, you might be interested to know not just about the *levels* of stress experienced by the mothers in this study, but also the stress *factors*: what were the sources of stress and were they related? These questions could be tackled by the use of a questionnaire, but thinking about our own experiences of responding to questionnaires in daily life we might reasonably be sceptical about how informative the responses would be. Fortunately, the Home-Start evaluators had thought about these issues and had incorporated a qualitative component in their research design.

The procedure which was developed for the evaluation is described in the research report (McAuley et al., 2004, p. 4). It began with a semi-structured face-to-face interview with all the mothers, asking them questions about their own and their child's well-being. In the second interview 12 months later, the researchers also asked questions about the mothers' experiences of Home-Start and how it had helped them. These semi-structured interviews were followed immediately by asking the mothers to complete the various measures.

You will recognise that the methodology thus combined a qualitative research method (semi-structured interview) with a quantitative method (validated self-report measures). This, then, is an example of a mixed-methods research project. Although the authors of the research report do not actually draw attention to this feature of their evaluation, it is highlighted in a subsequently published journal paper entitled: 'Young families under stress: Assessing maternal and child well-being using a mixed-methods approach' (McAuley et al., 2006). In that paper, the authors point out some important features of their use of mixed methods (p. 45): that the qualitative and quantitative data were collected from all the participants at the same time; that the interviews and measures covered the same domains; and that the analyses were carried out in a complementary manner so that agreement and disagreement between the approaches could be explored. We shall examine the findings from this mixed-method study later in the chapter. But next we need to be clear about the basic concepts before considering the variety of mixed-method designs.

Basic concepts

Definition

What do we mean by 'mixed methods'? In practice, the term seems to be used rather loosely – and not just in social work research. Look at the abstract of a paper published in the *British Journal of Social Work* (Exercise 13.2).

Exercise 13.2: Is this a mixed-methods study?

Read the following abstract.

The Strengthening Families (SF) child protection conference model attempts to address some of the weaknesses of traditional conferences by helping families participate more easily and by enhancing risk assessment. This study examined the impact and feasibility of implementing the SF model across one local authority. A mixed-methods design was adopted. Data collection included: semi-structured interviews with professionals and parents; non-participant observation of SF and traditional conferences; and anonymised child protection plans. (Appleton et al., 2015).

How do the 'mixed methods' in this study compare to those in our 'Research in practice' case study, the Home-Start evaluation introduced above?

In this chapter we will use the term 'mixed methods' to mean both a methodology (an overall philosophical framework that governs our approach to the research) and a research design which uses a mixture of quantitative and qualitative research methods. At its core is a belief that the use *and integration* (mixing) of quantitative and qualitative methods can produce findings which are of greater value than using one method on its own. (You will note that this definition thus excludes the example in Exercise 13.2, which uses a mix of qualitative methods only.)

Mixed methods as methodology is pragmatic. Answering the research questions is of primary importance. Some research questions are best answered using quantitative methods and others using qualitative methods. As we have indicated in the instances in the introduction to this chapter, in social work research we often we need a combination of both. The corollary is that mixed methods should only be used when the purpose of the research demands it.

Purposes of mixed methods

It is important to be clear from the beginning of any research project about purpose of the research methods chosen. This is particularly important in the case of mixed-method research. Greene, Caracelli and Graham (1989, p. 5) offer five key purposes:

1 *Triangulation* seeks convergence, corroboration, correspondence or results from different methods.

2 *Complementarity* seeks elaboration, enhancement, illustration, clarification of the results from one method with the results from another.

3   *Development* seeks to use the results from one method to help develop or inform the other method, where development is broadly construed to include sampling and implementation, as well as measurement decisions.

4   *Initiation* seeks the discovery of paradox and contradiction, new perspectives or frameworks, the recasting of questions or results from one method with questions or results from the other method.

5   *Expansion* seeks to extend the breadth and range of enquiry by using different methods for different enquiry components. (Greene et al., 1989, p. 259)

You may already have spotted that our 'Research in practice' case study used mixed methods (semi-structured interviews and quantitative measures) for the first purpose in this list, *triangulation*. The researchers investigated the same domains of mother and child well-being in both, intending to see if the findings converged. The evaluation of Strengthening Families used mixed (qualitative) methods to extend the breadth of the enquiry using semi-structured interviews, observation and analysis of child protection plans; this is an example of *expansion*.

Chaumba (2013) employed Greene and colleagues' framework to analyse the stated purpose of 47 mixed-method social work research studies identified through a systematic review of the English language literature published between 1995 and 2010. The primary purpose was given as 'triangulation' in well over half the studies (27). Next most frequent were the 10 studies where the purpose was stated to be '*complementarity*'. One of these is a case study conducted five years after a devastating flood in a small town in North Carolina, USA which investigated the process of rebuilding communities (an example of macro social work) (Yoon, 2009). The researcher was interested in how community assets played a role in rebuilding. A survey using quantitative measures was used to assess respondents' retrospective perceptions of community assets – elected leadership and community cohesion; these were positively associated with indices of financial recovery. Concurrently, semi-structured interviews were conducted with 'key informants' recommended by local residents. These included a religious leader, the leader of a voluntary rescue agency and the former mayor. These interviews revealed community assets which were 'invisible' to the survey method, specifically the community's symbolic meaning as the first town chartered to African-American people in the US. Its historical legacy attracted politicians, including the president, and volunteers, but more importantly strengthened the resolve of its residents not to forsake their town. The interviews complemented the survey to give a fuller picture of the rebuilding process.

The third most frequent purpose (five studies) was '*expansion*', illustrated by Carpenter et al.'s (2006) evaluation of a postgraduate programme of interprofessional education for community mental health professionals in England. In addition to quantitative measures of attitudes, the evaluation included participant observation of teaching, focus groups and individual interviews with participants and their managers. Different methods were used to assess different learning outcomes, within an overall framework of levels from participants' reactions to implementation of learning in practice and outcomes for service users.

'*Development*' was represented by just one study, which used focus groups in the development of a survey. '*Initiation*' did not feature. In the final two studies in the review the purpose was not stated, although it could be inferred.

Having considered the purposes of mixed-method research studies, we can give our attention to the types of research design which can be used to realise these purposes.

Mixed-method research designs

Bryman (2006) remarked on a proliferation of typologies of mixed-method research and wondered whether their variety and range had reached the point where they had 'become almost too refined, bearing in mind that the range of concrete examples … is not great.' (p. 98). We have much sympathy with this view: one influential North American textbook (Tashakkori and Teddlie, 1998) presents no fewer than 35 different mixed-method designs. Chaumba's (2013) systematic review employed a much more straightforward fourfold typology developed by Creswell and Plano Clark (2007). There are triangulation, embedded, exploratory and explanatory designs.

But first we think it would be helpful to note three criteria which distinguish designs quite clearly: time, whether the quantitative and qualitative data are collected concurrently or sequentially; the stage of the research process at which mixing takes place (research question formulation, data collection, data analysis or data interpretation); and which method and data have priority, qualitative or quantitative. These criteria will be evident the studies we are about to review.

Exercise 13.3: Applying criteria to the Home-Start evaluation

Apply the three criteria to classify the Home-Start evaluation:

1. When were the two types of data collected?

2. What stage(s) of the research process did mixing happen?

3. Did quantitative or qualitative data have priority?

Explanatory mixed-method designs

We begin with the straightforward case in which qualitative methods are used to add depth to the findings of quantitative research. A typical study involves a questionnaire survey distributed to a large sample of a given population. At the same time, a smaller sample is selected for the collection of qualitative data.

The 'Research in practice' example introduced in Chapter 9 investigated the causes of stress in social workers and care managers. In that chapter we described how validated measures were used to collect quantitative data from 249 partici-pants in a survey and explained how these data were analysed statistically. In addition, concurrent interviews were carried out with 48 participants, four each from the 12 pilot sites. The researchers explained that these interviews were used to 'further clarify the findings of the main questionnaire, and to explore the mechanisms through which the IB pilots contributed to social worker per-ceptions of job pressures, discretion and support' (Wilberforce et al., 2014, p. 817). In this study, the quantitative (QUAN) component had priority over the qualitative element (qual). This may be represented according to Creswell and Plano Clark (2007) as:

QUAN → qual → Interpretation based on QUAN → qual

As is often the case in qualitative research, the sample was selected purposively so that the researchers could explore possible differences between social work-ers experienced with IBs and others with little or no such experience. Findings from the qualitative component of this study provided further information with which to understand the results of the quantitative analysis. As the researchers explained:

> This [primarily quantitative] study found that being part of the IB pilots was associ-ated with a doubling of the likelihood of being at risk of high strain, which suggests that the new processes added to existing burdens of work and reduced discretion. … [The] qualitative interviews revealed a number of common tensions relating to the new policy, most notably the difficulties and pressures of administering the new pro-cesses. … Furthermore, a number of social workers reported concerns over being held accountable for risks that may not be properly managed under IBs, including financial abuse. (Wilberforce et al., 2014, p. 826)

The mixing of methods in this study occurred at the design stage and in the data interpretation. Here, the interpretation was facilitated by the use across both quantitative and qualitative components of the same theoretical frame-work, the Job Demand/Control Model derived from organisational psychology.

A more elaborate version of this model employs a *sequential* design in which the quantitative data are collected and analysed prior to a follow-up investigation using a qualitative method. For example, the evaluation of the programme of interprofessional education for community mental health mentioned above (Barnes et al., 2000) included a theoretically driven investigation of interprofessional stereotypes and stereotype change using a previously validated rating scale. The stereotypes included: academic rigour; interpersonal skills; communication skills; leadership; practical skills; breadth of life experience; and professional competence. The key research hypothesis was that at the end of the programme, which involved getting to know and work with members of the other professions, negative stereotypes would be diminished and positive stereotypes enhanced. However, statistical analysis determined that the null hypothesis should be accepted – there was no evidence of change. Why should this be?

The researchers decided that an explanatory qualitative investigation using ethnographic methods should be employed. This component of the evaluation would employ the same theoretical framework so that, once the qualitative data had been analysed, it could be interpreted in the light of the quantitative findings.

We can summarise the design as:

QUAN $\rightarrow$ QUAN results $\rightarrow$ QUAN interpretation $\rightarrow$

qual study design $\rightarrow$ qual results $\rightarrow$ Interpretation: QUAN $\rightarrow$ qual

One of the research team joined the course as a participant observer for nine full-day teaching sessions. She noted that much of the teaching was presented in a whole-group didactic style; the latter part of sessions then allowed participants an opportunity to discuss the information among themselves in small groups. She observed that the course participants themselves, not the presenters, usually decided membership of these small groups. The participants typically chose those sitting around them who were colleagues from the same team or service with whom they may also have travelled to the programme venue. If group membership was actually determined by the presenter, it was usually done on the basis of existing team or service membership. In other words, there were no structured opportunities for participants to interact with members of other teams and professions and have their stereotypes challenged. Furthermore, outside the teaching sessions, there was little evidence of interprofessional mixing due to difficulties with structural and environmental factors, such as lack of time and the layout of the building. These qualitative findings added support to quantitative data which indicated that the programme was not providing sufficient opportunities for interprofessional learning (i.e. learning about working together), as opposed to shared learning (i.e. merely learning in the same environment). In this study, the quantitative component predominated, with the qualitative element helping to explain its (unexpected) findings.

Exercise 13.4: When did mixing of methods take place?

At what stages did mixing take place in the evaluation of the programme of interprofessional education for community mental health?

In a second variant of the sequential explanatory mixed-method design, the qualitative component rather than the quantitative component predominates. This is sometimes known as the participant selection model. Here a sample is surveyed using appropriate measures with which to identify a purposive sample of participants for a qualitative interview study. For example, Yusof surveyed social workers, psychologists and other professionals who were also registered as family therapists in the UK. She was interested in exploring the relationships between their adult attachment style and their practice (Yusof and Carpenter, 2015). The (online) survey employed a validated self-report measure of experiences in close relationships as adults. The analysis determined whether respondents could be categorised as having 'secure', 'preoccupied', 'dismissing' or 'fearful' adult attachment styles. At the conclusion of the questionnaire, respondents had been asked to express their interest in the possibility of participating in a follow-up interview to explore their past experiences, interactions between their personal self and their professional self, and the meanings that those experiences had for them. It was explained that it would not be possible to interview everyone who volunteered. Yusof invited participants representing each of the adult attachment styles identified by the measure. She was successful in recruiting 11 participants for an in-depth interview: three each were 'secure', 'preoccupied' and 'fearful', and two were 'dismissing'. The data were analysed using an intensive qualitative method, Interpretive Phenomenological Analysis (Smith et al., 1999). We can summarise this sequential explanatory design as:

quan data collection → quan data analysis → QUAL purposive sample selection →

QUAL data collection → QUAL analysis → Interpretation: quan → QUAL

Exploratory mixed-method designs

Exploratory designs begin with an initial qualitative investigation, the results of which inform a subsequent quantitative study. They are indicated when we want first to explore a new topic or area in order to establish the focus and content of a survey. This may involve generating appropriate questions to include in a questionnaire and may be an initial stage in the process of developing a research instrument (a validated scale). Alternatively, the emphasis may be on using the qualitative data to develop hypotheses which can be tested on a large sample.

For example, Bryan, Flaherty and Saunders (2010) wanted to evaluate an innovative parent-led adoption support programme in Kentucky, USA. Their goal was to gain insight into the adoption experiences of participants in the support groups and their satisfaction with the programme; as the authors explained, little was known about this matter. Consequently, they set up a total of six focus groups, purposefully selected as representative of the rural and urban areas where the support groups were being run; 42 members took part. Analysis of the focus group data identified six themes that were used to develop questions for the survey. These included motivations for adopting, reasons for attending the support groups, barriers to participation and so on. The researchers included four open questions about participants' adoption experiences and whether the participants had any specific recommendations for improving the programme. As they explained, these questions would allow other important themes to emerge from the substantially larger sample they proposed to survey. We can summarise the design:

qual data collection → qual analysis → qual results (themes) → develop questionnaire →

QUAN survey → QUAN analysis → QUAN results → Interpretation: qual → QUAN

The researchers mixed the qualitative and quantitative findings for interpretation. They concluded that the results largely converged, but that there was divergence in one important respect. In the focus groups there had been serious concerns expressed by some participants about 'the honesty and fairness of the state in its interactions with adoptive families' (p. 109). The majority of the 251 survey respondents disagreed. The authors commented: 'This may illustrate potential risks of relying exclusively on focus group methods, in which outspoken members may create a bandwagon atmosphere for opinions that are not widely held in the population of interest' (p. 109). Clearly, this points up the potential limitations of qualitative research methods and the advantages of mixing quantitative and qualitative methods. Here the mixing was evident in research question formulation, data collection and interpretation, and the purpose of the mixing was clear from the start. Such clarity is especially important in the final two designs we consider, embedded designs and triangulation designs.

Embedded designs

Embedded designs are similar to explanatory sequential designs in that qualitative data are collected and analysed to help interpret predominantly quantitative studies; the difference is that the data collection is concurrent. They are commonly used in experimental intervention studies in health care services, but are beginning to appear in social work research as well. These are generally described as a process study which is embedded in an outcome study, typically a case-randomised controlled trial (RCT) (Chapter 6). For example, Barlow and her colleagues (2013) have embedded qualitative components in the RCT of Parents under Pressure, an intensive home-based programme designed to support parents dependent on drugs or alcohol by providing them with methods of managing their emotional regulation and supporting their new baby's development. Given the likely challenges of providing a service to this particular user group, the authors explained that the research design would embed a qualitative component designed:

> to enhance understanding of the user and provider experiences of the new service. A range of data will be collected from participants who refuse to take part in the study or drop out of the intervention or study; this will include quantitative demographic data and qualitative data to explore the reasons for non-participation or discontinuation. In-depth interviews will also be conducted with practitioners and supervisors following the training and during the delivery of the intervention … and a purposive sample of participating parents. The latter will be selected using quantitative outcome data to identify study participants who show change and those who show no change, and the aim of the interviews will be to gain a better understanding of the factors that contributed to these outcomes. (Barlow et al., 2013, p. 7)

What's important to appreciate in an embedded design is that one method, usually the qualitative component, is supplementary. Creswell and Plano Clark (2007, p. 69) recommend asking the question: 'Would the results of the secondary data type be useful or meaningful if they were not embedded within the other data set?' In the above example, they clearly would not.

Triangulation

We have already mentioned that 'triangulation' was the most common purpose of mixed-method studies in social work research, the goal being convergence, corroboration, or correspondence of results from different quantitative and qualitative methods. Our 'Research in practice' example has this as a specific aim, as McAuley et al. (2006) explained. We also use triangulation to refer to a form of research *design*, following Creswell and Plano Clark (2007) who define it as obtaining different but complementary data on the same topic. They explain that it is a 'one-phase design in which researchers implement the quantitative and qualitative methods during the same timeframe and with equal weight' (pp. 62–64). This distinguishes it from exploratory and explanatory sequential designs and from the embedded design.

Our 'Research in practice' example employed the most straightforward triangulation where the quantitative data were collected using validated measures and the qualitative interview data were collected during the same interview with the same people. We shall return to that shortly. A similar example is Lee and Eaton's (2009) investigation of financial abuse of elderly Korean immigrants in California. In this study, participants were asked to respond to a case study vignette as part of the interview; qualitative responses to the vignettes were quantified (data transformation) and a sophisticated statistical analysis was conducted which explored the associations between help seeking and adherence to traditional cultural values using multivariate analyses. The authors also presented a thematic analysis of the qualitative data and developed an integrated interpretation of the reasons why the Korean elders would not seek external help in dealing with financial abuse.

A more complex triangulation design involves the concurrent collection and analysis of data from two or more sources; the researcher draws the findings together aiming to produce a holistic appreciation of the research problem. Campbell (2008) provides an example of this approach. In order to gain an understanding of the views of a range of stakeholders about compulsory psychiatric hospital admission in Northern Ireland, he facilitated service user and carer focus groups, interviewed lawyers and members of Mental Health Review Tribunals and hospital managers and surveyed a large sample of solicitors who were involved in tribunals work. In this case, the extent of mixing of qualitative and quantitative methods is not clear. The published presentation of the findings contains substantial qualitative data, but no report of analyses of the quantitative survey responses. It may be that the survey was undertaken primarily for pragmatic purposes.

We should emphasise that since the goal of triangulation is convergence, the data must be analysed using the same conceptual framework. For example, if you are using a theoretical framework of family resilience to underpin an investigation of how families cope when one member has been diagnosed with a life-limiting condition, you will want to use a validated measure of family resilience in your quantitative component. Let's suppose that you also collect qualitative data through interviews with family members. Clearly it makes sense to develop a semi-structured interview schedule which enables you to explore the various dimensions of family resilience, so that you can bring the findings together for analysis. Your efforts would not be helped if you analysed your qualitative data inductively using grounded theory, for example, because the themes which emerged may be quite different.

Test your understanding

Think back to the introduction to this chapter and the three situations outlined where, we suggested, the numbers (quantitative methods) are unlikely to tell us enough. We also made suggestions about qualitative research methods which could enhance a quantitative approach. These are only suggestions and you may have ideas of your own. To test your understanding, consider how you would plan a study using mixed social work research methods. Be sure to:

- Define the *purpose* of your mixed-methods study using Greene et al.'s (1989) framework (p. 221–222).

- Select the most appropriate mixed-methods *design* and categorise it according the framework used in this chapter. State the methods to be used.

- Identify the stages at which the mixing of methods would take place.

Just to remind you, the three situations were:

1   Design and conduct a survey of the circumstances and social care needs of a 'new' population (e.g. young people with a life-limiting condition living unexpectedly into adulthood because of advances in medicine and surgery).

2   Investigate children's resilience to adverse events, in particular children who have proved exceptionally resilient.

3   The effectiveness of 24-hour services versus day-only (8am to 5pm) assertive outreach teams in preventing people with severe mental illness from psychiatric admissions.

Critical Thinking Box

We return to our 'Research in practice' example for the critical thinking exercise.

The researchers asked the mothers to complete validated measures of well-being for themselves and their children at baseline and follow-up, which was approximately 11 months later. We have extracted from Chapter 4 of the research report (McAuley et al., 2004) a summary table of data from the main measures used. Mean scores and standard deviations for both Home-Start recipients and the comparison group are shown in Table 13.1. Details about the measures themselves may be found in the report. At this stage, you just need to know that the scales used are not scored in the same way: for

▶

three scales marked,* a lower score indicates an improvement; for the other two, a higher score indicates improvement.

Table 13.1 Mothers' and children's mean scores on well-being measures at baseline and follow-up for Home-Start and comparison groups

	Home-Start (N = 80) Mean (SD)		Comparison (N = 82) Mean (SD)	
Mothers	Baseline	Follow-up	Baseline	Follow-up
Parenting stress*	97.97 (20.33)	88.13 (20.16)	100.54 (21.34)	88.93 (20.14)
Self-esteem*	25.24 (5.74)	22.03 (5.55)	24.85 (4.71)	22.66 (6.00)
Social support	20.63 (4.78)	22.33 (5.59)	21.26 (5.41)	23.10 (5.60)
Children	(N = 30)		(N = 19)	
Problems*	14.70 (7.11)	10.97 (8.00)	13.47 (9.90)	12.58 (10.45)
Competence	16.17 (3.17)	16.63 (3.39)	15.00 (3.46)	16.53 (3.39)

* Note lower scores indicate improvement
Source: data extracted from McAuley et al. 2004

1. Take a look first at the mean scores on the measures at baseline and follow-up for the Home-Start group. What do these figures suggest happened between baseline and follow-up? Next compare the mean scores at baseline and follow-up for the comparison group. What is your provisional conclusion?

   Unfortunately, the report does not include details of the statistical tests used to test whether the differences between means for the groups and over time were statistically significant or not. The authors do, however, report their conclusions on the basis of their analyses; we will come to these shortly.

2. We now turn to the qualitative interview data, which are reported in Chapter 5 of the research report. The authors focused on 42 mothers 'who had the average number of stress factors at the initial interview to gain an in-depth understanding of the changes over time' (p. 28). These were drawn from the Home-Start group and the comparison group. In general, the findings were that the mothers in both groups felt that they were experiencing less stress, had higher self-esteem and fewer mothers felt isolated compared to one year previously. There were no simple conclusions to be drawn

about their children's behaviour. The Home-Start recipients were generally very positive about the help they had received:

> Many of the mothers described how they valued the support of and contact with their Home-Start volunteers. Many indicated that the relationship between themselves and the volunteers had developed into a friendship. (p. 32)

> More than four-fifths of the mothers considered that Home-Start '… had made a difference in relation to the stresses they were experiencing at the time of the first interview. They tended to portray Home-Start support as providing a general sense of relief from overwhelming pressure'. (p. 33)

At this point we can tell you that the authors' conclusions from the quantitative component of the study were that:

a. In general, mothers were experiencing less parenting stress and had higher self-esteem and greater social support at follow-up compared to their baseline scores.

b. There were no (statistically) significant differences in the improvements between the Home-Start and comparison groups over time.

Remember that the purpose of this mixed-method triangulation design was 'convergence'. On the basis of the information you have so far:

● How do you think the findings of the quantitative and qualitative components of this study converge and diverge?

● Write down the reasons you can think of to account for the findings of the quantitative component.

● Why do you think that the mothers in the qualitative interviews were so positive about Home-Start?

3. Now we suggest that you access the report and read Chapter 5, which presents the results of the qualitative study. What additional information does this provide to help you understand the outcomes for these families?

4. Finally, you can then turn to Chapter 9 where you will see the authors' own reflections on the findings of their study. Do you agree with their conclusions?

Summary

We have acknowledged in this final chapter that quantitative research methods alone may not tell us the full story. In social work research, some questions are best answered using quantitative methods and others using qualitative methods. Frequently, we need a combination of both. We used a number of examples to demonstrate how mixed quantitative and qualitative methods can greatly enhance our understanding of the kinds of questions of interest to social work practice and policy.

Mixed methods is a pragmatic methodology. The purposes to which it is suited include: the corroboration, clarification and elaboration of findings from one method with the results from another; the development of research topics, questions and measurement; discovering new perspectives or frameworks by recasting the results from one method with questions or results from the other method. We have presented the four main types of mixed-methods designs: explanatory and exploratory designs, embedded and triangulation designs. You will have seen how the quantitative concepts and methods discussed in the previous chapters of this book are an essential foundation for the mixed methods described here. So, too, are the principles of evaluation and ethical research, and the methods of statistical analysis. In addition, the use of mixed methods requires a level of proficiency in qualitative research methods of design, data collection and analysis. It is also generally more work to carry out, analyse and interpret than a single method study. That must be allowed for in planning a mixed-method study as part of a dissertation or thesis. Nevertheless, we hope that the examples in this chapter provide a model and a source of inspiration to the next generation of social workers and social work researchers.

Further resources

Brannen, J. (2005). Mixed methods research: A discussion paper. *Methods Review Papers No. 5.* National Centre for Research Methods. Economic and Social Research Council. Available from http://eprints.ncrm.ac.uk/89/1/MethodsReviewPaperNCRM-005.pdf (30 pages) (accessed 7 July 2016).

ANSWERS TO EXERCISES AND CRITICAL THINKING BOXES

Chapter 2

Exercise 2.1: Is my work good enough?

You were asked to consider your mark of 62% for a piece of coursework. The lecturer had provided the class with information relating to the class average and the range of marks in the class. Would you prefer to be student A or student B? Why?

Student A achieved a mark of 62%. The class average was 68% with a range of 55% (being the lowest mark in the class) to 75% (being the highest mark in the class).

Student B achieved a mark of 62%. The class average was 58% with a range of 35% (being the lowest mark in the class) to 75% (being the highest mark in the class).

In this instance you would prefer to be student B, who has achieved a grade higher than the class average. In addition, in class B, there is greater variation in the range of marks achieved and therefore the student is achieving closer to the top of the class.

Exercise 2.2: Numbers and social work practice

1. In giving evidence in court the decision maker must weigh up the likelihood of whether a child will suffer future harm. It is very hard to give a precise numerical value to the risk, so we need to use descriptors that convey meaning. Using terms such as 'possible' and 'probable' indicates the likelihood of such harm occurring. In using the term 'probable' the social worker is stating that it is more likely for the child to experience future harm, whereas the term 'possible' implies that it is just as likely that the child will not experience harm.

2. The community mental health team need to balance the benefits of electroconvulsive therapy with the drawbacks. We know that some individuals do benefit from electroconvulsive therapy, but not everyone. Conversely, we know that there are side effects from electroconvulsive therapy for most recipients. In considering whether the known side effects are outweighed by the potential benefits, we need to be able to understand from the research literature the indicators of who might receive most benefit, and in what circumstances.

3. In undertaking a community profile of the need for a service, some key information is likely to include:

- the size of the population of interest and where they live;

- their demographics (such as age, gender);

- the views and wishes of potential beneficiaries of the service about whether they need a service, and what that service should provide.

Critical Thinking Box

Why are the findings from this study important?

Practitioners seldom come across young females with sexually abusive behaviour, and interventions have often not differentiated the responsivity to interventions by the gender of the recipient.

What are the similarities and differences in the age and gender of victims of the females compared to males in the study, and why is this important to understand? What other differences are there between the types of sexually harmful behaviour displayed by females and by males?

Compared with the males in the study sample, the young females were likely to be referred at a younger age, they were much less likely to have any criminal convictions at the point of referral, they had higher rates of sexual victimisation in their histories and they tended to have fewer victims drawn from a more narrow age range. In terms of similarities, the female sample had much the same and indeed as high levels of reported learning disability as the male group, and both groups displayed similar kinds of sexually abusive behaviours (although in somewhat different proportions). They were also quite likely to abuse victims of both genders and, in most cases, their victims were known to them, whether related or not. Rates of sexual violence or the use of physical force were relatively low in both groups.

Better understanding these similarities and differences supports practitioners to assess and work with young females.

What are the limitations of the sample size of this study?

The study drew data from 24 young females in contact with services, and therefore is unlikely to be representative of all young females with sexually abusive behaviour. However, this is an important study in drawing out what might be the particular characteristics and needs of this service user group.

Chapter 3

Exercise 3.1: Surveying alcohol use

Consider the example of adult alcohol dependency. You are interested in undertaking a survey of the levels of alcohol misuse within your community to inform service development:

- *Who is your study population?*

- *Which community members might be more difficult to reach with a survey?*

- *What would you do to ensure that the survey was more inclusive of the entire range of individuals within the community?*

In undertaking a survey of levels of alcohol misuse within your community you need to be able to identify:

- Who the study population are – is this everyone, to ensure that you capture everyone who might misuse alcohol, whether known to services or not, or just those who are in contact with services? The former is a larger and therefore more costly study, whereas the latter is likely to miss individuals not in contact with services, who might be an interesting group to know more about.

- Some community members might be more difficult to reach – for example, individuals who do not recognise that their alcohol use is problematic; individuals not in contact with services; individuals who might need to keep their use of alcohol secret, such as young people, individuals who are worried about whether employers or social care professionals might draw adverse conclusions about their suitability for employment or to care of their children.

- To ensure that the survey had the potential to reach everyone in the community it would be important to have a profile of the entire population and to ensure that everyone had an equal opportunity to participate. This would be supplemented by additional measures to reach the groups who might be more reluctant to take part, such as targeting youth groups, or to ensure that the survey is accessible, for example having it translated into the languages in use in the community.

Exercise 3.2: Using routinely collected data

- *Should the permission of service users be sought to allow a researcher to access the information held by an organisation about them for a research study?*

- *Would your answer change if the researcher only had information that was anonymised?*

- *What might be some of the implications for the robustness of the research if some information was withheld from secondary analysis because a service user or gatekeeper declined access to particular case files?*

Ordinarily the information held by organisations (whether a bank, a GP or a shop) on individuals who use that service should only be used for the purposes for which it was supplied. We also expect that this information is held securely, and not shared with anyone else without our permission. This is particularly the case with information which may be seen as sensitive – such as health information and information relating to the involvement of social services. However, the law recognises that organisations need to regularly review what they are doing, and whether they need to do anything differently. This can sometimes involve undertaking audits, evaluations or research. As such, organisations need to be able to use information about individuals beyond simply providing the individual with a specific service. In most instances it is important, and possible, to ask service users for their permission for their personal data to be used for research purposes. In Chapter 11 we explore the ethical issues involved in research, including the importance of consent.

However, there may be circumstances where it may not be possible or practicable to seek permission, for example when looking at historical information. In other cases service users may not provide consent for a whole range of reasons, which may not be related to their views on whether they wish to be part of the research (e.g. they may have moved address). In trying to better understand the needs and experiences of some of the most vulnerable individuals, their experiences may be less well understood if as complete a picture as possible is not established. One way of addressing the twin objectives of protecting the identity of service users and allowing all files to be examined is to anonymise the data made available to researchers. While this can be costly, it also ensures that the research is undertaken ethically and lawfully.

Critical Thinking Box

What additional information might assist you to make a judgement about whether the sample chosen to be surveyed was representative of social workers in each of the countries?

It would be helpful to know information about the numbers of social workers in each country from which the sample is drawn, along with their gender, age, level of qualification, length of time in role and employment details. This would help readers to make a judgement about whether samples are more similar or dissimilar to the whole social work population within each country.

What additional information might assist you to make a judgement about whether the response rate of the survey would support the generalisation of findings to the whole social work profession in each country?

It would be helpful to know whether the non-respondents differed in any specific ways from respondents. For example, might some social workers working in particular roles/ sectors be more inclined to respond, or be less available to complete a survey? Might respondents of a particular age be more likely to reply to the survey? By knowing this additional information we can have greater confidence in extrapolating the study findings beyond the participants in the survey.

Chapter 4

Exercise 4.1: Validated research instruments in practice

Why, in general, do you think psychologists often use such instruments but social workers rarely do?

Of course this is actually an empirical question – a subject that could be researched – though to our knowledge it is not thus far been explicitly researched. There are therefore lots of potential answers. It may be that a lack of confidence in quantitative research and a lack of knowledge about validated instruments might be a factor. However, when we have discussed this with workers lack of knowledge is only a part of the picture. Other factors, such as a belief that each individual is unique and a tendency to therefore discount generalisable knowledge is one issue. A more pragmatic fact may be that often social workers work with people who are reluctant to receive a service and using standardised instruments may be more difficult than with people who are actively seeking help for a particular issue. An important practice issue is that there are many instruments, and many different types of problem, and knowing what to use with whom may be an issue.

Do you think these reasons are good reasons for not using them?

This is a matter of personal judgement. However, our biased opinion is that once validated instruments are understood by a social worker it is hard to see why they would not use them at least in some of the work they do, as set out in answer to the next point.

How might you use them in your practice?

Validated instruments have three major potential contributions to social work practice. The most obvious is as an aid to assessment. Often as social workers we are assessing a potential issue or problem but may struggle to be sure how serious the issue is. Validated instruments provide a useful adjunct for such assessment. Thus, for instance, parents may feel a child's behaviour is a problem, and it is important to understand their real subjective experience of parenting, but if the Strengths and Difficulties Questionnaire is completed by them (and perhaps also by the young person and/or the school) it is far easier to compare the severity of the behaviours being described. And of course this applies to most issues that a worker might be dealing with. A second role is to help us evaluate our work. Changes in validated instruments are a very useful way of gauging change. Indeed, with standardised validated instruments scores can indicate the proportion of the population with more or less serious problems. Thus if a focus of work is a particular issue then measuring that issue before and after work with the individual or family may be helpful. Finally, validated instruments can be useful as an intervention to help people. Providing more objective feedback in a respectful way is at the heart of effective brief interventions, and standardised instruments provide an opportunity to do so. Thus, for instance, many people who drink heavily do not think that they do because heavy drinking is the norm amongst their friends or family. Completing a standardised instrument such as the AUDIT or the Maudsley Addiction Profile can allow feedback on the proportion of the population who drink less than them or have fewer problems. Validated instruments therefore have a potential contribution to make to assessment, effective helping and evaluating our work.

Exercise 4.2: Screening for alcohol problems – are you at risk of having an alcohol problem?

How easy or difficult was this process?

To some extent the answer to this is less important than the following point: it is usually a good idea to complete an instrument yourself before asking someone else to. It provides an 'insider' understanding of the process.

Would it provide you or others with useful information about alcohol use?

Completing the AUDIT can often come as a shock to people – as many of us drink more than we tend to think we do. It can therefore be a useful indicator of whether an individual is at risk of developing alcohol problems. As such, the AUDIT would be of limited use for some purposes (for instance as part of an assessment of whether an individual was dependent on alcohol). However it might be very helpful with other groups. For instance, as an activity with a young person or perhaps even a group of young people to raise awareness and begin conversations about alcohol use.

What are the pros and cons of this way of exploring alcohol use?

There are two obvious advantages. One is that the information is more objective than individual stories. A second is that the conversation is less personal and this can make answering easier; everyone is asked the same questions and that is obvious. On the other hand using standardised instruments is very prescriptive and provides a limited amount of information. It can never, therefore, be a replacement for a proper, individualised assessment. Rather, such measures may provide useful adjuncts or elements of work.

Chapter 5

Exercise 5.1: Performance measurement

Are these reasonable things for the government to count?

There is no right or wrong answer to this question, but on the face of it these are not unreasonable things to collect information about.

What are their strengths or weaknesses?

The importance of collecting such data is that it provides important information on services and experiences of families and children. Yet the primary weakness is that even important quantitative data such as these provide no object information about child or family welfare. We do not know if the children who entered care benefited from the experience, whether families whose assessments were not completed on time had a worse or better service experience or whether child protection plans actually protected children.

What better things to measure can you suggest?

This is in some senses the key question. It is easy to critique government and other public agencies for collecting a lot of unhelpful information, but it is difficult to know what information would be better to collect in a way that is practicable. If you can help answer this question you would be helping to have a positive influence on social work in years to come…

Critical Thinking Box

How confident can we be from the data presented that the number of children entering care through care proceedings since the Act was put into place is increasing? Are there any other explanations for some or all of this change? How might you explore them?

The data show fairly clearly and unequivocally that the number of children being removed from home has increased substantially, and this shift has continued in the years since the study was published. What is unclear is why this is happening. Here it might be interesting to look at variations within the overall pattern. For instance, are there authorities or regions or even countries within the UK where this is less of a pattern? How has the pattern looked over time? Are there other factors that might explain what is happening? How does it compare with other countries' rates? Answers to these questions would not definitively tell you why this is happening – but they would help you to understand a complex and important area.

What can you not conclude from this increase? Can you think of any ways in which additional data might help shed more light on whether this increase is a good or bad outcome?

What cannot be concluded is that this is a bad thing – or a good thing. To know that we would need to know far more about the outcomes of children in care, and of children who might or would have come into care. Furthermore, it can be persuasively argued that it is not solely the impact on children that needs to be considered. What of the impact on parents, on siblings, on other family members, on communities and on society as a whole of removing more children? There are never simple answers to such complex questions, but exploring the well-being of children in care and what happens to families after children are removed, studying the effectiveness of services aimed at keeping children at home and analysing longer-term outcomes would all be helpful.

Chapter 6

Critical Thinking Box

A key first question is: do you feel this RCT is ethical? What might make you think it was or was not ethical?

Traditionally it has been argued that we cannot do an RCT of children entering care for ethical reasons. The arguments against it are that the harm caused by leaving children at home may be so serious that to do an RCT is impossible. (This is the same argument as outlined in a light-hearted spoof article of the impact of falling out of planes with or without a parachute which concludes by suggesting that what is now needed is an RCT (Smith and Pell, 2003).) Yet what the article found is that the intervention prevented care and children suffered no obvious harm. The key question here is whether it is genuinely unknown if care is the better option. As for many RCTs, if the evidence is already very clear then an RCT is likely to be unethical. Where we genuinely do not know, then not evaluating either care or the alternative seems to be the unethical option.

How would you judge this study in relation to:

* *Internal validity?*

A bit of a trick question here: you need a lot more information. And this study does not seem to have been published in an academic journal. Which raises questions about why not: was the quality of the study good enough? There are all sorts of questions about the way samples were selected, randomisation, attrition and other factors that cannot be answered without a lot more information.

- *External validity?*

A key question is whether this would apply in other contexts, such as another country. Often interventions that work in one setting do not work as well in others. Equally, control groups often do better in non-US studies – perhaps because of the lack of a strong welfare state in the US.

How applicable do you think it would therefore be to you if you were the manager tasked with setting up a new service for children at risk of entering care?

It would be foolish to rely too heavily on this piece of evidence, because it is not reported in detail, does not seem to have been replicated and may not apply in a different setting. Nonetheless, it does suggest that an intensive service aimed at children who would have entered care may result in a reduced need for care. Therefore learning lessons about how this was done while carefully evaluating the specific intervention might be appropriate.

Chapter 7

Exercise 7.1: Categorical and continuous variables

1. Continuous

2. Continuous

3. Categorical

4. Categorical

5. Continuous

Exercise 7.2: Levels of measurement

1. Ratio

2. Nominal

3. Ratio

4. Ordinal (although, as discussed, some researchers may treat as interval)

5. Nominal

6. Ordinal

7. Ratio

8. Ordinal (although, as discussed, some researchers may treat as interval)

9. Nominal

10. Interval

Exercise 7.3: Measures of central tendency

1. Level of satisfaction

    a. Mean = 2.09

    b. Median = 2

    c. Mode = 1 and 2 as both values occur four times

    d. Could report as follows: The mean level of satisfaction is 2.09 indicating that the people in the sample are generally unsatisfied.

2. Assessment score

    a. Mean = 60.33

    b. Median = 60

    c. Mode = 74

    d. Could report as follows: The mean assessment score is 60.33.

3. Years in care

    a. Mean = 3.9

    b. Median = 4.5

    c. Mode = 5

    d. Could report as follows: The mean years in care is 3.9, with a median of 4.5 and a mode of 5.

4. Local authority

    a. Mean = Cannot calculate as the variable is nominal level

    b. Median = Cannot calculate as the variable is nominal level

    c. Mode = 3 (Bristol City Council)

    d. Could report as follows: The mode is 3, which means that Bristol City Council was the most commonly represented amongst the sample.

5. Units of alcohol per week

    a. Mean = 7.22

    b. Median = 3

    c. Mode = 3

    d. Could report as follows: The mean units of alcohol per week is 7.22, yet the median and mode is 3. The mean has been influenced by an outlier of 35.

Test your understanding

1. **Sex:** The level of measurement of this variable is 'nominal'. In terms of descriptive statistics, you can provide a measure of central tendency of 'mode' (female). You can also provide the percentage and frequency of males, females and intersexed [60% female (f = 6); 40% male (f = 4); and 0% intersexed (f = 0)].

2. **Age:** The level of measurement of this variable is 'ratio'. In terms of descriptive statistics, you can provide measures of central tendency of 'mode' (45), 'median' (43), and/or 'mean' (43.67). You can also report the 'range' (31) [60–29].

3. **Ethnicity:** The level of measurement of this variable is 'nominal'. In terms of descriptive statistics, you can provide a measure of central tendency of 'mode' (White British). You can also provide the percentage and frequency of White British, Black British and Asian British [66.67% White British (f = 6); 22.22% Black British (f = 2); 11.11% Asian British (f = 1)].

4. **Depression assessment score:** The level of measurement of this variable is 'ratio'. In terms of descriptive statistics, you can provide measures of central tendency of 'mode' (30; and 50), 'median' (47), and/or 'mean' (42.33). You can also report the 'range' (25) [55–30].

5. **Summary:** An example summary of the information above could be as follows:

> Of the individuals who are currently attending the group, 60% are female and 40% are males and the mean age is 43.67 with a range of 31 years (60–29). In terms of ethnicity, 66.67% are White British, 22.22% are Black British, and 11.11% are Asian British. The mean depression assessment score is 42.33 with two modes of 30 and 50 and a range of 25 (55–30).

Critical Thinking Box

1. *Provide an example of frequency, percentage, mean and standard deviation and indicate what this tells you about the sample*

   The following variables for both the MST and YOT samples are presented as:

   a. **Frequencies** – Female gender (9; 10); Ethnicity (White British/European 24; 13; Black African/Afro-Caribbean 15; 20; Asian 2; 3; Mixed/Other 11; 15); Number with custodial sentences (0; 0)

   b. **Percentages** – Female gender (16.4%; 19.2%); Ethnicity (White British/European 49.1%; 25.5%; Black African/Afro-Caribbean 27.3%; 39.2%; Asian 3.6%; 5.9%; Mixed/Other 20%; 29.4%); Number with custodial sentences (0; 0)

   c. **Means** – Age in months (182.7; 180.6); Socio-economic status (SES) (2.5; 2.0); Offences in year before referral (Total number 2.5; 2.4; Violent offences 0.75; 0.73; Non-violent offences 1.8; 1.7); IPPA score (94.2; 100.3)

   d. **Standard deviations** – Age in months (12.3; 12.9); SES (1.6; 1.7); Offences in year before referral (Total number 1.6; 1.8; Violent offences 1.0; 0.9; Non-violent offences 1.6; 1.7); IPPA score (24.6; 19.6)

2. *Create an argument for where and why the authors should have presented the median or mode when reporting.*

The authors only provide the means and standard deviations for the interval/ratio level variables. There could be outliers within the range of values for these variables and providing the median and mode could give different measures of central tendency than merely providing the mean. The IPPA score has a standard deviation of 24.6 for the MST sample, which indicates that the values among the sample deviate from the mean by 24.6 units on average. Providing the median and mode could provide additional information about the extent to which the values are spread across this sample.

3. *Is the table clear and would you suggest any amendments to the presentation of the findings?*

We would suggest the table could be constructed to be more explicit in whether the values are means, frequencies (n), standard deviations or percentages. These could possibly be separated out into columns with the appropriate labels at the top of the table. We would also suggest presenting the range for age, offences in year before referral and IPPA score.

4. *Provide an overall picture of the sample of young people assigned to MST and YOT.*

The individuals assigned to the MST group (*n* = 56) were primarily male (83.9%), with a mean age (in months) of 182.7 (*SD* = 12.3). The largest percentages of individuals were associated with the ethnicity of 'White British/European' (49.1%). They had a mean of 2.5 total number of offences in the year before the referral with a mean of 0.75 violent offences and 1.8 non-violent offences. Their mean IPPA scores was 94.2 (*SD* = 24.6). The individuals assigned to the YOT group (*n* = 52) were primarily male (80.8%), with a mean age (in months) of 180.6 (*SD* = 12.9). The largest percentage of individuals associated were with the ethnicity of 'Black African/Afro-Caribbean' (39.2%). They had a mean of 1.8 total number of offences in the year before the referral with a mean of 0.9 violent offences and 1.7 non-violent offences. Their mean IPPA scores was 100.3 (*SD* = 19.6).

Chapter 8

Exercise 8.1: What's the probability?

1. .14 or 14% chance

2. .285 or 28.5% (we would round this up to 29%)

3. 1.0 or 100%

Exercise 8.2: The area under the normal curve

1. 47.72%

2. Nearly 50 times out of 100 or 49.87% of the time

3. .6826 or 68.26% or 68 times out of 100

4. 81.85%

Exercise 8.3: Research and null hypotheses and statistical significance

1. There is no relationship between amount of supervision social workers receive and level of job satisfaction.

2. There is a difference in young people's reoffending based on whether they had custodial or noncustodial sentences

3. False. The alpha level is set by the researcher prior to the data analysis; the p-value is generated by the statistical test.

4. False. Because the p-value ($p = .06$) is greater than the α level ($\alpha = .05$), we cannot reject the null hypothesis of no difference and therefore need to assume that any observed relationship or difference between variables is due to chance (sampling error).

5. A 5% chance or 5 times out of every 100 that any observed relationship or difference is actually due to chance (sampling error).

6. (a) statistically significant – because .03 is less than the set α level of .05; (b) statistically significant – because .001 is less than the set α level of .01; (c) not statistically significant – because .50 is greater than the set α level of .05.

Test your understanding

1. *What does $\alpha = .05$ mean and why is it important in interpreting the results in the table?*

   $\alpha = .05$ is the level of probability the researcher has set where the null hypothesis can be rejected with confidence and, thus, the research hypothesis of a relationship or difference can be supported. By setting the alpha level at .05, the researcher decides to reject the null hypothesis only if the probability of falsely rejecting the null hypothesis is .05 or 5% or 5 times in 100. There is a 5% chance that any findings of relationships or difference between variables in the sample is actually due to chance and not to any true differences in the population.

   Important in interpreting the results of the table – if the researcher has set $\alpha = .05$, then we use this to interpret the results of the table by seeing if the p-value is higher or lower than .05. If $p > .05$, then we reject the research hypothesis and have to accept the null hypothesis of no difference. If $p \leq .05$ then we can reject the null hypothesis and accept the research hypothesis of a difference between two variables.

2. *Which geographical areas produced a 'statistically significant' reduction in mean hours from entry to exit? How do you know?*

Area A and Area C produced a statistically significant reduction in the mean hours from entry to exit. We know this because the p-values for each area is less than our set $\alpha = .05$.

3. *What are the chances that the difference between the 9.50 mean hours of entry and 7.00 mean hours of exit for Area C is due to chance and, therefore, most likely does not reflect a difference in the population?*

There is a .03 or 3% or 3 times in 100 chance that the difference reflected in this sample would not be reflected in the true population. Otherwise stated, there is a 3% chance our findings of a difference is due to chance or sampling error.

4. *From the research findings, what can you conclude about the reablement programmes in each of the three geographical areas? As a social worker, would you refer to the programme in each of the areas? Why or why not?*

We can conclude that the reablement programme leads to a decrease in number of care hours needed from entry to exit; thus, the programme appears to work! Although there was not a statistically significant difference in Area B, we still see a decrease in number of hours of care from entry to exit. As a social worker, we would use this information to refer people to the programme as it appears to reduce the number of care hours needed.

Critical Thinking Box

What would you say is the likelihood that Adele may 'slip' or 'relapse' during the first four weeks of treatment? What information and evidence from the article did you use to answer this question?

The study found through bivariate analyses that those individuals more likely to slip/relapse within the first four weeks of treatment had a higher rate of secondary substance use, which includes cocaine (p. 45), and a DSM-IV Axis II Cluster B diagnosis of personality disorder (PD) (p. 46) – both of which are characteristics of Adele. The study then found through multivariate analyses that although the secondary drug use was no longer statistically significant in predicting slip/relapse during the first four weeks, the diagnosis of PD remained statistically significant (p. 46). Therefore, as a social worker, you might see the likelihood of Adele slipping/relapsing during the first four weeks of treatment as highly likely.

What would you say is the likelihood that Adele will remain abstinent after treatment if she experiences a 'slip' or 'relapse' during treatment? How confident are you in your answer?

The study found that those individuals who slipped/relapsed during the first four weeks of treatment were more likely to use alcohol at 12 weeks. Therefore, if Adele does slip/relapse during the first four weeks, the chances that she will use alcohol at 12 weeks is high.

As her social worker, based on the findings from this research, what resources and interventions could you put into place to increase her chances of remaining abstinent during and after treatment? How could you help to prepare Adele for the future?

The study found that the diagnosis of PD was the largest contributor to having a slip/relapse during the first four weeks, and having a slip/relapse during the first four weeks was a predictor of alcohol consumption at 12 weeks. The authors explain that PD is often associated with impulsivity – as per the DSM-IV diagnostic criteria. Therefore, interventions that aim to tackle Adele's impulsivity might prevent her from using alcohol. The study also found that cocaine use was a predictor of a slip/relapse. As a social worker, you might want to work with Adele on her relationship with and use of cocaine in addition to alcohol. Your work with Adele will most likely focus on the social, behavioural and emotional aspects of both her alcohol and cocaine use with the knowledge that impulsivity may play a role in whether or not she will remain abstinent.

Chapter 9

Exercise 9.1: Correlation and causation

1. A visual interpretation indicates a strong negative relationship. Based on the information we have about the data, we cannot infer causation because we are only able to meet one of the three assumptions required to infer causation. We are able to say that two variables are related/correlated, but we are not able to say that one variable came before the other, or that the relationship cannot be explained by extraneous variables.

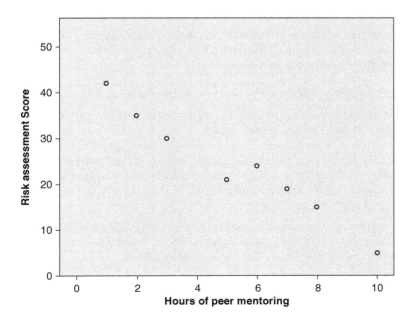

2. For the example, $r(162) = .15$, $p = .06$:

   a. r = the Pearson's product moment correlation, which is .15. This indicates a weak positive relationship between level of stress and amount of time spent writing research reports.

   b. (162) = the sample size.

   c. $p = .06 = p$-value or level of significance. This indicates that the probability of obtaining the result of a weak positive relationship by chance is 6 times in 100. As $\alpha = .05$, and p of .06 is > than .05, we would interpret the results as not statistically significant.

3. The results indicate a strong negative relationship that is statistically significant at $p <$ .001. We would write the results as: $r(15) = -.82$, $p < .001$.

Exercise 9.2: Is there a difference between the means?

1. **Research hypothesis** – There is a difference in number of days abstinent from alcohol among service users from Treatment A and Treatment B over 30 days following treatment.

   Null hypothesis – There is no difference in number of days abstinent from alcohol among service users from Treatment A or Treatment B over 30 days following treatment.

   Research question – Is there a difference in number of days abstinent from alcohol among service users who received Treatment A and service users who received Treatment B over 30 days following treatment?

2. **Independent variable** – Treatment A or Treatment B. **Level of measurement** – nominal.

   Dependent variable – Number of days abstinent from alcohol (over 30 days following treatment). **Level of measurement** – ratio.

3. The second box indicates the descriptive statistics and reports the mean of days abstinent for Treatment A as 26.50 ($SD = 9.00$), which is more days than the mean of days abstinent for Treatment B, which is reported as 10.55 ($SD = 12.56$). The sample size is 40 with 20 individuals in each group.

   The first box indicates a statistically significant finding for 'Levene's test of equality' ($p = .01$), which means we cannot assume equal variances. Therefore, we have to interpret the second row of the output. The findings are as follows:

   Individuals who received Treatment A remained abstinent for more days ($M = 26.50$; $SD = 9.00$) than individuals who received Treatment B ($M = 10.55$; $SD = 12.56$), $t(34) = 4.62$, $p < .001$. The mean difference of days abstinent between Treatment A and Treatment B is 15.95 with a 95% confidence interval of 8.93–22.97.

The statistically significant findings indicate that we can reject the null hypothesis of no difference and assume our results are highly unlikely (1 time in 1,000) to be due to chance (sampling error).

Exercise 9.3: The perceived effectiveness of social work methods: ANOVA

- Levene's test for equality of variances is not significant ($p = .63$) indicating we can accept the null hypothesis of no difference between variances and thus assume there is equal variance.

- The mean effectiveness score for SFP is 7.96, for CBT is 4.72, and for psychoanalysis is 3.40.

- There is a statistically significant difference in perceived effectiveness of social work methods based on the type of method, $F(2, 72) = 10.05$, $p < .001$. Post hoc comparisons using Tukey HSD test indicated that the mean effectiveness score for SFP ($M = 7.96$; $SD = 5.22$) was significantly different from CBT ($M = 4.72$; $SD = 2.53$) ($p = .01$) and psychoanalysis ($M = 3.40$; $SD = 2.72$) ($p < .001$). There was no statistically significant difference in effectiveness score between CBT and psychoanalysis ($p = .42$).

Exercise 9.4: Differences in type of stress relief based on profession: chi-square

The first box indicates that of those who enjoy running as a stress reliever, 52.9% are nurses, and 47.1% are social workers; of those who enjoy meditation as a stress reliever, 47.2%, are nurses and 52.8% are social workers. A chi-square test was performed and indicated no difference between type of stress relief based on profession, $\chi^2(1, N = 70) = .23$, $p = .63$.

Test your understanding

1. **Parametric tests** – (1) the level of measurement of the dependent variable should be at least interval level, and when examining the extent to which two variables are correlated then both variables must have at least an interval level of measurement; (2) the sample should be from a population that is normally distributed, thus the sample data should be normally distributed; (3) homogeneity of variance; (4) no extreme scores.

2. **Infer causality** – (1) the two variables are related (correlated); (2) the variable assumed to be the causal variable must have occurred prior to the outcome variable; (3) the relationship between the two variables cannot be explained by any extraneous variables.

3. Bivariate analysis:

a. *t*-test

b. χ^2 test of independence

c. Correlation analysis (*r*)

d. ANOVA

Critical Thinking Box

Note: There are several ways in which you could design an evaluation of this programme. Below is one possible response.

1. **Hypothesis** – There is a difference in participants' total difficulties score, as measured by the SDQ, from beginning to end of the 10-week arts-based group.

   Null hypothesis – There is no difference in participants' total difficulties score, as measured by the SDQ, from beginning to end of the 10-week arts-based group.

2. We propose using the 'one-sided SDQ for parents or teachers of 4–17 olds', which is a shorter form that could be easy to distribute, complete, analyse and use to test the research hypothesis.

3. We propose a parent fill out the SDQ form before the start of the 10-week programme and then again at the end of the 10 weeks.

4. We would score the SDQs at the beginning and the SDQs at the end for each participant. We will ensure they are matched by using a unique identifying code (to ensure confidentiality) to enable comparisons from pre-group to post-group. We might first want to run descriptive statistics to determine the mean and standard deviation of the scores from pre-group and post-group. A decrease in mean scores would point to the effectiveness of the programme, while an increase in mean scores would point to the programme potentially not working or even causing harm. We will then run a paired samples *t*-test to see if there is a statistically significant difference in scores from pre-group and post-group. If we set $\alpha = .05$ and the *p*-value from our *t*-test is less than .05, we can reject the null hypothesis of no difference and accept our research hypothesis of a difference. Again, do be sure to look at the means of the scores from pre- to post-group as we would want to see the means decrease from pre- to post-group.

Chapter 10

Exercise 10.1: Bivariate linear regression analysis

1. Yes. $R = .93$.

2. ($R^2 = .86$) 86% of variance in final test results can be explained by hours spent studying.

3. 1 in 1,000 times ($p < .001$). The ANOVA table provides the F-value of 113.36, which is reported to be statistically significant at $p < .001$. This means that we can now interpret the value of b for the regression equation.

4. $y = 48.83 + 2.74(x)$

5. A student who studied four hours = 59.79 or 60%; A student who studied 12 hours = 81.71 or 82%.

6. The results from the bivariate linear regression analysis indicates that hours spent studying explains 86% of the variance in final test results, $R^2 = .86$, $F(1,18) = 113.36$, $p < .001$. The results indicate that for every one additional hour of time spent studying, final test results will increase by 2.74 points. Confidence intervals indicate that the population slope (b) is between 2.20 and 3.28 with 95% confidence.

Variable		*B*	*SE B*	β	*t*	*p*
Constant		48.83	3.08			
Hours spent studying		2.74	.26	.93	10.65	.000*
Adjusted R^2	.86					
F	113.36*					

*$p < .001$.

Exercise 10.2: Multivariate linear regression analysis

1. **Predictor variables** – motivation score; number of social supports; and number of days in treatment. **Outcome variable** – number of sobriety days.

2. 88% ($R^2 = .88$)

3. Yes. Because the ANOVA table indicates the F-value is statistically significant at $p < .001$.

4. Number of social supports and motivation score significantly influence number of sobriety days. Number of days in treatment is not statistically significant and, therefore, will not be included in the regression equation.

5. The multiple linear regression analysis indicates that 88% of the variance in number of sobriety days can be explained by number of social supports and motivation score, $R^2 = .88$, $F(3,56) = 140.49$, $p < .001$. The results indicate that for every one additional social support, number of sobriety days will increase by 17.51 days, and for every one increase in motivation score, number of sobriety days will increase by 1.36 days. Standardised coefficients indicate that motivation score (β = .442) is slightly more influential in predicting number of sobriety days than number of social supports (β = .440).

Variable		B	SE B	β	t	p
Constant		-65.59	12.36			
Number of days in treatment		.73	1.18	.08	.62	.54
Number of social supports		17.51	4.23	.440	3.96	.000*
Motivation score		1.36	.54	.442	2.50	.015*
Adjusted R^2	.88					
F	140.49*					

*$p < .001$; *$p < .001$

Test your understanding

1. **Regression equation**

   a. $y = a + bx$

   b. y = the outcome (or dependent) variable; x = the predictor (or independent) variable; a = the intercept (or constant); b = slope

2. **Regression equation**

   a. $y = a + b_1x_1 + b_2x_2 + b_3x_3 + b_4x_4 + b_5x_5 + b_6x_6$

   b. y = the outcome (or dependent) variable; x_1, x_2, x_3, x_4, x_5, and x_6 are the predictor (or independent) variables; a = the intercept (or constant); b_1, b_2, b_3, b_4, b_5, and b_6 are the slope for each predictor variable.

3. Whereas bivariate linear regression analysis seeks to predict the change in one outcome variable (y) given a change in one predictor variable (x), multivariate linear regression analysis seeks to predict the change in one outcome variable (y) given a change in more than one predictor variable (for example, x_1, x_2, and x_3). It is able to do this by providing information about how all the predictor variables together contribute to a change in the outcome variable, but also the influence of each individual predictor variable on the outcome variable.

4. In bivariate linear regression analysis, 'R' is Pearson's product moment correlation coefficient (r) (because there were only two variables in the analysis). In multiple linear regression analysis, 'R' is truly a 'Multiple R' as it is the correlation between the predictor variables (two or more variable) and the outcome variable. The value of R indicates the correlation between the variables. If we square R (R^2), then we can see how much of the variance in the outcome variable is made up of the predictor variables.

5. b indicates the extent to which the outcome variable will change with one unit increased in the predictor variable. The standardised coefficient (β) is particularly important in multiple linear regression analysis. This is because we cannot actually compare the values of b for two or more variables when they are not measuring the same thing (they do not operate in the same units of measurement). This is why the standardised coefficient of b (β) is provided, which standardises all the predictor variables according to standard deviations and, thus, makes them comparable in terms of which predictor variable is more or less likely to influence the outcome variables compared to other predictor variables.

Critical Thinking Box

1. This piece of research provides evidence of the factors that have been found to be associated with the use of direct payments (DPs). As a social worker, you can see that from the sample of families in England, those more likely to use DPs are those who are highly educated, from White British backgrounds, have younger children, are from areas of lower levels of deprivation, have access to service and social networks, and use short breaks. Although this doesn't mean that families that meet these characteristics will definitely take up DPs, it means they are more likely to. Therefore, you may want to target families who do not hold these characteristics (the characteristics the research found to be associated with *not* taking up DPs) to see how you can support them in using DPs, or explore with them the barriers (or reasons) that are preventing them from using DPs.

2. This research could be problematic if you, as a social worker, assume that all families who meet certain characteristics will automatically take up DPs and other families who do not meet these characteristics will automatically *not* take up DPs. This could lead to stereotyping and approaching families with pre-set ideas of how they might respond to the use of DPs. Social workers should acknowledge that not all families are the same despite sharing similar characteristics.

3. Similar to answer 2 above, if you, as a social worker, believe that the research applies to every family who have these characteristics (of both taking up DPs and those not taking up DPs) then you could lead to stereotyping and oppressive practice. The research should be helpful in identifying what is generally found in the population, thus providing some direction for how you should approach your social work practice. The research is helpful in gaining a 'general' idea of the profile of those families who do and do not take up DPs and can help you, as a social worker, in how or where to focus your work. But not all families are the same and believing this research is the truth for all families could lead to stereotyping and families not getting the services they need or deserve. Research helps to tailor and guide social work practice, but not to strictly direct social work practice in a particular direction.

Chapter 11

Exercise 11.1: US National Association of Social Workers code of ethics

Certainly (a) and (b) are relevant as they concern evaluation and monitoring of interventions and surveying service user satisfaction is an important part (though only part) of that process. Item (d) is relevant insofar as there should perhaps have been independent ethical review of the survey. In relation to (d), (e) and (j) it would be important to make it clear to respondents that their completed questionnaires would be anonymous (provided there are no indicators of risk of immediate harm – see item [l]) and that their responses would not be linked to any decisions about service provision – in other words, reassure them they can be critical of services if they want to be, without any detrimental impact on their care. Items (k), (l) and (m) are relevant to the careful anonymising and secure handling of data. Item (n) is relevant to accurate and fair analysis and write-up. Item (o) may be relevant if the research was being conducted by staff within the social work agency, who may need to consider any influence of their own interests.

Exercise 11.2: To what extent is it acceptable for researchers to chase non-response?

Certainly there should be nothing that could be construed as harassment. If anyone says they do not want to take part in a study then you should leave them alone, even if this does threaten the validity of the study. A grey area, however, is where you are unsure that information has reached someone. This could be the case when approaching children in foster care as you might have to go through several people before reaching them directly – for example a social worker or foster carer. The correct approach would perhaps be to check if the follow-up information has been seen and deliberately ignored, or just not seen. If the latter is true, then to repeat an invitation would certainly be a legitimate approach. Turning up at someone's door without warning might seem intrusive, but it does depend on the context. If you have, for example, interviewed a young person at home before and sought their permission on that occasion to call to the house for the follow-up then it would be acceptable, especially if you have written in advance offering a specific time and date.

Exercise 11.3: What are the ethical implications of secondary analysis?

Ethical conduct here depends very much on what was agreed when participants signed up to the study and how the data are handled. If the data are not anonymised and there was no original agreement to reanalysis by others, then the secondary analysis is unethical. If, however, it was clear to the survey respondents that their identities would be removed from the data set for future use by other researchers, or that no identifying details were required in the first place, thus facilitating wider use of the data set, then for others to reuse the data could be acceptable. There is nothing intrinsically unethical about analysing the relationship between responses in different parts of the question-naire (e.g. stress and educational background) when this specific analysis was not explic-itly listed in the original study information. Good practice would be to make clear that a data set might be used by others in future, beyond the original research team; if this is the intention, and if for some reason respondents cannot be anonymised, then it is essen-tial that this is clearly understood and consented to.

Critical Thinking Box

Item (g) in the NASW code of ethics (see Exercise 11.1) states:

> Social workers should never design or conduct evaluation or research that does not use consent procedures, such as certain forms of naturalistic observation and archival research, unless rigor-ous and responsible review of the research has found it to be justified because of its prospective scientific, educational, or applied value and unless equally effective alternative procedures that do not involve waiver of consent are not feasible.

This advises against research without consent but does not rule it out, if no alternative is possible and the study is of scientific, educational or applied value.

There may be legal prescriptions as well, however. In the UK there is the Data Protec-tion Act to navigate. This does not apply to data already anonymised, but the Gibbons et al. study took place in an era where most records were on paper only, so it would not have been practically possible for all case files to be anonymised before they were seen by the research team. This will probably still be the case today, even in an era of elec-tronic records, assuming that established recording practices are largely qualitative and text-based.

To give the UK's legal framework as an example, under the Data Protection Act the Information Commissioner would need to be satisfied that:

- processing the data is in the substantial public interest and necessary for the research;
- data are not being used in a way which would affect any particular individuals;
- data are not processed in a way which would cause substantial damage or distress to the data subject;
- processing for research purposes should not be incompatible with the purposes for which the data were originally obtained.

According to these conditions, the Gibbons et al. research could be considered legal. Regardless of the specifics of UK law, it could be considered ethical anyway insofar as the study is furthering the interests of families in the child protection system by uncovering the extent to which they are missing out on services. That finding could of course not have been predicted at the outset, but whatever the finding the study should be consid-ered relevant to preventing child maltreatment and therefore in the public interest. Given the highly sensitive context of child protection registration, the study would not have been practically possible if consent were required from every child or parent. In the light of this reality, insisting on prior consent for every case file would not be in the public interest. Researchers should be aware that social work organisations may not understand the law and may err on the side of caution in refusing access (see Hayes and Devaney, 2004), so it is advisable to be armed with legal knowledge in advance.

Chapter 12

Exercise 12.2: Exploring the Longitudinal Study of Young People in England

You will see that 85 young people in the study are reported by parents to currently be in care. Unfortunately there are a further 256 parents who were not interviewed in wave 1 and 356 who 'refused' this section. However, the fact that a further one parent is recorded as 'refused' might suggest that the 356 simply skipped the section as it did not apply to them and only one parent actually refused to complete it. But given the stigma (in the UK) of a child being in care, we could speculate there might indeed be some under-reporting.

Critical Thinking Box

1. *What does this study tell us and what does it not tell us?*

   The study gives us a picture from a general population sample about how people with intellectual disabilities compare with the rest of the population. It also provides a reasonably representative picture of the population of people with intellectual disabilities (see below on sample). Some qualitative research would also be useful to find out why people with learning difficulties have lower levels of social participation and why they regard their neighbourhoods less favourably.

2. *What are the benefits and disadvantages of this kind of secondary analysis?*

   The sampling is much more robust than anything a social work student or researcher could generate on their own. However we are of course limited by the questions asked in the Understanding Society questionnaire. Understanding Society does not have any specific questions about social work, unlike its predecessor the British Household Panel Study. It can, however, be used for research which is very relevant to social work, such as this study which looks at issues such as social participation and perception of neighbourhood.

3. *What are likely to be the implications of using a general population sample for coverage of people with intellectual disabilities?*

   There is only indirect evidence in this study that cognitive impairments may have originated in childhood. The questionnaire did not require literacy, but rather the questions were delivered verbally by a fieldworker. However, because the survey relies on self-report, respondents are unlikely to have severe intellectual disabilities. Despite some limitations, this is a probability sample of the general population so, unlike many studies of intellectual disabilities, it reaches beyond those people in touch with services.

Chapter 13

Exercise 13.1: Evaluating Home-Start

1. *To what extent do you consider that the claims made by the charity about its effectiveness could be addressed by this research project?*

   The claims are that parents (1) learn to cope (2) improve their confidence (3) build better lives for their children (4) that parents and volunteers can develop a trusting relationship and (5) that this can lead to powerful change in the family.

   We need to consider whether these claims can be addressed by the quantitative methods (the use of the validated scales) and qualitative methods (interviews) mentioned. To assess the former, we would have to examine the scales themselves, but on the face of it, it is plausible that the 'parenting stress' measure gives at least some information about ability to cope and that the 'self-esteem' measure assesses confidence. For these claims, the information elicited in the interviews could provide corroboration. There is also a measure of 'child development', but this sounds much more limited than 'a better life', which could be defined along many different dimensions which would be complex to measure. Responses to the interview questions could be helpful (e.g. 'You say that you feel able to build a better life for your children. Can you explain, in which ways "better"? What has enabled you to do this?').

   The relationship between the mother and the volunteer is not measured in this research design, although there are instruments which have been developed to assess the 'therapeutic alliance' which would have to be adapted. The interviews could certainly explore this topic.

   Note that the researchers also measured mothers' social support but that no claims are made about this.

2. *Do you agree with that the outcomes chosen could reflect 'change in the family'? What other members of the family might have been included?*

   The researchers only measure changes in the mother and to a lesser extent, the child. Fathers are also parents and carers may be grandparents. The family may also include other children.

3. *Why is it important to have a comparison group in the evaluation? What is the weakness of this quasi-experimental design?*

   Considering the children first, they are certain to grow and develop during the study whether or not the family receives volunteer support. The question is, whether they do any better with the support; the same goes for the mothers. The weakness of this quasi-experimental design is that participants have not been randomly allocated to the intervention (Home-Start) or comparison groups and that the families live in different areas. So, we cannot unreservedly attribute differences between the groups at follow-up to the intervention effect.

4. *Do you think there are any significant ethical issues raised by this design?*

A research ethics committee is unlikely to be concerned about the design; the comparison group is not being denied a 'treatment' which is already known to be effective and can still receive support from health visitors.

5. *Can you suggest a research hypothesis and a null hypothesis concerning the relationship between the intervention status (Home-Start vs. comparison group) and the outcome 'maternal stress'?*

The research hypothesis is that mothers who receive additional Home-Start support will be less stressed after the intervention than a comparison group of mothers who receive 'treatment as usual' from health visitors and other services. The null hypothesis is that Home-Start does not have any greater impact on maternal stress, for better or worse, than 'treatment as usual'. This is best expressed as a two-tailed hypothesis because it's possible that the volunteer visits might make mothers more stressed if they felt criticised.

Exercise 13.2: Is this a mixed-methods study?

The Home Start evaluation used mixed methods (semi-structured interviews and quantitative measures) for the purpose of triangulation: it investigated the same domains of mother and child well-being in both, intending to see if the findings converged. The evaluation of Strengthening Families used mixed qualitative methods to extend the breadth of the enquiry using semi-structured interviews, observation and analysis of child protection plans; this is an example of expansion.

Exercise 13.3: Applying criteria to the Home-Start evaluation

Apply the three criteria to classify the Home-Start evaluation:

1. *When were the two types of data collected?*

Concurrently

2. *What stage(s) of the research process did mixing happen?*

Design, data collection, interpretation

3. *Did quantitative or qualitative data have priority?*

Neither

Exercise 13.4: When did mixing of methods take place?

Interpretation (only): the observation was not part of the original design and it happened after the quantitative data collection.

Test your understanding

1. **Circumstances and social care needs of a 'new' population.**

   Purpose: development; **Design**: sequential – focus groups (or interviews) followed by a survey (postal/online or as part of a semi-structured interview); **Mixing**: at question formulation, data analysis and interpretation.

2. **Children's responses to a measure of resilience.**

   Purpose: expansion; **Design**: sequential explanatory – survey using validated measure, data analysis, sample selection and semi-structured interviews; **Mixing**: at data analysis and interpretation.

3. **Preventing psychiatric admissions.**

   Purpose: Initiation; **Design**: sequential explanatory – survey using validated measures and non-participant observation and semi-structured interviews; **Mixing**: at qual design and interpretation. (Note, if qual had been included in the design from the beginning and carried out at the same time, this would be embedded.)

Critical Thinking Box

1. We asked you first to examine the data presented in Table 13.1. Comparison of the mean scores suggests that the mean scores for mothers' parenting stress and self-esteem had decreased between baseline and follow-up, indicating improvements in both the Home-Start and comparison groups. Mothers' mean ratings of social support had increased between baseline and follow-up.

   Mothers' mean ratings of their children's problems had decreased in both the Home-Start and comparison groups. There was a larger difference in mean scores for Home-Start children (3.73) compared to the comparison group (0.89) which may suggest a statistically significant difference in change scores between the two groups. Interestingly, there is very little difference in mean scores on the measure of children's competence for the Home-Start group over time and an increase in mean scores for the comparison group – but note the follow-up scores. We might be tempted to draw a preliminary conclusion that Home-Start had a positive effect in reducing children's problem behaviour. But note that the number of children for whom data are reported was only 30 out of 80 families (i.e. 38%) for the Home-Start group and 19 out of 81

(23%) in the comparison group. The large amount of missing data should warn us about drawing conclusions about the samples as a whole. Further, it is essential that any apparent differences be tested for statistical significance. In this study, no statistically significant differences were found.

2. Next, we asked whether you thought the findings of the quantitative and qualitative components of this study converged and diverged. It's clear that the findings from the interviews and the self-report measures of mothers' stress, self-esteem and social support were the same. But what about the children? In the chapter we summarised the results of the qualitative data analysis as follows: 'There were no simple conclusions to be drawn about their children's behaviour.' This would also be convergent with the quantitative findings which did not find a difference between the two groups. How can we account for these?

The mothers who were interviewed at follow-up were generally very positive about Home-Start, but there were no statistically significant advantages for this intervention compared to the comparison group who did not receive this service. Why? A possible reason is that while the mothers appreciated the weekly two-hour visits of Home-Start volunteers, this intervention was not especially influential in their lives. Other factors, such as becoming more confident in mothering through experience gained over the year of the study and making friends with other mothers through participation in play groups etc. may have been important factors, factors shared by both groups in the study. But why were the mothers in the qualitative interviews so positive about Home Start? This could be 'selection bias', those interviewed were presumably willing volunteers who were more likely to have favourable views. It might have been an example of 'social desirability' – interviewees wanting to give the answers that they thought the interviewer wanted to hear.

3. If you read Chapter 5 of the report, you will see the mothers' own thoughts about the changes in their lives which had made a difference to their stress, self-esteem, social support and views on their children. What they have to say is very interesting and is a nice illustration of the value of qualitative research in a mixed methods study.

4. Finally, the authors' conclusions presented in Chapter 9 of the report have a lot to say about the difficult circumstances of these families. Indeed, these rather than the outcomes of Home-Start are the concern of the journal article (McAuley et al., 2006) which was published after the report we have been examining. You will see their conclusion about outcomes that the results 'did not support the view that Home-Start had made a significant difference to the mothers … relative to the experiences of the families in the Comparison group. Interviews with the mothers suggested that the intensity and type of support may have contributed to this' (p. 61).

You will also notice that the researchers carried out an economic evaluation, concluding that 'the evidence does not…point to a cost-effectiveness advantage for Home-Start'.

An overall conclusion would be that this particular study does not support the charity's claim that Home-Start can produce a 'powerful change within the family'.

REFERENCES

Alcohol Concern (2014). *Statistics on Alcohol* [online]. Available at: www.alcohol concern.org.uk/help-and-advice/statistics-on-alcohol/ (accessed 15 October 2015).

Ambroz, A., Shotland, M. and Siddiqui, H. (2013). *Randomized Control Trial.* Better Evaluation [online]. Available at: http://betterevaluation.org/plan/approach/rct (accessed 15 October 2015).

Appleton, J., Terlektsi, E. and Coombes, L. (2015). Implementing the Strengthening Families approach to child protection conferences. *British Journal of Social Work*, 45(5), 1395–1414.

Association of Directors of Adult Social Services (2012). *Social Work in Adult Social Services* [online]. Available at: www.adass.org.uk/workforce-development-policy-page (accessed 15 October 2015).

Australian Association of Social Workers (AASW) (2015). Australian Social Work Education and Accreditation Standards (ASWEAS) 2012 V1.4 [online]. Available at: www.aasw. asn.au/document/item/3550 (accessed 17 April 2016).

Babor, T., De la Fuente J., Saunders J. and Grant M. (2001). *AUDIT: The Alcohol Use Disorders Identification Test. Guidelines for Use in Primary Health Care*, 2nd edn. Geneva: World Health Organization.

Bailey, D. and Liyanage, L. (2012). The role of the mental health social worker: Political pawns in the reconfiguration of adult health and social care. *British Journal of Social Work*, 42(6), 1113–1131.

Barlow, J. Sembi, S. Gardner, F., Macdonald, G., Petrou, S., Parsons, H., Harnett, P. and Dawe, S. (2013). An evaluation of the parents under pressure programme: A study protocol for an RCT into its clinical and cost effectiveness. *Trials*, 14, 210. www. trialsjournal.com/content/14/1/210 doi: 10.1186/1745-6215-14-210.

Barnes, D., Carpenter, J. and Dickinson, C. (2000). Interprofessional education for community mental health: Attitudes to community care and professional stereotypes, *Social Work Education*, 19, 461–475.

Baynes, P. and Holland, S. (2010). Social work with violent men: A child protection file study in an English local authority. *Child Abuse Review*, 21(1), 53–65.

BBC News [online] (2012, 11 May). Children in Hackney wait longest for adoption. Available at: www.bbc.co.uk/news/uk-england-london-18031119 (accessed 15 October 2015).

Beauchamp, T. and Childress, J. (2013). *Principles of Biomedical Ethics*, 7th ed. New York: Oxford University Press.

Bebbington, A. and Miles, J. (1989). The background of children who enter local authority care. *British Journal of Social Work*, 19(1), 349–368.

Beckett, C. (2001). The great care proceedings explosion. *British Journal of Social Work*, 31(3), 493–501.

Benedictus, L. (2013, 29 December). Unreliable statistics of 2013. *The Guardian.* Available at: www.theguardian.com/lifeandstyle/2013/dec/29/unreliable-statistics-of-2013 (accessed 15 October 2015).

Biehal, N., Ellison, S., Baker, C. and Sinclair, I. (2009). Characteristics, outcomes and meanings of three types of permanent placement-adoption by strangers, adoption by carers and long-term foster care. *Department of Children, Schools and Families, London Research Brief,* DCSF-RBX-09-11.

Blease, C. R. (2013). Electroconvulsive therapy, the placebo effect and informed consent. *British Medical Journal,* 39, 166–170.

Blomberg, H., Kallio, J., Kroll, C. and Saarinen, A. (2015). Job stress among social workers: Determinants and attitude effects in the Nordic countries. *British Journal of Social Work,* 45(7), 2089–2105.

Blythe B. and Jayaratne, S. (1999). *Michigan Families First Effectiveness Study: A Summary of Findings.* Michigan: State of Michigan Family Independence Agency.

Boxall, K. and Ralph, S. (2009). Research ethics and the use of visual images in research with people with intellectual disability. *Journal of Intellectual and Developmental Disability,* 34(1), 45–54.

British Academy (2012). *Society Counts.* London: British Academy.

Brown, G. W. and Harris, T. O. (eds) (1978). *Social Origins of Depression: A Study of Psychiatric Disorder in Women.* London: Tavistock.

Bryan, V., Flaherty, C. and Saunders, C. (2010) Supporting adoptive families: Participant perceptions of a statewide peer mentoring and support program. *Journal of Public Child Welfare,* 4(1), 91–112.

Bryman, A. (2006). Integrating quantitative and qualitative research: How is it done?' *Qualitative Research* 6, 97–113.

Bryman, A. (2012). *Social Research Methods,* 4th ed. Oxford: Oxford University Press.

Butler, I. (2002). A code of ethics for social work and social care research. *British Journal of Social Work,* 32, 239–248.

Butler, S., Baruch, G., Hickey, N. and Fonagy, P. (2011). A randomized controlled trial of multisystemic therapy and a statutory therapeutic intervention for young offenders. *Journal of the American Academy of Child & Adolescent Psychiatry,* 50(12), 1220–1235.

Bywaters, P. (2015). Inequalities in child welfare: Towards a new policy, research and action agenda. *British Journal of Social Work,* 45(1), 6–23.

Bywaters, P., Brady, G., Sparks, T. and Bos, E. (2016). Child welfare inequalities: New evidence, further questions. Child and Family Social Work, 21 (3): 369–380.

Cafcass (2015). *Care Applications in December 2015: December 2015 Statistics from Cafcass* [online]. Available at: www.cafcass.gov.uk/leaflets-resources/organisational-material/care-and-private-law-demand-statistics/care-demand-statistics.aspx (accessed 15 October 2015).

Campbell, J. (2008). Stakeholders' views of legal and advice services for people admitted to psychiatric hospital. *Journal of Social Welfare & Family Law,* 30(3), 219–232.

Carmichael, M. (2008). *Experience of Domestic Violence: Findings from the 2006/07 Northern Ireland Crime Survey.* Belfast: Northern Ireland Office, Statistics and Research Branch.

Carpenter, J., Barnes, D., Dickinson, C. and Wooff, D. (2006). Outcomes of interprofessional education for community mental health services in England: The longitudinal evaluation of a postgraduate program. *Journal of Interprofessional Care,* 20(2), 145–161.

Carpenter, J., Patsios, D., Wood, M., Shardlow, S., Blewett, J., Platt, D., Scholar, H., Haines, C., Tunstill, J. and Wong, C. (2011). *Newly Qualified Social Worker Programme Evaluation Report on the Second Year (2009–10)*. London: Department for Education.

Carpenter, J., Shardlow, S., Patsios, D. and Wood, M. (2015). Developing the confidence and competence of newly qualified child and family social workers in England: Outcomes of a national programme. *British Journal of Social Work*, 45, 153–176.

Catchpole, R. and Greeton, H. (2003). The predictive validity of risk assessment with violent young offenders: A 1-year examination of criminal outcome. *Criminal Justice and Behavior*, 30(6), 688–707.

Chakrabarti, S., Grover, S. and Rajagopal, R. (2010). Electroconvulsive therapy: A review of knowledge, experience and attitudes of patients concerning the treatment. *World Journal of Biological Psychiatry*, 11, 525–537.

Charney, D. A., Zikos, E. and Gill, K. J. (2010). Early recovery from alcohol dependence: Factors that promote or impede abstinence. *Journal of Substance Abuse Treatment*, 38, 42–50.

Chaumba, J. (2013). The use and value of mixed methods research in social work. *Advances in Social Work*, 14(2), 307–333.

Children's Commissioner for England (2015). *Protecting Children from Harm: A Critical Assessment of Child Sexual Abuse in the Family Network in England and Priorities for Action*. London: Children's Commissioner for England.

Children's Workforce Development Council (2008). *NQSW Handbook*. Leeds: CWDC.

Children's Workforce Development Council (2009). *NQSW Outcome Statements and Guidance (2008)*. Leeds: CWDC. Available from www.gov.uk/government/publica tions/newly-qualified-social-worker-programme-2011-2012-outcome-statements-and-guidance.

Coe, R. (2014, 9 January). Classroom observation: It's harder than you think [online]. Available at: www.cem.org/blog/414/ (accessed 15 October 2015).

Colombo, G., Burnap, P., Hodorog, A. and Scourfield, J. (2016). Analysing the connectivity and communication of suicidal users on Twitter. *Computer Communications*, 73 (Part B), 291–300.

Council on Social Work Education (CSWE) (2015). *2015 Educational Policy and Accreditation Standards* [online]. Available at: www.cswe.org/File.aspx?id=81660 (accessed 17 April 2016).

Craig, L. and Beech, A. (2010). Towards a guide to best practice in conducting actuarial risk assessments with sex offenders. *Aggression and Violent Behavior*, 15, 278–293.

Creswell, J. W. and Plano Clark, V. L. (2007). *Designing and Conducting Mixed Methods Research*. Thousand Oaks, CA: Sage Publications.

Croisdale-Appleby, D. (2014). *Re-Visioning Social Work Education. An Independent Review*. London: Department of Health.

Crime Survey for England and Wales (CSEW) (2015). Crime Survey for England and Wales [online]. Available at: www.crimesurvey.co.uk (accessed 1 September 2016).

Crown Prosecution Service (2012). *Violence Against Women and Girls Strategy 2008–2011: An Assessment of Success*. London: CPS.

Dancey, C. P. and Reidy, J. (2011). *Statistics Without Maths for Psychology*, 5th ed. Harlow: Pearson Education.

Dartington Social Research Unit (1995). *Child Protection: Messages from Research*. London: HMSO.

Davies, M. (1994). *The Essential Social Worker: An Introduction to Professional Practice in the 1990s*, 3rd ed. Farnham: Ashgate.

Department for Education (2011). *Outcomes for children looked after by LAs: 31 March 2011*. London: Department for Education [online]. Available at: www.gov.uk/govern ment/statistics/outcomes-for-children-looked-after-by-local-authorities-in-england-31-march-2011 (accessed 15 October 2015).

Department for Education (2012). *Adoption Scorecards*. London: Department for Education [online]. Available at: www.gov.uk/government/publications/adoption-scorecards (accessed 15 October 2015).

Department for Education and Skills (2006). *Care Matters: Transforming the Lives of Children and Young People in Care*. London: Department for Education and Skills [online]. Available at: www.gov.uk/government/publications/care-matters-transforming-the-lives-of-children-and-young-people-in-care (accessed 15 October 2015).

Devaney, J. (2014). Male perpetrators of domestic violence: How should we hold them to account? *The Political Quarterly*, 85(4), 480–486.

DHHS (2002). *Evaluation of Family Preservation and Reunification Programs: Final Report* [online]. Available at: https://aspe.hhs.gov/execsum/evaluation-family-preservation-and-reunification-programs-final-report (accessed 15 October 2015).

Dickerson, F. (2007). Women, aging, and schizophrenia. *Journal of Women and Aging*, 19(1–2), 49–61.

Dingwall, R. (2008). The ethical case against ethical regulation in humanities and social science research. *Twenty-first Century Society*, 3(1), 1–12.

Dixon, J., Biehal, N., Green, J., Sinclair, I., Kay, C. and Parry, E. (2014). Trials and tribulations: challenges and prospects for randomised controlled trials of social work with children. *British Journal of Social Work*, 44(6), 1563–1581.

DrinkLess (2015). *What is a Standard Drink?* [online]. Available at: www.drink-less.com/global/am-i-drinking-too-much/what-is-a-standard-drink (accessed 15 October 2015).

Dyer, J. S. and Hoffenberg, M. (1975). Evaluating the quality of working life. In L. Davis and A. Cherns (eds), *The Quality of Working Life: Problems, Prospects and State of Art*, 134–149. New York: Macmillan/Free Press.

Emerson, E., Hatton, C., Robertson, J. and Baines, S. (2014). Perceptions of neighbourhood quality, social and civic participation and the self-rated health of British adults with intellectual disability: cross-sectional study. *BMC Public Health*, 14(1), 1252–1259.

Emery, C. (2011). Disorder or deviant order? Re-theorizing domestic violence in terms of order, power and legitimacy: A typology. *Aggression and Violent Behavior*, 16, 525–540.

Engelhardt, T. (2007, 5 September). Seven years in hell: On body counts, dead zones, and an empire of stupidity. *Common Dreams* [online]. Available at: www.commondreams.org/views/2007/09/05/seven-years-hell-body-counts-dead-zones-and-empire-stupidity (accessed 15 October 2015).

Field, A. (2009). *Discovering Statistics Using SPSS*, 3rd ed. London: SAGE Publications Ltd.

Forrester, D., Cocker, C., Goodman, K., Binnie, C. and Jensch, G. (2009). What is the impact of public care on children's welfare? A review of research findings and their policy implications. *Journal of Social Policy*, 38(3), 439–456.

Forrester, D., Fairtlough, A. and Bennet, Y. (2008a). Approaches to defining need in children's services. *Journal of Children's Services*, 2(2), 48–60.

Forrester, D. and Harwin, J. (2008). Parental substance misuse and child welfare: Outcomes for children two years after referral. *British Journal of Social Work*, 38, 1518–1535.

Forrester, D., Pokhrel, S., McDonald, L., Copello, A., Binnie, C., Jensch, G., Waissbein, C. and Giannou D. (2008b). *Final Report on the Evaluation of "Option 2"*. Cardiff: Welsh Government [online]. Available at: http://gov.wales/docs/caecd/research/080411-option-2-evaluation-en.pdf (accessed 15 October 2015).

Francis, J., Fisher, M. and Rutter, D. (2011). Reablement: A cost-effective route to better outcomes. *Research Briefing 36*. London: Social Care Institute for Excellence.

Frost, N. (2002). A problematic relationship? Evidence and practice in the workplace. *Social Work and Social Sciences Review*, 10, 38–50.

Gibbons, J., Conroy, S. and Bell, C. (1995). *Operating the Child Protection System*. London: HMSO.

Gibbs, A. (2001). The changing nature and context of social work research. *British Journal of Social Work*, 31, 687–704.

Gillon, R. (1994). Medical ethics: Four principles plus attention to scope. *British Medical Journal*, 309, 184–188.

Goldberg, D. and Williams, P. (1988). *A User's Guide to the General Health Questionnaire*. Windsor, UK: NFER-Nelson.

Goldberg, E. M. and Warburton, R. W. (1979). *Ends and Means in Social Work*. London: Allen and Unwin.

'Goodhart's Law' (2016). *Wikipedia* [online]. Available at: https://en.wikipedia.org/wiki/Goodhart%27s_law (accessed 22 August 2016).

Goodman, A. and Goodman, R. (2011). Population mean scores predict child mental disorder rates: Validating SDQ prevalence estimators in Britain. *Journal of Child Psychiatry*, 52(1), 100–108.

Graham, B. (2005, 14 October). Enemy body counts revived. *The Washington Post* [online]. Available at: www.washingtonpost.com/wp-dyn/content/article/2005/10/23/AR2005102301273.html (accessed 15 October 2015).

Green, C. (2006). Gender and use of substance abuse treatment services. *Alcohol Research & Health*, 29, 55–62.

Greene, J. C., Caracelli, V. J. and Graham, W. F. (1989). Toward a conceptual framework for mixed-method evaluation designs. *Educational Evaluation and Policy Analysis*, 11(3), 255–274.

Guo, C. and Saxton, G. D. (2014). Advocacy tweeting social change: How social media are changing non-profit advocacy. *Nonprofit and Voluntary Sector Quarterly*, 43(1), 57–79.

Haapala, D. and Kinney, J. (1979). Homebuilders approach to the training of in-home therapists. In S. Maybanks and M. Bryce (eds), *Home Based Services for Children and Families: Policy, Practice and Research*, 248–259. Springfield, IL: Charles C. Thomas.

Harnett, P. H. (2007). A procedure for assessing parents' capacity for change in child protection cases. *Children and Youth Services Review*, 29(9), 1179–1188.

Hayes, D. and Devaney, J. (2004). Accessing social work case files for research purposes: Some issues and problems. *Qualitative Social Work*, 3(3), 313–333.

Health and Care Professions Council (HCPC) (2012). *Standards of Proficiency. Social Workers in England* [online]. Available at: www.hpc-uk.org/publications/standards/index.asp?id=569 (accessed 17 April 2016).

Hedgecoe, A. (2008). Research ethics review and the sociological research relationship. *Sociology*, 42(5), 873–886.

Henderson, M., Scourfield, J., Cheung, S. Y., Sharland, E. and Sloan, L. (2016). The effects of social service contact on teenagers in England. *Research on Social Work Practice*, 26(4) 386–398.

Henry, S. (2009). Social construction of crime. In J. Miller (ed.), *21st Century Criminology: A Reference Handbook*, 296–305. Sage Publishing.

Hodge, D. R., Lacasse, J. R. and Benson, O. (2012). Influential publications in social work discourse: The 100 most highly cited articles in disciplinary journals: 2000–09. *British Journal of Social Work*, 42(4), 765–782.

Home-Start (2015). *About Us* [online]. Available at: www.home-start.org.uk/about-us (accessed 6 August 2015).

Institute for Family Development (n.d.). *Programs HOMEBUILDERS – IFPS*. Available at: www.institutefamily.org/programs_IFPS.asp (accessed 15 October 2015).

International Association of Schools of Social Work and International Federation of Social Workers (IASSW/IFSW) (2004). *Global Standards for Education and Training of Social Workers*. [online]. Available at: www.iassw-aiets.org/global-standards-for-social-work-education-and-training (accessed 17 April 2016).

Jackson, C. (2007). The General Health Questionnaire. *Occupational Medicine*, 57(1), 79.

Karasek, R. (1979). Job demands, job decision latitude, and mental strain: Implications for job redesign. *Administrative Science Quarterly*, 24(2), 285–308.

Kellogg Foundation (2004). Evaluation Handbook [online]. Available at: www.wkkf.org/resource-directory/resource/2010/w-k-kellogg-foundation-evaluation-handbook (accessed 15 October 2015).

Kershaw, C., Nicholas, S. and Walker, A. (2008). *Crime in England and Wales 2007/08*. London: Home Office.

Kinney, J., Madsen, B., Fleming, T. and Haapala, D. A. (1977). Homebuilders: Keeping families together. *Journal of Consulting and Clinical Psychology*, 45, 667–673.

Kiteley, R. and Stogdon, C. (2014). *Literature Reviews in Social Work*. London: Sage Publications.

Klevens, J., Sadowski, L., Kee, R., Trick, W. and Garcia, D. (2012). Comparison of screening and referral strategies for exposure to partner violence. *Women's Health Issues*, 22(1), e45–e52.

Kratochwill, T. R., McDonald, L., Levin, J. R., Young Bear-Tibbetts, H. and Demaray, M. K. (2004). Families and schools together: an experimental analysis of a parent-mediated multi-family group program for American Indian children. *Journal of School Psychology*, 42, 359–383.

Kreisberg, N. and Marsh, J. C. (2016). Social work knowledge production and utilisation: An international comparison. *British Journal of Social Work* 46(3), 599–618.

Kroeber, A. L. and Kluckhohn, C. (1952). *Culture: A Critical Review of Concepts and Definitions*. Cambridge, MA: Peabody Museum.

Laing, L., Humphreys, C. and Kavanagh, K. (2013). *Social Work and Domestic Violence: Developing Critical and Reflective Practice*. London: Sage Publishing.

Lazenbatt, A. and Devaney, J. (2014). Older women living with domestic violence: Coping resources and mental health and wellbeing. *Current Nursing Journal*, 1(1), 10–22.

Lee, H. and Eaton, C. K. (2009). Financial abuse in elderly Korean immigrants: Mixed analysis of the role of culture on perception and help-seeking intention. *Journal of Gerontological Social Work*, 52(5), 463–488.

Lindsey, D., Martin, S. and Doh, J. (2002). The failure of intensive casework services to reduce foster care placements: An examination of family preservation studies. *Children and Youth Services Review*, 24 (9–10), 743–775.

Lothen-Kline, C., Howard, D. E., Hamburger, E. K., Worrell, K. D. and Boekeloo, B. O. (2003). Truth and consequences: ethics, confidentiality, and disclosure in adolescent longitudinal prevention research. *Journal of Adolescent Health*, 33, 385–394.

Lubet, S. (2015, 3 June). Alice Goffman's denial of murder conspiracy raises even more questions. *New Republic.* Available at: www.newrepublic.com/article/121958/ sociologist-alice-goffman-denies-murder-conspiracy-run (accessed 15 October 2015).

Masson, H., Hackett, S., Phillips, J. and Balfe, M. (2015). Developmental markers of risk or vulnerability? Young females who sexually abuse – characteristics, backgrounds, behaviours and outcomes. *Child & Family Social Work*, 20(1), 19–29.

Maxwell, N., Scourfield, J., Gould, N. and Huxley, P. (2012). UK panel data on social work service users. *British Journal of Social Work*, 42(1), 165–184.

McAuley, C., Knapp, M., Beecham, J., McCurry, N. and Sleed, M. (2004). *Young Families Under Stress. Outcomes and Costs of Home-Start Support.* Joseph Rowntree Foundation, York. Available at www.jrf.org.uk/sites/default/files/jrf/migrated/files/1859 352189.pdf (accessed 4 May 2016).

McAuley, C., McCurry, N., Knapp, M., Beecham, J. and Sleed, M. (2006). Young families under stress: Assessing maternal and child well-being using a mixed-methods approach. *Child & Family Social Work*, 11(1), 43–54.

McCord, J. (1978). A thirty-year follow-up of treatment effects. *American Psychologist*, 33(3), 284–289.

McLaughlin, H. (2012). *Understanding Social Work Research,* 2nd edn. London: Sage Publications.

Moher, D., Tetzlaff, J., Tricco, A. C., Sampson, M. and Altman, D. G. (2007). Epidemiology and reporting characteristics of systematic reviews. *PLoS Med*, 4(3), e78.

Moseley, A. and Tierney, S. (2005). Evidence based practice in the real world. *Evidence and Policy*, 1(1), 113–119.

Munro, E. (2011). *The Munro Review of Child Protection: Final Report. A Child Centred System.* London: Department for Education.

National Association of Social Workers (2008). *Code of Ethics* [online]. Available at: www. socialworkers.org/pubs/code/code.asp (accessed 15 October 2015).

Nevo, I. and Slonim-Nevo, V. (2011). The myth of evidence-based practice: Towards evidence-informed practice. *British Journal of Social Work*, 41(6), 1176–1197.

O'Higgins, A., Sebba, J. and Luke, N. (2015). *What is the Relationship Between Being in Care and the Educational Outcomes of Children? An International Systematic Review.* Oxford: University of Oxford.

Oakley, A., Strange, V., Toroyan, T., Wiggins, M., Roberts, I. and Stephenson, J. (2003). Using random allocation to evaluate social interventions: Three recent U.K. examples. *The Annals of the American Academy of Political and Social Science*, 589, 170–189.

Ofcom (2013). *Adults' Media Use and Attitudes Report* [online]. Available at: http:// stakeholders.ofcom.org.uk/binaries/research/media-literacy/adult-media-lit-13/2013_Adult_ML_Tracker.pdf (accessed 15 October 2015).

Office of National Statistics (2013). *Focus On: Violent Crime and Sexual Offences, 2011/12.* London: Office for National Statistics [online]. Available at: www.ons.gov.uk/ons/ dcp171778_298904.pdf (accessed 15 October 2015).

Office of National Statistics (2014). Intimate personal violence and partner abuse. In *Focus on Violent Crime and Sexual Offences 2012/13.* London: Office for National Statistics [online]. Available at: www.ons.gov.uk/ons/rel/crime-stats/crime-statistics/

focus-on-violent-crime-and-sexual-offences--2012-13/rpt---about-this-release.html (accessed 15 October 2015).

Overbeek, G. and Andershed, A. K. (2011). Introduction: Girls' problem behaviour: From the what to the why. In M. Kerr, H. Stattin, R. Engels, G. Overbeek and A. Andershed (eds), *How Girls' Delinquency Develops in the Context of Maturity and Health, Co-Occurring Problems, and Relationships*. Chichester: Wiley-Blackwell.

Pawson, R. and Tilley, N. (1997). *Realistic Evaluation*. London: Sage Publications.

Peled, E. and Leichentritt, R. (2002). The ethics of qualitative social work research. *Qualitative Social Work*, 1(2), 145–169.

Petrosino A., Turpin-Petrosino C., Hollis-Peel, M. and Lavenberg J. (2013). 'Scared straight' and other juvenile awareness programs for preventing juvenile delinquency. *Cochrane Database of Systematic Reviews*, 4, Art. No.: CD002796.

Police Service of Northern Ireland (2014). *Domestic Abuse Incidents and Crimes Recorded by the Police in Northern Ireland: Quarterly Update to 31 March 2014* [online]. Available at: www.psni.police.uk/globalassets/inside-the-psni/our-statistics/domestic-abuse-statistics/archive/quarterly_domestic_abuse_bulletin_apr-mar_13_14.pdf (accessed 15 October 2015).

Potter, J. and Wetherell, M. (1987). *Discourse and Social Psychology: Beyond Attitudes and Behaviour*. London: Sage Publications.

Punch, K. (2013). *Introduction to Social Research Quantitative and Qualitative Approaches*, 3rd ed. London: Sage Publications.

Reidy, H., Webber, M., Rayner, S. and Jones, M. (2013). *Evaluation of the Southwark Reablement Service* [online]. Available at: www.york.ac.uk/media/spsw/documents/cmhsr/Southwark%20Reablement%20Service%20Evaluation%2021.6.13.pdf (accessed 15 October 2015).

Robling, M., Bekkers, M-J., Kerry, B., Butler, C., Cannings-John, R., Channon, S., Martin, B., Gregory, J., Hood, K., Kemp, A., Kenkre, J., Montgomery, A., Moody, G., Owen-Jones, E., Pickett, K., Richardson, G., Roberts, Z., Ronaldson, S., Sanders, J., Stamuli, E. and Torgerson, D. (2016). Effectiveness of a nurse-led intensive home-visitation programme for first-time teenage mothers (Building Blocks): A pragmatic randomised controlled trial. *The Lancet*, 387(10014), 146–155.

Rogers, S. (2011, 31 October). Adoption statistics for England: get the data. *The Guardian*. Available at: www.theguardian.com/news/datablog/2011/sep/29/adoption-statistics-england (accessed 15 October 2015).

Rushton, A. and Monk, E. (2010). A 'real-world' evaluation of an adoptive parenting programme: Reflections after conducting a randomized trial. *Clinical Child Psychology and Psychiatry*, 15(4), 543–554.

Scourfield, J. and Maxwell, N. M. (2009). Social work doctoral students in the UK: A web-based survey and search of the index to theses. *British Journal of Social Work*, 40(2), 548–566.

Sebba, J., Berridge, D., Luke, N., Fletcher, J., Bell, K., Strand, S., Thomas, S., Sinclair, I. and O'Higgins, A. (2015). *The Educational Progress of Looked After Children in England: Linking Care and Educational Data*. Oxford: University of Oxford and University of Bristol.

Selwyn, J., Wijedasa, D. and Meakings, S. (2014). *Beyond the Adoption Order: Challenges, Interventions and Adoption Disruption*. London: Department for Education [online]. Available at: www.gov.uk/government/uploads/system/uploads/attachment_data/file/301889/Final_Report_-_3rd_April_2014v2.pdf (accessed 15 October 2015).

Sharland, E. and Teater, B. (2016). Research teaching and learning in qualifying social work education. In I. Taylor, M. Bogo, M. Lefevre and B. Teater (eds), *Routledge International Handbook of Social Work Education*, 144–156. London: Routledge.

Shaw, I., Arksey, H. and Mullender, A. (2004). *ESRC Research, Social Work and Social Care.* London: Social Care Institute for Excellence.

Sheldon, B. and Macdonald, G. (2008). *The Textbook of Social Work.* London: Routledge.

Silverman, D. (2010). *Doing Qualitative Research: A Practical Handbook*, 4th ed. London: Sage Publications.

Simkiss, D. E., Snooks, H. A., Stallard, N., Kimani, P. K., Sewell, B., Fitzsimmons, D., Anthony, R., Winstanley, S., Wilson, L., Phillips, C. J., Stewart-Brown, S. (2013). Effectiveness and cost-effectiveness of a universal parenting skills programme in deprived communities: Multicentre randomised controlled trial. *BMJ Open*; 3:e002851.

Slater, T., Scourfield, J. and Greenland, K. (2015). Suicide attempts and social worker contact: Secondary analysis of a general population study. *British Journal of Social Work*, 45(1), 378–394.

Slater, T., Scourfield, J. and Sloan, L. (2012). Who is citing whom in social work? A response to Hodge, Lacasse and Benson. *British Journal of Social Work*, 42(8), 1626–1633.

Smith, J. A., Jarman, M. and Osborn, M. (1999). Doing interpretative phenomenological analysis. In M. Murray and K. Chamberlain (eds), *Qualitative Health Psychology: Theories and Methods*. London: Sage.

Smith, K., Osborne, S., Lau, I. and Britton, A. (2012). *Homicides, Firearm Offences and Intimate Violence 2010/11: Supplementary Volume 2 to Crime in England and Wales 2010/11*. London: Home Office.

Stevens M., Liabo K., Witherspoon S. and Roberts H. (2009). What do practitioners want from research, what do funders fund and what needs to be done to know more about what works in the new world of children's services? *Evidence and Policy*, 5(3), 281–294.

Stevenson, L. (2015, 12 October). Care demand could reach highest ever levels this year, figures indicate. *Community Care* [online]. Available at: www.communitycare.co.uk/2015/10/12/care-demand-reach-highest-ever-levels-year-figures-indicate/ (accessed 15 October 2015).

Stewart-Brown, S., Anthony, A., Wilson, L., Winstanley, S., Stallard, N., Snooks, H. and Simkiss, D. (2011). Should randomised controlled trials be the 'gold standard' for research on preventive interventions for children? *Journal of Children's Services*, 6(4), 228–235.

Strega, S., Fleet, C., Brown, L., Dominelli, L., Callahan, M. and Walmsley, C. (2008). Connecting father absence and mother blame in child welfare policies and practice. *Children and Youth Services Review*, 30(7), 705–716.

Tashakkori, A. and Teddlie, C. (1998). *Mixed Methodology: Combining Qualitative and Quantitative Approaches*. Thousand Oaks, CA: Sage.

Tharyan, P. and Adams, C. E. (2005). Electroconvulsive therapy for schizophrenia. *Cochrane Database of Systematic Reviews*, 2, Art. No.: CD000076.

Thyer, B. (2015). A bibliography of randomized controlled experiments in social work (1949–2013): Solvitur ambulando. *Research on Social Work Practice*, 25(7), 753–793.

Times of India (2011, 2 February). *Third Gender Gets a Place in Census 2011* [online]. Available at: http://timesofindia.indiatimes.com/city/ahmedabad/Third-gender-gets-a-place-in-census-2011/articleshow/7428098.cms (accessed 15 October 2015).

Twain, M. (1907). Chapters from my autobiography – Chapter XX. *North American Review*, DXCVIII [online]. Available at: www.gutenberg.org/ebooks/19987 (accessed 15 October 2015).

Vaswani, N. and Merone, L. (2014). Are there risks with risk assessment? A study of the predictive accuracy of the Youth Level of Service-Case Management Inventory with young offenders in Scotland. *British Journal of Social Work*, 44, 2163–2181.

Velleman, R. and Orford, J. (1999). *Risk and Resilience: Adults who were the Children of Problem Drinkers*. Reading: Harwood Academic.

Waite, J. and Easton, A. (2013). *The ECT Handbook*, 3rd ed. London: Royal College of Psychiatrists.

Ward, H., Brown, R. and Hyde-Dryden, G. (2014). *Assessing Parental Capacity to Change when Children are on the Edge of Care: An Overview of Current Research Evidence*. London: Department for Education.

Washington State Institute for Public Policy (2006, Revised 2007). *Intensive Family Preservation Programs: Program Fidelity Influences Effectiveness* [online]. Available at: www.wsipp.wa.gov/ReportFile/938 (accessed 15 October 2015).

Webb, S. (2001). Some considerations on the validity of evidence-based practice in social work. *British Journal of Social Work*, 31, 57–79.

Welch, V., Hatton, C., Emerson, E., Collins, M., Robertson, J., Langer, S. and Wells, E. (2012). Using direct payments to fund short breaks for families with a disabled child. *Child: Care, Health and Development*, 38(6), 900–909.

Wilberforce, M., Jacobs, S., Challis, D., Manthorpe, J., Stevens, M., Jasper, R., Fernandez, J., Glendinning, C., Jones, K., Knapp, M., Moran, N. and Netten, A. (2014). Revisiting the cause of stress in social work: Sources of job demands, control and support in personalised adult social care. *British Journal of Social Work*, 44, 812–830.

Wikimedia Meta-Wiki (2010). *Fundraising 2010/Banner Testing* [online]. Available at: https://meta.wikimedia.org/wiki/Fundraising_2010/Banner_testing (accessed 15 October 2015).

Winter, K. and Connolly, P. (2005). A small-scale study of the relationship between measures of deprivation and child-care referrals. *British Journal of Social Work*, 35(6), 937–952.

World Health Organization (2005). *WHO Resource Book on Mental Health, Human Rights and Legislation* [online]. Available at: www.who.int/mental_health/policy/legislation/Resource%20Book_Eng2_WEB_07%20(2).pdf (accessed 15 October 2015).

World Medical Association (2013). *WMA Declaration of Helsinki – Ethical Principles for Medical Research Involving Human Subjects* [online]. Available at: www.wma.net/en/30publications/10policies/b3/ (accessed 15 October 2015).

Yoon, I. (2009). A mixed-method study of Princeville's rebuilding from the flood of 1999: Lessons on the importance of invisible community assets. *Social Work*, 54 (1), 19–28.

Young, J. M. and Solomon, M. J. (2009). How to critically appraise an article. *Nature Reviews Gastroenterology and Hepatology*, 6, 82–91.

Youth in Mind (2012). *Selected SDQ Publications*. Available at: www.sdqinfo.org/f0.html (accessed 28 July 2016).

Yusof, Y. and Carpenter, J. (2014). The impact of family therapists' adult attachment styles on their career choice and approach to therapy: An interpretive phenomenological analysis. *Journal of Social Work Practice*, 29(4), 395–412.

INDEX